T0323644

Social Enterprise Law

Social Enterprise Law

Trust, Public Benefit, and Capital Markets

DANA BRAKMAN REISER

and

STEVEN A. DEAN

OXFORD
UNIVERSITY PRESS

OXFORD
UNIVERSITY PRESS

Oxford University Press is a department of the University of Oxford. It furthers
the University's objective of excellence in research, scholarship, and education
by publishing worldwide. Oxford is a registered trade mark of Oxford University
Press in the UK and certain other countries.

Published in the United States of America by Oxford University Press
198 Madison Avenue, New York, NY 10016, United States of America.

© Oxford University Press 2017

CIP data is on file at the Library of Congress
ISBN 978-0-19-024978-6

1 3 5 7 9 8 6 4 2

Printed by Sheridan Books, Inc., United States of America

For Jeff and Charley

For Jen and John

CONTENTS

ACKNOWLEDGMENTS

Over the past few years, we poured ourselves into writing SOCIAL ENTERPRISE LAW. Those efforts would have proven fruitless without countless contributions and sacrifices both from people we know well and from others we hardly knew. Our gratitude to all of them is powerful. We could never hope to thank everyone who deserves it but we particularly acknowledge the help, comments, and insights of Benjamin Alarie, Susan Block-Lieb, Brad Borden, Cass Brewer, Allen Bromberger, Deborah Burand, Adam Chodorow, Allison Christians, Kate Cooney, Sarah Dadush, Harvey Dale, Nestor Davidson, Rob Esposito, Jim Fanto, Brian Galle, Joan Heminway, Ted Janger, Roberta Karmel, Carol Liao, Anthony Luppino, Johanna Mair, Dan Medwed, Haskell Murray, Minor Myers, Jonathan Ng, Shu-Yi Oei, Dan Osusky, Alan Palmiter, Seth Perlman, Alicia Plerhoples, Mark Sidel, Linda Sugin, Anne Tucker, John Tyler, and Dennis Young on drafts of the book as well as the articles that preceded it.

Those earlier efforts laid important groundwork for SOCIAL ENTERPRISE LAW. Not only do those articles, *Financing the Benefit Corporation, SE(c)(3): A Tax Regime to Catalyze Social Enterprise Crowdfunding, Creative Financing for Social Enterprise, Hunting Stag with FLY Paper: A Hybrid Financial Instrument for Social Enterprise, and Theorizing Forms for Social Enterprise*, form the heart of this book, those we wrote together also refined our co-authoring relationship. We thank the staffs of the Seattle University Law Review, the Indiana Law Journal, the Stanford Social Innovation Review, the Boston College Law Review, and the Emory Law Journal, for their efforts on those articles, which in turn improved this book. Our sincere thanks go as well to Patrick Bannon and Christie McGuinness for their valuable research assistance.

We also thank the participants in the many conferences and workshops at which we were able to present parts of this book, including numerous annual meetings of the Association for Research on Nonprofit Organizations and Voluntary Action, Law and Society Association Conferences and Annual Social Enterprise Conferences, two symposia of The Adolf A. Berle, Jr. Center on Corporations at Seattle University School of Law, the Harvard Seminar on Current Issues in Tax Law, the University of Colorado Leeds School of Business Crowdfunding Conference, the EMES International Research Conference, the NYU Nonprofit Forum, the 4th Annual Midwest Symposium on Social Entrepreneurship, and faculty workshops at Arizona State University Sandra Day O'Connor College of Law, Brooklyn Law School, Fordham University School of Law, The Lilly Family School of Philanthropy at Indiana University, University of Miami School of Law, and West Virginia University College of Law. The comments and suggestions we received during these presentations improved the work tremendously.

We are lucky to be not only co-authors but also colleagues at Brooklyn Law School, and we have been buoyed by the support of the rest of its faculty, administration, and staff. In particular, we thank Bill Araiza, Chris Beauchamp, Miriam Baer, Heidi Brown, Susan Herman, David Reiss, Jayne Ressler, and Larry Solan for their help and advice. Thanks go as well to Beth Pollastro, Marva Skeene, and Joanne Tapia, for helping us in innumerable small and large ways, to Kathy Darvil, our indomitable reference librarian, and to Dean Nick Allard and Brooklyn Law School for their support of our research.

We will be forever grateful to William Birdthistle, Scott Parris, and Cathryn Vaulman, without whom this book would not have found a home at Oxford University Press (OUP). We also appreciate OUP's David Pervin, Emily Mackenzie, and David McBride for their editorial assistance, Richard Isomaki for his stalwart copyediting, Prabhu Chinnasamy for guiding us through the production process, and Ina Gravitz for excellent indexing.

Family and our family of friends also worried and celebrated with us throughout the process of writing this book, and they tolerated late nights, early mornings, canceled plans, and interrupted vacations as we honed the manuscript. Thank you to Anita, Bob, and Pat Brakman, Anthony Dean, Ruth Dean, Erin Dow, Linda Feldman, Roberta Griff, Claire Kelly, and Ingrid Luchsinger, and above all to Jeff and Charlotte Reiser and Jennifer Wingate and John Dean.

Social Enterprise Law

Introduction

Social Enterprise Law: Trust, Public Benefit, and Capital Markets reveals the law's power to bring impact investors and social entrepreneurs together to nurture hybrid ventures that collapse the traditional barrier between for-profit and non-profit. In keeping with the productively disruptive spirit of social enterprise, the core of the book consists of defiantly unconventional, but practical, legal tools designed to connect capital with ideas. These concepts, situated at the "intersection of a big problem, a radical solution, and breakthrough [legal] technology,"[1] demonstrate that, rather than a threat to be neutralized, the law can be a vital ally for social enterprise.

The final chapters offer a different perspective, highlighting the importance of precision and of planning for contingencies. Chapter 6 shows how emerging metrics allow entrepreneurs and investors to use the law to find partners with similar appetites for profit and social mission. Chapter 7 demonstrates that corporate governance and contract can ensure that even an exit reinforces rather than undermines a social enterprise's amalgamation of profit and social mission. Together, they demonstrate that the law helps to bring bold visions to life, not by restricting choice, but by providing investors and entrepreneurs with the capacity to reveal their preferences and the tools to enforce them.

By exploring a range of innovative examples of social enterprise law in action, *Social Enterprise Law* not only provides practical advice for investors and entrepreneurs but serves as a comprehensive guide for everyone from policymakers to students. While couched in terms of US law, the book's core insights regarding the promise of social enterprise law should resonate in every country in which double-bottom-line ventures have taken root.[2] The book is not just for experts, but is intended to reach anyone with an interest in social enterprise and curiosity about how the law can be harnessed to achieve unlikely victories.

A Double Bottom Line

To say that a social enterprise's calling cannot be distilled to either unfettered greed or pure altruism conveys little about the role such organizations play in today's economy and less about what they might become in the future. Even Goldman Sachs—a paragon of financial success—touts its "commitment to finding effective and innovative ways to tackle economic, social and environmental challenges."[3] Concluding that Goldman Sachs pursues a social mission alongside its profit imperative, or that it maintains a dual or blended mission, would render the concept of social enterprise meaningless. While maximizing profits can seem a calling, mission here suggests the pursuit of public benefit.

Social Enterprise Law recognizes the transformational potential of for-profit ventures dedicated to generating both social good and financial returns. Such firms want to earn profits for their owners (who are their founders, at least initially) but also have a deeply rooted commitment to benefiting society or the environment. More important, unlike a merely ethical for-profit venture, they (at least sometimes) demonstrate a willingness to trade profit gains for gains in social good.

Etsy.com may be the best-known such venture. A virtual marketplace emphasizing handmade goods, Etsy proudly declares that it stands "committed to using the power of business to create a better world through our platform, our members, our employees and the communities we serve."[4] Without more, that affirmation would be hard to distinguish from the Goldman Sachs statement above and countless others. In describing its insistence on balancing profit ambitions with its other aims, though, Etsy goes further, maintaining that

> [a]s we grow, commitment to our mission remains at the core of our identity. It is woven into the decisions we make for the long-term health of our ecosystem, from the sourcing of our office supplies to our employee benefits to the items sold in our marketplace.[5]

Unsurprisingly, Goldman Sachs does not make a comparable claim regarding the depth of its devotion to mission.

A venture such as Etsy can assert that its mission—here shorthand for social mission—plays a central role in its decision-making process in a way that Goldman Sachs could not. Without that commitment to mission, Etsy might not even be Etsy. Both TOMS Shoes and Warby Parker differentiate themselves with their one-for-one approach to combining private profit with public purpose. By pledging that "[e]very time a TOMS product is purchased, a person in need is helped"[6] or that "for every pair of glasses sold, a pair is distributed to someone in need"[7] these for-profit companies distinguish themselves from competitors and attract customers. Of course, many customers will buy their shoes or eyeglasses without caring—or even knowing—about those commitments, but those that do care may make a crucial difference in the success of each business.

Social enterprises really abound, however, at the smaller end of the spectrum of businesses—far from household names like these. Harvest Power, a for-profit sustainable waste processor and organic consumer products manufacturer, describes its founding vision as "[c]reat[ing] a more sustainable future by help-ing communities meet challenges at the intersection of waste, agriculture and energy in the 21st century."[8] Nisolo, an apparel- and shoe-manufacturing busi-ness, offers employees in Peru above-fair-trade wages, healthcare benefits, and skills, health, and financial literacy training, as part of its goal to produce "ethi-cally made" fashion items.[9] Seeds Green Printing Company offers 100 percent eco-friendly printing solutions to preserve forests and reduce energy consump-tion and pollution.[10] A quick browse through the next airline magazine, com-munity newspaper, or business case competitor list you encounter will reveal additional examples of medium-sized, small, and microbusinesses blending profit and purpose to varying degrees.

Rather than focusing on the question of what quantum of social mission war-rants the label, *Social Enterprise Law* tackles the more concrete matter of access to capital. Since social enterprises, like their for-profit and nonprofit counter-parts, need capital to fuel their ambitions, labels remain important. Nobody expects actors that supply and deploy capital to be indifferent to whether the recipient is a for-profit venture or a charity. For the same reason, albeit within a narrower range, investors and entrepreneurs in social enterprises face the same questions. *Social Enterprise Law* will, we hope, increase access to capital by offer-ing a range of legal tools designed to promote transparency, allowing investors and entrepreneurs to broadcast—and commit to—their desired blend of profit and mission.

The legal interventions introduced below also address a distinct set of con-cerns. As any business lawyer can tell you, when you talk to entrepreneurs and tell them you are a lawyer, they are pretty sure you are out to kill their dreams. Lawyers have terrible reputations in lots of ways, and this is one of the worst. We are seen as the people who say No, who say, "You can't do that," who say, "It's not possible." And, entrepreneurs, of course, see themselves as the ones who say, "Yes, why not?" and "Anything is possible"—and they are right. But we reject that dichotomy. In fact, the law can be an incredibly powerful tool, and one that should be harnessed to help social enterprises thrive.[11]

Legal innovation has struck the world of social enterprise before. In particu-lar, new legal forms (the low-profit limited liability company first, and now the benefit corporation, public benefit corporation, and social purpose corporation) aim not only to house social enterprises but to free them from the concern that the law will conspire with market forces to strip them of their social missions. Those hybrid forms ensure that a legal imperative to maximize shareholder value at all costs does not preclude for-profit ventures from operating as social enterprises. Even if the notion that the law poses a threat to mission tends to be overblown, that first generation of social enterprise legal interventions served a valuable purpose by attacking the notion at the roots.

Unfortunately, despite their success in helping social enterprises gain acceptance, those hybrid forms do little to enhance their access to capital. The legal tools described below offer more than mere freedom from legal interference. They provide affirmative protection for mission in order to build trust between entrepreneurs and investors. These second-generation innovations take a variety of forms, ranging from hybrid financial instruments to traditional regulatory mechanisms. Collectively, these legal devices demonstrate that the law can be a potent and nimble ally of social enterprise rather than a threat to be neutralized.

Social Enterprise Law Rebooted

For many, the words *trust* and *corporation* hardly belong in the same sentence. Nevertheless, the relationships among shareholders, managers, and board members hinge on the duties they owe to one another. Corporate law can be seen as an effort not only to clearly articulate those obligations but to elevate them into enforceable rights. The result forms an intricate system of burdens and entitlements designed to build trust among investors and managers. While far from infallible, that network of checks and balances broadly delivers on its promise of profits for investors by harnessing the efforts of employees in executing the vision of the board.

Given its relatively recent vintage, it is no surprise that social enterprise lacks a comparably robust legal infrastructure. Unfortunately, time alone will not close that gap. Current efforts to adapt existing tools to serve the needs of double-bottom-line ventures have gathered momentum, particularly with the rise of the hybrid forms described in chapter 3. State legislators have planted many seeds, but to date those hybrid forms have produced only a few fragile shoots. More of the same will produce equally meager results.

The chapters that follow this introduction show why. They present a series of solutions anchored by a central theme. They illustrate how the law can nurture trust between social enterprise investors and entrepreneurs just as it has inspired the confidence necessary to match the supply of capital with the demand for capital by both traditional for-profit and nonprofit ventures. Collectively, they offer a vision of a possible future in which trust—and the investment it makes possible—fuels the growth of social enterprise. Distinguished by the hallmarks of transparency and precision, that second generation of legal interventions proves that the law can be a servant of social enterprise as well as an obstacle.

In one sense, the law governing for-profit and charitable ventures demands little subtlety. Profit and social mission dominate those respective fields. While a traditional corporation need not mindlessly pursue every available dollar of short-term profit, it does emphasize shareholders' financial interests. A charity can generate enormous profits, but none of those profits may find their way into the hands of owners or insiders. Their unambiguous dedication to profit and social mission renders superfluous a precise demarcation of the boundaries of their respective territories.

Chapter 1 proceeds from the premise that social enterprise, by contrast, calls for a delicate balance between social mission and profit. This binary nature presents a critical obstacle and makes precision essential. Lacking a lodestar of either profit or charity, a social enterprise must chart its own path. In a very real sense, unlike a traditional for-profit corporation or a charity, each social enterprise must make an affirmative choice not just as to what it does but as to what it is. Entrepreneurs and investors must reach a consensus along this dimension at the same time they construct the venture itself. Making that collective choice presents a challenge, but broadcasting the result and making it stick loom even larger. A muddy message and a watered-down commitment to balancing mission and profit may not be an inevitable byproduct of blending mission and profit, but without new thinking from the legal community, the risk remains intolerably high.

Fortunately, canvassing the expansive toolbox the law provides for the task of facilitating the flow of capital from investors with deep pockets to entrepreneurs with bright ideas yields a panoply of versatile implements. Across the next four chapters, *Social Enterprise Law* will explore how social entrepreneurs and impact investors can deploy three different types of legal tools to generate trust: potent organizational forms, hybrid financial instruments, and targeted tax regimes. Using these mechanisms to identify mission-focused counterparties and enforce shared commitments over time can unlock the capital needed to grow and scale social enterprises.

In a world free of resource constraints, the mission-protected hybrid (MPH) described in chapter 2 would build on the success of the first-generation hybrid entities. Benefit corporations and their kin can be thought of as an open declaration that when investors and entrepreneurs reach a consensus to balance mission and profit, state law will not interfere. Unfortunately, that first generation of hybrids does little to ensure that any such consensus will endure. The MPH, as its name suggests, goes further.

This new legal form would integrate two principal layers of security for a social enterprise's mission. The significance of the first, the fact that an MPH must prioritize mission, can be difficult to appreciate. That impact-first orientation establishes a presumption in favor of the enterprise's mission. Profit may still trump mission in any given particular, but not without reflection and an affirmative choice. In a sense, that emphasis on mission inverts the traditional corporate focus on profit. The second level of protection follows charities' lead in shielding mission by curbing payouts. Unlike a charity, the MPH imposes limits on distributions to owners rather than an outright ban. Exiting the MPH form would free a venture from the impact-first imperative but at the price of a portion of its assets, which would be transferred to an organization still committed to the MPH's former cause. Together, those protections not only permit but also protect a pairing of social mission with profit.

Having sketched the broad outlines of a robust social enterprise hybrid form, chapter 3 looks back at the first generation of hybrids. It acknowledges the significance of the commitment states have enthusiastically made to respect whatever idiosyncratic blends of social mission and profits that investors and entrepreneurs create. Unfortunately, that hands-off approach has done little to promote investment in social enterprise. The permissive stance embodied in benefit corporations and the other first-generation hybrids falls far short of the support and supervision the MPH would offer. Simply put, those first-generation hybrids make it easy to cast mission aside, leaving those investors and entrepreneurs committed to an impact-first approach to social enterprise without the tools necessary to signal their resolve and rally compatible fellows to their cause.

Without such a reliable signal, investors and entrepreneurs remain on the sidelines, understandably reluctant to find themselves left holding the proverbial bag should their counterparts trade mission for money. While the MPH offers one possible solution to that trust deficit, it is by no means the only remedy. Chapter 4 suggests just how far the pool of possible options truly extends. It bypasses the need to create a second-generation hybrid form by focusing directly on the challenge social enterprises face in accessing the capital they need to launch and grow.

The flexible low-yield debt (FLY paper) instrument it proposes, which is neither conventional debt nor pure equity, allows investors to identify Potemkin social enterprises owned by entrepreneurs with their sights set on a quick (and lucrative) exit. In the event such a transaction occurs, the investors would have the right to convert their debt investment into the lion's share of the venture's equity. As a result, no such sale would occur without first securing the consent of the FLY paper holders. Unlike the first- and second-generation hybrid forms, FLY paper makes no attempt to offer comprehensive protection for a venture's mission, instead eliminating a single—albeit significant—threat.

Sophisticated financial instruments like FLY paper could accomplish much that the first generation of hybrid forms has not, but they might never be within the reach of investors and entrepreneurs of modest means. New federal regulations targeted at crowdfunding seem tailor made for small-scale social enterprises to raise equity capital, but those rules offer no mechanism investors can use to identify committed social enterprises. Chapter 5 presents a third strategy for preserving a balance between social mission and profit that would fill that gap.

The proposal bears no more resemblance to chapter 4's hybrid financial instrument approach than it does to prior chapters' proposed and existing legal forms. Its SE(c)(3) tax regime pairs an elective tax benefit for mission-related expenditures with increased taxation of dividends and capital gains. This combined tax benefit and tax increase rewards fidelity to mission while putting a price tag on faithlessness. Opting into SE(c)(3) would allow even a shoestring social enterprise to signal its resolve to prioritize mission. A higher tax burden on profit-taking makes shareholder greed its own punishment. Although the application of SE(c)(3)'s stick raises few questions, the role of its carrot serves to highlight what may be the central social enterprise puzzle. Demanding that an SE(c)(3) demonstrate that it has earned the promised benefit poses a significant challenge.

Having elaborated three distinct forms the second generation of social enterprise law could take, with chapter 6 *Social Enterprise Law* focuses specifically on that critical question of measurement. Like traditional charities and for-profit ventures, social enterprises fill almost every conceivable niche. Because of that diversity, crafting a single yardstick to measure each venture's commitment to mission presents a daunting task. Moreover, the stakes are high. A reliable metric could anchor every one of the proposals described here, from SE(c)(3) and FLY paper to the first- and second-generation hybrid forms. Fortunately, as this chapter details, parallel efforts to operationalize such tools have already begun to yield promising results.

The final chapter, appropriately, focuses on endings. The implications of exit weave throughout *Social Enterprise Law*, so examining exits in depth casts light on the preceding chapters. The fatal flaw in the first generation of hybrid forms lies in the ease with which ventures can embrace those forms only to cast aside the commitments they impose. The MPH borrows from the charitable playbook by embracing a modified nondistribution constraint to prevent those easy exits. FLY paper enhances mission's durability with financial engineering (and without government intervention) by inhibiting exits. But many, if not most, social enterprises will face the question of exit without these second-generation mechanisms already in place. Again, the law offers a variety of tools to assist entrepreneurs and investors navigating the shoals of exit. Contexts as diverse as venture capital finance, small-business sales, and even the misunderstood tale of Ben & Jerry's sale to Unilever offer lessons in using the law to prevent a sale from becoming a sellout.

Although not the end that investors or entrepreneurs dream of, failure can disrupt a commitment to mission as thoroughly as any other type of exit. Chapter 7 also grapples with the consequences of financial failure—including bankruptcy—for a social enterprise's mission. At a minimum, it is useful to consider what such an eventuality might mean for first-generation hybrid forms and for the tools that we propose.

The second generation of legal innovations targeted at the needs of social enterprise will not solve every problem faced by double-bottom-line ventures. It should, however, dispel the misconception that the best the law can do to help social enterprise is to stay out of the way. Well-designed legal interventions can affirmatively promote trust among investors and entrepreneurs, bringing together like-minded individuals with the resources and drive needed to build successful social enterprises. *Social Enterprise Law* boldly plants a flag on the territory first tamed by the initial wave of hybrid forms, demonstrating the breadth and power of the resources the law offers social enterprise.

1

The Social Enterprise Trust Deficit

The contours of the social enterprise concept resist a crisp consensus description. Some use the term to describe both nonprofits and for-profits, big and small. It might be understood to encompass any organization that can articulate a claim to generate both revenues and environmental or social benefits. Of course, such a sweeping definition yields a category too heterogeneous to be the subject of meaningful discussion. Our focus rests on a particular terrain. Here, social enterprise means a for-profit firm dedicated to achieving a blend of profits for owners and good for society (mission). The second-generation legal tools described in the following chapters not only embrace such ventures but grant them access to capital, the fuel they burn to advance both objectives.

Social purposes can be embedded in business models in myriad ways. A social enterprise may structure its supply chain to pursue social goals. For example, it may privilege particular types of suppliers, such as woman- or minority-owned businesses or environmentally friendly purveyors, and commit to do so even when such choices make production more costly. Likewise, employment decisions and production processes may be designed to achieve social good. Employing new immigrants or persons with disabilities will require greater outlays for training, but will produce gains for these groups, their families, and their communities. Choices also abound when selecting manufacturing or service delivery models, and a social enterprise may select local production or a reduced carbon footprint in service of its social mission. Indeed, even the particular product or service a business provides or the consumer population it intends to serve can further social commitments. Enterprises producing green technology or goods priced for consumers living in poverty in the developing world can make strides toward cleaner air or better lives for those at the base of the pyramid.[1] That double bottom line—along with profit for owners, social enterprises all seek to generate broader social value—represents the common thread in this diverse tapestry.

The entrepreneurs and investors behind these enterprises hardly resemble the caricature of rapacious capitalists out to enrich themselves alone. But neither do they pursue social goals as a mere sideline. Practitioners of corporate philanthropy make charitable donations out of surplus in order to curry brand or public relations advantages. Standard-issue corporate social responsibility addresses social issues to improve a firm's image or generate longer-term financial gain. Social enterprises instead target the true integration of a double bottom line; their (admittedly hackneyed) slogan is "doing well by doing good."

Social entrepreneurs and investors also reject the other extreme of selfless asceticism, only desiring to benefit the world around them. They pursue environmental conservation, poverty reduction, women's empowerment, or improved lives for children, but they do not aspire to be charities. They want to generate profits, to sustain their businesses, and to more than merely make a living. The organizations they form do not embrace the nonprofit commitment to reinvest all profits from their endeavors in continued pursuit of their identified social goals. The founders of social enterprises start businesses. They want a financial return as well as a return for society. And their investors too seek blended value—both financial gains and societal improvements.

Detractors may call this social enterprise vision pure fantasy, and claim entrepreneurs and investors in the real world do not seek blended value. But look around. Mark Zuckerberg and Priscilla Chan are funneling their billions in Facebook stock into a for-profit LLC rather than a traditional charity, in part to enable it to stake "innovative companies helping to solve big challenges in society such as education and health care."[2] Its first major investment, leading a $24 million funding round, went to Andela,[3] a two-year-old for-profit start-up that trains software developers in Africa for jobs with tech giants like IBM.[4] Andela aims to earn profits for its owners, but also to combat a particular social ill. In its words,

> While brilliance is evenly distributed around the world, opportunity is not. . . . Andela identifies the most talented software developers on the African continent and embeds them into engineering organizations as full-time, distributed team members.[5]

Like Andela before it hit the impact investment jackpot, social enterprises tend to be small, upstart companies begun on a combination of hardscrabble entrepreneurship and bright-eyed optimism.[6] Stories like Andela's stand out, but entrepreneurs like Colin and Karen Archipley of Archi's Acres—an organic, hydroponic farming business designed to provide entrepreneurial training to veterans and turn a profit[7]—start new ventures every day. Recognizing that, top business schools have launched social entrepreneurship programs at a rapid clip, responding to the demands of their elite student bodies.[8] Social enterprise may always be a niche, but it is also a real business category, and trends in consumer preferences and demographics suggest even greater promise for the future.[9]

The Importance of Capital

This promise will go unfulfilled, though, if social enterprises cannot access capital.[10] An entrepreneur can come up with her "big idea"—and in social enterprise, it can be big across the profit or the social-good dimension, or both—and pour her savings and personal credit into it. But this bootstrapping has obvious limits. Depending on the entrepreneur's personal network, friends and family may provide additional investment to help her get up and running, produce early proof of concept, or operate a single location. Other than for the independently wealthy and exceedingly well connected, though, a successful business will reach a point where it requires outside investment. When this moment arrives will depend on the industry in which a business operates as well as the entrepreneur's own balance sheet. Whether an entrepreneur needs to find investors to support prototype development, geographic expansion, increasing market share, or some other strategy, seeking scale requires access to capital. This chapter explores the unique challenges social enterprises face in solving this capital access problem, laying the foundation for the potential solutions later chapters propose.

Trust

To part investors from their money, and entrepreneurs from complete control, takes trust. Access to capital suffers when distrust is a problem, and faithlessness can run in either direction. An investor would be a fool to give her money to someone styling himself as an entrepreneur but with no assurances he would devote himself to creating value for the firm and, in turn, the investor herself. An entrepreneur would be just as foolish to give up control to investors he believed intended to use that power to appropriate for themselves all of the value he created in starting a company. If entrepreneurs and investors cannot trust each other, even in the traditional business realm, capital will not flow.

For social enterprises, the very dual-mission concept at their core makes this already vexing problem much harder. Investors need to be convinced not only of their ability to earn returns, but also that they can trust an entrepreneur's social commitments—and those of any fellow investors. The last thing an impact investor wants to be is a sucker—risking lower financial returns supposedly to generate social good and instead watching her funds being frittered away or padding the pockets of others. Social entrepreneurs not only worry that an investor might use control to pillage a venture's finances, but also need assurances that investors will not literally sell out or simply stop trying to change the world once big profits become attainable. If they cannot resolve these high-degree-of-difficulty trust problems, capital will remain elusive.

Stag Hunt

While not known for evocative imagery, economists do in some instances resort
to using it to capture a particularly slippery concept. Game theory relies heavily
on such conceits. The most recognizable example might be the notion of mutually assured destruction, which may have helped stave off nuclear strikes during
the Cold War by making their consequences palpable. On a more intimate scale,
the prisoner's dilemma captures the anguish of the choice between cooperation
and defection among accused conspirators.

The stag hunt game represents something of a variation on this better-known
prisoner's dilemma. Although hunting for stag may not be the staple in popular culture that a pair of suspects in separate police interrogation rooms has
become, its broad outlines can be understood easily enough.[11] Two hunters set
their sights on a major prize (the stag), but each will go home hungry unless they
both remain focused on the stag. On their own, they have the ability to snare
smaller game (hares). And, unless each has some way to verify the commitment
of the other hunter—to trust each other—they will do just that.

If one of the hunters knows from personal experience, for example, that
the other has a profound allergy to hare, she will not waver (although she herself could safely eat hare). Her confidence ensures the hunt's success just as
her doubts would have doomed it. Presumably her insight came as the result
of her relationship with her companion. Their familiarity with one another
might result from the fact that they grew up as neighbors. Importantly, they
need not be friends or even particularly like one another. Assurances are
everything. So long as they remain confident in one another's commitment
to the stag hunt, the hunt will succeed. Because of that, the stag hunt is an
"assurance game."[12]

The Social Enterprise Assurance Game

Social enterprise founders and investors confront their own version of the stag
hunt. Rather than a stag, their big prize combines social and financial returns.
Temptation—the hare—will come in the form of opportunities to remove or
reduce the enterprise's social commitment and thereby generate greater financial returns. Although each investor might prefer a stag and may even believe
that each other investor shares that preference, unless they have compelling evidence to support that belief, it would be all too easy (and perhaps smart) to yield
to temptation.

An owner could ensure that a social enterprise will pursue his unique vision
of the balance between mission and profit by forgoing the involvement of other
investors. At the risk of stating the obvious, if a founder retains all of a social
enterprise's equity, he can rest easy. Of course, excluding the presence of outside investors means doing without the capital they might provide. Without

that capital, the social enterprise's mission will be preserved, but it will not flourish.

When circumstances make a sale of some or all of a venture's equity necessary, understanding potential investors and trusting their intentions becomes paramount.[13] Parting with a significant equity stake in a double-bottom-line venture means parting with an equal measure of control over its future.[14] For the founder of an incorporated social enterprise, yielding a majority stake means ceding the ability to elect directors that share his vision of a balance of a profit and mission.

When retaining that control ceases to be a viable option—just as when a hunter recognizes that he cannot catch the stag on his own—the owner of a social enterprise must give careful consideration to who answers his call for help. Perhaps the most straightforward way to ensure that the new owner will offer more than empty assurances about a commitment to preserving the venture's mission would be to find a like-minded purchaser with a proven track record. A microfinance entrepreneur, for example, might seek out another microfinance entrepreneur as an investor. Selling to a party she has worked alongside for years would offer the seller "longstanding knowledge of the buyer and its reputation."[15] No different than considering only hunters with a hare allergy, the obvious downside to such an approach lies in the constraints it places on the pool of potential purchasers.

That limited universe of prospective buyers does, of course, represent a source of capital that could allow a founding social enterprise investor to expand a social enterprise's reach or simply to redeploy her capital elsewhere. The fact that a buyer has demonstrated over time her commitment to both mission and profit offers meaningful reassurance that a sale would not be tantamount to selling out. Whether any of those proven investors would have an appetite for the specific investment in question at the time the would-be seller hopes to strike a deal would be a more difficult question. If intimacy alone can build the trust required to access outside capital, double-bottom-line ventures have quite limited growth potential. But while casting a wider net would increase the likelihood of a successful capital injection, it could simultaneously put the venture's mission in jeopardy.

Law's Assurances

Legal regimes often develop around a key tension the way a pearl grows around a grain of sand. Tort law attempts to persuade actors to balance self-interest against the safety of others. Success might mean greater accountability for those with decision-making authority and fewer accidents as a result. Intellectual property rules aim to promote creativity—producing music and literature as well as inventions and brand names—but run the risk of stifling innovation by putting a fence around the ideas creators metabolize.

The assurances embedded in two distinct species of corporate law function in much the same way, working to refine anonymous capital into a safe fuel for for-profit corporations while assuring contributors that nonprofit ventures will remain faithful to their avowed social missions. The for-profit corporation provides a focal point that serves that end by allowing entrepreneurs to attract capital in the form of equity investments. Nonprofit corporate law treads a parallel path, reassuring donors and beneficiaries that their dollars and aspirations for the future can be entrusted to charities beyond their control. Corporate law traffics in such promises, allowing parties to overcome what might otherwise be crippling suspicions to pursue gains for society and for themselves. Yet both of these options ill-serve social enterprise.

The For-Profit Legal Landscape

For-profit corporate law provides assurance of a shared vision to traditional investors and finance-first entrepreneurs. Indeed, the corporate form makes trust all but irrelevant. Investors and entrepreneurs do not need to trust—or even know—one another so long as they have faith in the rights and obligations corporate law specifies. Investors receive limited liability and the protection of fiduciary obligations that direct firm management to pursue the interests of the corporation and its shareholders with loyalty and care. State corporate law— bolstered by the disclosure requirements and antifraud safeguards imposed by federal securities law—makes it easy for willing investors and entrepreneurs to say yes without first building the trust such a relationship would otherwise demand. Together, they facilitate cooperation and deter defections, shaping behavior and expectations. With these rules of fair play and honest brokering in place, investors' and entrepreneurs' self-interest in the single focal point of business success largely obviates the need for further safeguards.

The methods through which state law controls corporate activity can be as direct as rejecting an initial filing of formative documents of a venture that fails to fit within conventional parameters. In other cases, states exert a more subtle form of control. Their authority to regulate poison pills and other privately crafted takeover defenses powerfully illustrates this indirect influence over corporate behavior.

After all, as chapter 7 demonstrates, nothing affects a for-profit corporation's fate like an acquisition. At the stroke of a pen, a venture's management can be replaced and its scale and scope dramatically altered. Takeover defenses do not preclude a corporate acquisition. Instead, they simply buttress the power of a board to decide whether to permit a corporation to be acquired. A poison pill—also known as a shareholder rights plan—accomplishes that by diluting the ownership stake of a would-be acquirer when that unwelcome stake reaches a given threshold.[16] That dilution might result, for example, from discount purchases of stock by other shareholders. Knowing that a target has adopted a shareholder rights plan, a potential acquirer would first negotiate with the board to persuade it to "disarm" the plan. Only once an acquirer reaches an understanding with the target's board regarding its intentions will the acquirer make an appeal to the target's shareholders.

Such antitakeover strategies emerged not from state legislatures but from the offices of law firms and other advisers. Initially challenged in state courts, but ultimately upheld as a legitimate exercise of a board's authority, poison pills have become an accepted, state-sanctioned tool of corporate control.[17] Today, courts and legislatures determine which types of takeover defenses are permitted in a given jurisdiction, some providing boards with more discretion and others giving shareholders greater control.

Whatever the specific balance a jurisdiction strikes with respect to unsolicited takeover bids and other corporate inflection points, the overall dynamic remains consistent. Legislators establish basic ground rules while private actors police compliance. Frustrated shareholders, for example, might sue to recover potential gains lost to a board's refusal to defuse a poison pill in response to a takeover offer. While state laws and state courts play key roles in empowering or constraining boards, shareholders, and management, they do not bear the primary responsibility for monitoring or enforcing boundaries. No state actor weighs in on the suitability of an acquisition or of a new strategic initiative. They do not need to. Clear and privately enforceable rules of the road suffice to allow a for-profit corporation's founder and investors to come together around their easily identifiable focal point of profit.

An Unfortunate Mismatch

Alas, adopting the same market mechanism that stabilizes purely market-driven for-profit corporations by rewarding profitability and punishing its opposite would inevitably steer widely held social enterprises off course. The tectonic upheaval that accompanies corporate acquisitions can be precipitated by what would in isolation be inconsequential stock sales. Gaining control of a corporation means buying its shares. A would-be acquirer of a for-profit has a vision of the venture's future that it believes to be more profitable than its current path. Whether right or wrong, so long as the purchaser offers the corporation's shareholders a premium over the market price for their shares, current holders have little choice but to sell.

Even—perhaps particularly—a shareholder confident that the acquirer will fail in its ambitions would be foolish to refuse. Unless she can be certain that a sufficient number of shareholders share her view (and her courage), resisting the acquisition by refusing to sell will not impede the acquisition. Aside from the grim satisfaction that might accompany a share price decline she alone foresaw, holding out offers no upside. As a result, even a skeptical shareholder will sell, and what she believes to be a star-crossed acquisition will be consummated.

Corporate boards can, in theory, prevent such outcomes. But in practice, a patient acquirer with a sufficiently generous offer can simply wait until shareholder elections install a more sympathetic slate of board members.[18] For the same reason, even the stoutest takeover defenses will not frighten away a sufficiently determined suitor.

In the for-profit context, such an outcome does not pose an existential threat. The overconfident acquirer (and any remaining preacquisition shareholders unwise or unlucky enough to remain in possession of their shares) will suffer the fallout of an ill-fated transaction. But shareholders who sell will be better off than they would have been had no acquisition occurred since they receive a premium for their shares.

If the for-profit were instead a social enterprise, this would produce a more troubling result. If each of the enterprise's shareholders prefers a double-bottom-line approach, an acquirer's generous offer might appear doomed. Unfortunately, even if the offer's terms presuppose the venture's postacquisition transformation into a traditional for-profit venture, it is still likely to succeed. The fact that the board and each shareholder would prefer to preserve the social enterprise's mission will—without more—simply not matter.

For any individual shareholder to remain faithful to the venture's double bottom line, she must be as confident of the convictions of the *other* shareholders as she is of her own. If she resists while her peers, even reluctantly, yield, the shareholder could find herself having the venture's mission stripped away without compensation. In place of shares representing a stake in a double-bottom-line venture, she could find shares that constitute a risky bet on the acquisition's future profitability.

If the acquirer's vision falls short, the marooned shareholder will enjoy neither mission nor profit. Even if the acquirer pays cash for the target's stock or the gamble proves to be lucrative, it may still be unsatisfying to a shareholder who had consciously chosen two bottom lines over one. That truly committed impact investor might take her windfall and plow it into another double-bottom-line venture, but can never recapture what was lost.

Corporate law provides investors and entrepreneurs in traditional for-profit ventures the confidence to join forces and funds. But the blend of social mission and profit-seeking at the core of social enterprises is too complex for for-profit corporate law's structural tools to tame the distrust of its key players. Assuring social entrepreneurs and investors that they share a genuine commitment to balancing mission and profit demands more robust mechanisms. Without such tools, social enterprises will be consigned to the strategy of limiting ownership—a poor substitute for the ready security corporate law provides to standard for-profits.

Nonprofit Law's Assurances

The corporate form also embraces a fundamentally different type of venture. Your alma mater, your nearest teaching hospital, and your local food pantry are almost certainly formed as nonprofit corporations. So too the Ford Foundation, which has long operated as a Michigan nonprofit corporation. It has an endowment of more than $10 billion and makes over 1,000 grants per year to "reduce poverty and injustice, strengthen democratic values, promote international cooperation, and advance human achievement."[19] The Ford Foundation presents a stark contrast to for-profit multinationals like Microsoft and even the tiniest start-ups or neighborhood small businesses, yet all of these entities comfortably inhabit a corporate shell.

Nonprofit corporations face many of the same challenges as their for-profit counterparts. The fundamental issues of charting and navigating a course differ superficially more than they do in substance. Conflicts over priorities and strategies do not become less passionate when mission replaces a profit motive. Given that, perhaps it should not be surprising that organizations as far from the world of high finance as the Sierra Club and the UK Royal Society for the Prevention of Cruelty to Animals (RSPCA) have found themselves faced with hostile takeover efforts and the inevitable questions they raise.[20]

Members in favor of adding an anti-immigration plank to the Sierra Club's platform tried to elect their director candidates to a majority of board seats in 2004. The anti-immigration faction appealed to other members to support its candidates, but was ultimately defeated—perhaps in part due to extraordinary efforts by incumbents to rally members to oppose the coup. Prohunting insurgents within the RSPCA engaged in a campaign to recruit new members when they saw an opening to push withdrawal of the Society's support for nationwide antihunting legislation. It too turned back the takeover efforts, by rejecting hundreds of new applications for membership and expelling the anti-hunting faction's leaders, but only after obtaining the protection of a sympathetic judicial advisory opinion.

Trading profit for mission changes the stakes for managers and suppliers of capital but does not lower them. Without shareholders in the picture to police wayward ventures, though, the enforcement landscape changes considerably. Absent shareholders able to serve as private attorneys general by filing self-interested lawsuits in cases of corporate fraud or malfeasance, the task of providing accountability for nonprofits falls squarely on public actors. Directors, of course, remain the most important bulwark against management failures and malfeasance, just as in the for-profit context. They bear the primary responsibility for preserving both a nonprofit's mission and its financial integrity. When they cannot—or simply do not—state attorneys general possess the authority and the responsibility to step in.[21]

In an ideal world, that difference might be inconsequential. In reality, the absence of a robust system of private enforcement almost certainly results in reduced levels of scrutiny compared to that faced by for-profit corporations and their boards. State attorneys general possess limited resources and an expansive array of responsibilities, extending well beyond policing nonprofit behavior.[22]

The reliance on public enforcement affects the nature of the attention devoted to nonprofit oversight as well as the overall amount.[23] Attorneys general facing re-election will tend to pursue the types of matters likely to result in clear findings of wrongdoing, such as fraud or embezzlement. Even though questions of how faithfully managers adhere to an organization's mission might ultimately be more significant to voters, translating a successful effort to refocus a charity's resources into votes would be no easy matter. As a result, even those charged with policing nonprofits may not be particularly interested in the subtle distinctions that matter most to those supplying capital. When deciding how they might deploy the time and effort available for charitable enforcement, it would be natural for them to pursue and punish a clear case of financial misconduct by a particular actor rather than gauging the collective fidelity of nonprofits to their respective missions.

Fortunately, in the nonprofit context the resulting vulnerability does not threaten nonprofits' charitable nature. The nondistribution constraint ensures a purity no other entity attempts to provide. Simply put, this centerpiece of nonprofit corporate law demands that the assets of a charity remain permanently and exclusively devoted to charitable uses.[24] Despite their moniker, nonprofit corporations can be profitable! The label nonprofit has less to do with whether a charity can yield high returns than whether managers and board members may, in their individual capacities, profit from their relationships with those organizations. A certain degree of "drift" in an organization's charitable focus may be inevitable, but when insiders sacrifice a nonprofit's mission for their own ends, they cross a clear line of precisely the type that prosecutors excel at monitoring.

Again, this represents corporate law at work generating trust. The nondistribution constraint enshrined in nonprofit corporation statutes—and backstopped by federal tax law for section 501(c)(3) tax-exempt charities—reassures contributors that they are not lining the pockets of insiders. Donors large and small need not spend the energy and resources required to vet and monitor every nonprofit to which they give. Beneficiaries and the public too can more easily trust nonprofit institutions thanks to this limit. Nonprofits pose less risk of betraying their missions because the law blocks alternative uses of their funds. Although enforcement is certainly imperfect, stakeholders can rally around and be assured by the promise of singular dedication to charitable purpose.

The Problem of Serving Two Masters

Regrettably, nondistribution can no more solve the assurance game at the heart of social enterprise's capital access problem than the focal point provided by profit. Social enterprises reject the forbearance represented by the nonprofit form. This rebuff allows ventures the freedom to draw on the best of the non-profit and for-profit spheres, lending them a hybrid vigor. From an enforcement perspective, though, erasing the neat line between charity and investor profit exacts a steep price. Without that clearly defined boundary, the border largely disappears.

Just as in the charitable context, drawing distinctions between acceptable and unacceptable readings of a venture's mission would be difficult even if state attorneys general saw a compelling reason to attempt it. Social enterprises exist to simultaneously serve their mission and to generate profits for their owners, presenting an even more daunting enforcement task than purely mission-driven charities. Inviting public enforcement of a poorly defined blend of mission and profit—at least of the type provided by prosecutors—would be futile.

Crafting Assurances for Social Enterprises

For-profit and nonprofit corporations employ fundamentally different strategies in preserving their respective visions and reassuring suppliers of capital. Contributors to nonprofits outsource enforcement to attorneys general. Shareholders of for-profit corporations either do the work themselves by monitoring boards or selling their shares to others prepared to do so.

Double-bottom-line ventures fall into the gap that exists between these two well-developed areas of the law. They represent a challenge to convention not because they seek profits or because they devote resources to pursuing a social mission, but because they aim to do *both*. Corporate law has carved out a place for for-profits and nonprofits, but each is distinct. At the risk of understatement, the nonprofit and for-profit regimes are not interchangeable. Although they share a considerable percentage of their DNA—both are governed by a board of directors, for example—Microsoft could no more transform itself into a charity than the Ford Foundation could refashion itself into a for-profit business.

Social enterprise's comfort with profit distribution to owners makes it incompatible with the fundamental precept of nonprofit corporate law. The for-profit governance model, by contrast, can be retrofitted to accommodate social enterprise. Indeed, with the first generation of legal tools designed for social enterprises, state legislatures stepped boldly into this breach, fashioning modified for-profit forms empowered to broadly claim dual social and profit-making goals.

That innovation handed double-bottom-line ventures an important victory by having their dual mission officially sanctioned. Unfortunately, it offers little beyond this stamp of legitimacy. Critically, those hybrid forms suggest no particular balance of mission and profit to serve as a focal point for like-minded parties. Worse, they do too little to prevent one party from unilaterally sacrificing one bottom line for the other. This shortcoming—failing to secure the dual commitment these hybrid forms accommodate—means social enterprises cannot yet count on legal form to provide the assurances needed to access capital. In other words, the corporate law has not yet done for social enterprises what it has for both for-profits and nonprofits.

Fortunately, a second generation of legal tools can. Providing these assurances requires law to do more than get out of the way of dual-mission intentions. Pairing the pull of a focal point for like-minded entrepreneurs and investors with a firm push to prevent each from being able to unilaterally sacrifice mission for profit without the other's consent would do just that. Chapter 2 proposes the mission-protected hybrid (or MPH) to offer investors and entrepreneurs such a sheltered focal point. An MPH insists on a clear emphasis on mission that inverts the traditional corporation's emphasis on profit. The same could be achieved using unincorporated forms such as partnerships or limited liability companies, but we focus on the corporate form in part to underscore the fact that—however much of an oxymoron the notion of a corporate social mission might seem—balancing mission and profit does not require abandoning the corporate form. Chapter 3 explores the limitations of extant hybrid legal forms in detail. The remainder of this chapter articulates why for-profit corporate law will not generate sufficient trust between social entrepreneurs and their potential investors to make capital flow.

Symbolic Victories (and Worse)

Traditional legal doctrine has a long history of missing the mark when parties prioritize nonpecuniary interests. A staple of the first year of law school, *Peevyhouse v. Garland Coal & Mining Co.*,[25] offers a useful illustration. After property had been strip-mined, the coal company refused to meet its commitment to restore the property. The landowners sued and won. Unfortunately for the landowners, the victory proved hollow. Although it would have cost far more to "repair" the land as the contract required, the court awarded damages based on the increase in the land's market value those efforts would produce (or, more precisely, the decrease caused by the mining). The "win" left the landowners with $300 to accomplish the $2,940 worth of restoration that all acknowledged had been part of their bargain with the mining company.

Like those landowners, an investor in a social enterprise structured as a traditional for-profit corporation would find it difficult to restore a lost balance between mission and profit by invoking the remedies that corporate law offers. Were she to, for example, bring a successful lawsuit against the directors of a social enterprise for sacrificing mission in favor of profit, she would face the same quandary as Willie and Lucille Peevyhouse. In fact, the outcome might be even worse. There might actually be *no* decline in market value resulting from a breach of the directors' obligations to serve social mission. Without damages, the lawsuit offers neither a reward to encourage potential plaintiffs nor—except, perhaps, for the risk of a black mark by its corporate name—a deterrent for potential defendants.

Putting the question of damages to one side, even to obtain a judgment in her favor the shareholder would first have to navigate the many hurdles detailed in chapter 2 imposed by state law before bringing such a suit. Then she would have to prove that irresponsible actions on the part of its directors had steered the corporation off course. Poor, but well-intentioned choices by directors receive immunity from a business judgment rule that merely requires directors to show they considered the options with adequate information and exercised judgment in choosing one.

In the standard for-profit context, meeting each of those daunting burdens would at least result in directors being forced to pay compensation for the company's losses associated with forgone profits. A purely profit-oriented investor might accept cash returned to the corporation's coffers as an adequate substitute for profits left unearned. For social enterprise investors, monetary damages may well be unavailable—as privileging profit over social good will often increase profits and stock prices. If directors could somehow be tapped for money damages as a penalty for sacrificing social good, it will still be difficult to resuscitate a mission already scarred by malfeasance or incompetence.

The Power of the Marginal Shareholder

Of course, litigation only represents one means of preserving a social enterprise's mission. As highlighted by the remarkable contests over the missions of the Sierra Club and the RSPCA, exercising control over a board offers the clearest path toward controlling an incorporated (for-profit or nonprofit) entity. As a rule, those in the minority cannot exert control over directors on their own. Like the insurgents at the Sierra Club and the RSPCA, campaigns to unseat directors rely on winning support—votes—from fellow shareholders or members. A small shareholder convinced that a social enterprise's mission needs new oversight can advocate and even vote for change, but could accomplish nothing alone. Unilateral action would be an empty gesture. Like a stag hunt on a grand scale, an effort to bring the board of a widely held corporation to heel would require a shareholder to win cooperation from his peers. A challenge for a shareholder of any corporation, this path becomes even thornier when the venture has more than one bottom line.

If the board of a widely held social enterprise appears to be falling prey to the lure of profit, a vigilant shareholder could invest time and effort in campaigning for change. The success of those efforts would, of course, hinge on the willingness of other shareholders to join the campaign. The same would be true of its for-profit equivalent, but the presence of a second bottom line would, perversely, make it more difficult for shareholders committed to a double bottom line to rely on one another than it would be for shareholders in a venture focused on profit.

The board's shift toward profit may simply represent an acknowledgment that the market mechanism will tend to move any social enterprise's shares toward owners relatively uncommitted to balancing mission and profit. If shareholders have the power to jettison mission entirely in favor of profits and a decisive shift toward profits would raise the price of shares in tandem with the profitability of the underlying enterprise, it would be hard to imagine the process unfolding any other way. That flows not from a complete absence of committed investors or even an insufficient depth of commitment from the bulk of the venture's shareholders but from the inevitable existence of a weakest link.

Some number of shareholders with a relatively fragile commitment to preserving a social enterprise's mission will, in effect, be fatal to that mission. At the margins, shareholders with the most tenuous attachment to an enterprise's mission will find it difficult to resist offers inflated by a purchaser's still greater willingness to sacrifice mission for profit. Over the long term, the marginal, rather than the typical, shareholder will determine the fate of a corporate social enterprise.

Once a founder sells equity to a dispersed group of shareholders, investors' commitment to preserving its mission will necessarily fall across a range. Some will give a measure of priority to mission, others will gently emphasize profit, and still others will give them roughly equal billing. Even if most shareholders comfortably occupy a middle ground that accommodates both mission and profit, here it is the shareholders at the periphery that matter. Of a diverse group of shareholders, one will necessarily place the lowest value on mission and a corresponding premium on profits, relative to his peers. Even those not themselves inclined to trade mission for profit must expect that marginal shareholder to accept an offer from a purchaser with an even more profit-oriented vision of the social enterprise's future.

Such transactions pose a subtle existential threat to widely held corporate social enterprises. For a shareholder inclined to call on the support of his fellow owners to counteract a board's shift toward profit, the impact of those profit-focused sales by marginal shareholders need not be as cataclysmic as a bank run to persuade a would-be activist shareholder to stay on the sidelines. The speed with which the unraveling would occur matters less than the simple fact of the inexorable tug of profit at the edges of what might appear to be a close-knit community of shareholders. Each sale of shares in response to that pressure would shift the balance away from mission and make efforts to edge a board in the other direction more difficult and less rewarding.

Game theory acknowledges this entropic pressure. Backward induction describes the process through which the perceived inevitability of a future defection colors the expectations and influences the actions of shareholders.[26] At every decision point, a shareholder anticipates the fate of the social enterprise's mission and thereby speeds its demise. Not only will the shareholders least committed to an enterprise's mission willingly sacrifice it for greater profits, other shareholders—albeit grudgingly—will too.

Over the short term, shareholders may well succeed in swimming against the current in order to reverse an increased focus on profit. If they do, though, there is little reason to expect their success to endure. Shares will continue to drift into the hands of increasingly profit-motivated investors, tilting the electorate further from a focus on mission. This pattern may be no mystery, but its source tends to be misunderstood.

A Sustainable Balance between Profit and Mission

Asking shareholders to police a balance between profit and mission may not be as much of an invitation to disaster as putting foxes in charge of henhouses, but neither is it sustainable. So long as shareholders differ in the degree of their commitment to preserving a social enterprise's mission, a loose thread will cause a for-profit's commitment to mission to unravel. Heterogeneity will precipitate transactions that put shares in the hands of increasingly profit-oriented investors. Faced with the prospect of remaining faithful to their proverbial stag hunt while knowing that each new shareholder's commitment is likely to be more diluted than his predecessor's, even staunch supporters of a double bottom line will sooner or later find themselves ready to sell. Again, maintaining control and keeping stock in the hands of a few known and trusted parties remains a viable strategy, but only for firms and founders willing to trade the potential to scale for the security that intimacy provides.

As later chapters show, a sustainable balance could be struck with the aid of support—or, better yet, enforcement—from a source beyond the shareholders themselves. Although first-generation hybrid legal forms leave mission vulnerable, the second-generation MPH shields a social enterprise's commitment from those entropic pressures. FLY paper shows how those with sufficient resources could accomplish the same feat without help from government. SE(c)(3) envisions an unorthodox intervention by a public actor that would enable even a shoestring social enterprise to broadcast a reliable signal of commitment across its investor community.

All of these possibilities exist against a backdrop of efforts to create a robust set of performance measures for dual-mission enterprises. The evolution of that framework could help to make the MPH, FLY paper, and SE(c)(3) realities. In concert, reliable metrics and second-generation legal tools could offer dual-mission ventures the turnkey simplicity the law has long offered for-profits and nonprofits.

Conclusion

An off-the-shelf source of prospective enforcement of a balance between mission and profit for social enterprise remains a critical absence. For nonprofits, the puritanical clarity provided by the nondistribution constraint and the public enforcement it facilitates offers reassurance and stability (and, perhaps most importantly, modest enforcement costs). At the other end of the spectrum, for-profits rely on market pressures and costly, but potentially lucrative, shareholder lawsuits. Those mechanisms impose order where the freedom for-profits enjoy to embrace an idiosyncratic vision of the imperative to advance the interests of shareholders would otherwise create chaos. Both of these organizational forms allow ventures to attract and deploy capital without concern that those providing or utilizing it will upset settled expectations. They create trust.

Like their for-profit and nonprofit counterparts, social enterprises need capital to animate their unique visions of prosperity. And they, too, face a trust deficit. Without a bright-line prohibition to anchor public enforcement or an ability to harness private self-interest, however, social enterprises must rely on a different approach to generate trust. To attract the capital they require, social enterprises need a mechanism capable of reassuring investors and entrepreneurs of their shared commitment to a double bottom line.

The law offers numerous ways to fashion such mechanisms, and the chapters that follow turn to exploring these options. Chapter 2's MPH proposal demonstrates how a legal form could successfully bring social entrepreneurs and investors together. It adapts a range of proven enforcement mechanisms to improve on the first generation of legal technology represented by benefit corporation and other hybrid legal form statutes described in chapter 3. Chapters 4 and 5 offer more unorthodox alternatives that deploy commonplace legal tools— financial instruments and tax regimes—in novel ways. The proposals at the heart of those chapters address shortcomings of more traditional approaches and reveal potentially significant opportunities to be explored through innovations in measurement and exit-planning charted in *Social Enterprise Law*'s remaining chapters.

2

Prioritizing Mission with a
Mission-Protected Hybrid

Chapter 1 sets the stage for what follows by throwing a spotlight on the need for trust between social entrepreneurs and impact investors. Second-generation legal tools provide the assurances needed for capital to flow so social enterprises can grow in order to pursue their mutual goals. This chapter takes up that challenge by describing the contours of an ideal legal form for social enterprises to adopt, offering a counterpoint to the first-generation legal forms. Legislation creating a second-generation form for social enterprise solves the assurance game investors and entrepreneurs face by crafting a form that functions as a brand. Just as first-generation forms telegraph the aspirations of adopting ventures, this second-generation corporate form conveys trust.

The brand concept originated when western ranches permanently marked their cattle. It took off in the realm of consumer marketing, referring to a "[n]ame, term, design, symbol, or any other feature that identifies one seller's good or service as distinct from those of other sellers."[1] Today, brands as diverse as Walmart, Google, Uber, the Red Cross, Habitat for Humanity, and even our home borough of Brooklyn convey a sense of the businesses, nonprofits, and governments these brands market. Just any catchy or familiar name or symbol will not create a brand, however. "A brand exists when it . . . acquire[s] the power to influence the market."[2]

For a legal form to solve the assurance game experienced by social entrepreneurs and investors with a brand, it must do all of these things. The form must identify an adopting entity as one with a trustworthy commitment to a dual mission of profit and purpose. This would strongly differentiate entities adopting the branded form from others using traditional nonprofit or for-profit forms. To serve its intended function, the signal broadcast by the form would need to be powerful enough to influence the relevant market. Adoption of the form must engender confidence in founders and investors that they can trust each other's commitment because they believe this brand means their mutual interests will be protected.

Effective brands create a set of unique, strong, and favorable mental associations.[3] When founders adopt a nonprofit form, it communicates their deep
commitment to achieving social good, because the rules of the road for these
forms prohibit distribution of profits to owners. Any profits must be reinvested
toward pursuing mission. On the other hand, adopting a for-profit form signals a focus on financial returns. A specialized form for social enterprise will
be unique because of its core commitment to a double bottom line. Owners will
receive profit distributions, which clearly distinguishes these forms from nonprofit forms. Unlike for-profit forms, legislation will demand that adopting entities make social mission essential. For a specialized social enterprise form to
operate as an effective brand, this dual commitment must be explicit, staking
out an entirely new category of organization without lingering associations with
traditional nonprofit or for-profit forms.

While the importance of rhetoric here should not be understated, an expressive victory alone will not suffice. For a specialized legal form to function as a
brand on which investors and entrepreneurs will rely, the associations it creates
must be strong. For its adoption to persuade investors and entrepreneurs to
place their funds and their visions at risk, it must persuade each group that the
form will protect against the other's defection to a purely profit-driven approach.
The form should assure founders that adopting it will deter investors without a
deep commitment to maintaining the firm's social mission. Likewise, it should
reassure investors that neither those running the firm nor their fellow investors
would involve themselves with an entity formed in this manner if they were not
fully committed to social goals. Only then can a legal form function as a brand
capable of solving the trust problem inhibiting enterprise capital formation.

As an important first step to providing this reassurance, legislation creating the form would explicitly require adopting entities to espouse a dual mission. Legislatures must also include two other key components, however, for the
form to be capable of influencing the market of social enterprise founders and
investors. First, enabling legislation must impose a mandate that adopting entities not only pursue social good, but prioritize it. The brand will fail if it merely
instructs adopting entities to "do both" social good and profit generation and
leaves their leaders to figure out the trade-offs. This would communicate only a
weak, muddy signal. Instead, legislation must direct adopting entities to prioritize social good over their pursuit of profit. Second, and just as important, the
form must provide reliable mechanisms to enforce this prioritization mandate.
For the form to brand adopting social enterprises as safe spaces for entrepreneurs and investors to connect their ideas and capital, its mandate cannot be
merely aspirational. They must believe that entities adopting the form will live
up to it.

The rest of this chapter develops a model for such an ideal form: the mission-
protected hybrid, or MPH. Like the familiar *MPH* on roadside signs everywhere,

this MPH creates a speed limit, though here on avarice rather than velocity. The MPH begins with the for-profit corporate framework, but varies its standard components in important ways. Through its social good prioritization mandate, MPH legislation establishes a boundary beyond which adopting entities may not stray. Also like its namesake, the MPH form creates a norm of compliance through a range of enforcement mechanisms. In our MPH, rather than speed traps and red-light cameras, legislation installs a series of enforcement tools designed to assure investors and entrepreneurs that they can trust each other's commitments.

The Prioritization Mandate

Stakeholders may each want a very different balance of profit and social good from the social enterprise in which they invest. As discussed in chapter 1, the inability of social entrepreneurs and impact investors to send a reliable signal of their commitment generates instability and a lack of trust that hinders capital formation. The social enterprise concept's fluidity might appeal to an entrepreneur developing what she hopes will be a wildly profitable green-technology venture, to an investor committed to training individuals living at the "base of the pyramid" to become economically self-sufficient franchise operators without much concern for financial return, or to the founder of a small business producing artisanal products with a local, low-income labor force and expecting a modest return on investment. Prioritization of social good will not eliminate all of the nuances across widely divergent stakeholders like these. Research on both sides will remain paramount in determining with whom one wants to go into business. The MPH form's requirement that adopting entities prioritize social good will, however, create a sheltered focal point around which entrepreneurs and investors can come together, confident of each other's bona fides.

Additionally, prioritization of social good allows a specialized social enterprise brand to differentiate itself from other available forms. Differentiation is key to branding. By convincing consumers that one needs different products for washing plates and washing clothes, Procter & Gamble can market Dawn dishwashing liquid without fear it will cannibalize its sales of Tide laundry detergent. Legislatures creating legal forms of organization do not seek market share in the same way as consumer products powerhouses like P&G. For a specialized form to be a meaningful brand to social enterprise stakeholders, it must convince them to trust that the new entity will avoid the problems caused by existing products, here not unsightly streaks on dishes but an excessive emphasis on profits. Nonprofit forms suffer from an obvious flaw; the non-distribution constraint blocks the profit distribution social enterprises seek. Traditional for-profit forms, though, provide ample room to pursue social good when it maps onto profitability, and even bless reasonable charitable contributions. Accordingly, differentiation from for-profit forms is crucial. The MPH distinguishes itself from standard for-profit vehicles by requiring adopting firms to pursue profits but prioritize social good. Boldly emphasizing social mission offers a crisp mirror image of the focal point generated by traditional for-profit entities.

Prioritization is also crucial to enforcement. Regardless of the individual or institution tasked with enforcing the requirements of a specialized form for social enterprise, the dual-mission nature of these entities will impede its efforts. In a conundrum recognized at least since biblical times, serving two masters can lead to conflict and disappointment. The masters the Bible references are money and God—not too far removed from the profit and social good to be served by social enterprises—and it insists that a person simply cannot be devoted to both.[4] The social enterprise concept rests on the belief that, over the long term, pursuit of profit and social good can be mutually reinforcing. But, at many individual moments, one goal will need to be sacrificed for the other. If the form offers no guidance as to how to break a tie, it will be impossible to police these entities or their leaders.

If one goal must be first among equals, prioritizing social good becomes the only real option.[5] Selecting profit as the ultimate priority would leave too little daylight between social enterprise and traditional for-profit companies. From a branding perspective, it would also stymie any attempt to distinguish a new specialized legal form from existing for-profit forms. The mandate to prioritize social good differentiates the MPH from both nonprofit and for-profit alternatives. Further, it provides a baseline against which investors and entrepreneurs can build—and enforce—expectations.

Through Profit's Looking Glass: A For-Profit Form Prioritizing Mission

Legislators seeking models for the MPH prioritization mandate, however, will find very few. Existing for-profit and nonprofit legal forms rarely offer direct instruction on organizational objectives and furnish only limited guidance on the proper aims of their leaders. Profit is undeniably what most for-profit founders and investors seek from their involvement with their corporations. Yet for-profit corporate statutes are general in nature, allowing corporate formation for any lawful purpose. Further, their fiduciary duty provisions impose obligations of care and loyalty on directors and officers, but do not explicitly command them to seek profits. Indeed, this lack of clarity lies at the heart of one of the major debates in for-profit corporate jurisprudence: whether and to what extent for-profit corporations, and their directors, must pursue value maximization for shareholders.[6]

The issue was raised most famously in *Dodge v. Ford Motor Co.*[7] The Dodge brothers, early investors in Ford with their eyes on establishing a competing car company of their own, objected to Henry Ford's decision to reduce dividends paid to shareholders. Profits would be used instead to lower prices for products and expand manufacturing capacity. The Dodges brought suit seeking higher dividends than the board Henry Ford controlled had issued, and challenging his pricing and expansion plans. The plaintiffs argued that Ford was running the company for the benefit of its employees or perhaps society generally, and Henry Ford's statements about the company's excessive profitability and commitment to reducing auto prices and increasing employee wages tended to support them. Michigan's for-profit corporation statute did not identify the proper objectives of adopting entities. The Michigan Supreme Court's opinion in the case, however, declared that "a business corporation is organized and carried on primarily for the profit of the stockholders. The powers of the directors are to be employed for that end."[8] Proponents of the view that for-profit corporations and their directors must treat maximization of shareholder value as their lodestar obviously find comfort in this statement.

Yet the *Dodge* court only required Ford's board to reconsider its dividend decision, and it affirmed directors' broad discretion to set prices and make expansion and other business decisions. Advocates for a broader view of acceptable for-profit corporate objectives can simply reject the court's statement about the primacy of profit as mere "dicta": language of a court opinion that is not necessary to the decision it ultimately renders, and which therefore does not wield precedential force.[9] The decision can also be read narrowly, to articulate only special protections for minority shareholders at the mercy of a potentially tyrannical majority, rather than corporate objectives or fiduciary duties in general.

Although nearly 100 years old and creating binding precedent only for corporations formed under Michigan law, *Dodge* continues to drive a debate about corporate objectives that remains very much alive. In 2010, the influential Delaware Chancery Court used language reminiscent of *Dodge* in a case pitting eBay against craigslist.[10] Delaware plays an outsized role in US corporate law. For a variety of historical and other reasons, over half of all publicly traded companies incorporate in this second smallest state in the nation. Though it is home to fewer than a million people, 64 percent of Fortune 500 companies choose Delaware as their state of incorporation, and so did craigslist.[11] The state of a company's incorporation governs disputes over its fiduciaries' conduct and other internal affairs.[12] So, when the majority shareholders of craigslist took a number of actions to marginalize eBay, the company's minority shareholder, after eBay began competing in the online classified ad business, eBay brought its claims to the Delaware courts. The controlling shareholders defended some of their actions on grounds they were protecting the company's community-minded culture from the threat posed by eBay.

Like the Michigan court in *Dodge*, the Delaware court's opinion is subject to conflicting interpretations. In rejecting craigslist's claims that eBay's actions created a threat against which its directors could take action, the court said that the for-profit corporate form "is not an appropriate vehicle for purely philanthropic ends."[13] Despite this apparent embrace of the shareholder primacy norm, the very same sentence ends with the qualification "at least not when there are other stockholders interested in realizing a return on their investment."[14] Like *Dodge*, *eBay* can be read as staking out protections for minority shareholders rather than imposing generally applicable rules on the proper objectives for a for-profit corporation.

The case arose in the context of defensive actions—decisions made by a company's current leaders to shield the company from transactions with potential to shift control over it. Courts scrutinize these actions with particular zeal, as corporate fiduciaries face an inherent conflict of interest when they act defensively. Fiduciaries may be trying to protect the company; but adopting defenses will also help directors to protect their own positions. Just a few lines after the eBay decision appears to open the door to motivations other than profit, at least in some contexts, the pendulum seems to swing back toward shareholder value maximization, emphasizing that the duties of craigslist's fiduciaries "include acting to promote the value of the corporation for the benefit of its stockholders."[15] Notably, even in this charged defensive context, the court describes the profit imperative neither as exclusive nor primary.

And then there is *Hobby Lobby*. As corporations are creatures of state law, the US Supreme Court rarely makes pronouncements on their purposes or regarding corporate law more generally, but in the majority opinion of the 2013 watershed case on the Obamacare contraceptive mandate it did just that. In *Burwell v. Hobby Lobby Stores, Inc.*,[16] several closely held for-profit corporations challenged the requirement to provide contraceptive coverage as part of their employer-sponsored health plans, citing the Religious Freedom Restoration Act's free exercise guarantee. Defending the mandate, the government argued that for-profit corporations could not invoke free exercise protection for the exercise of religion, in part because of their profit-seeking nature. In rejecting this claim, Justice Samuel Alito properly looked to state law, under which the plaintiff companies could incorporate for any lawful business or purpose. He also went further, stating that "[w]hile it is certainly true that a central objective of for-profit corporations is to make money, modern corporate law does not require for-profit corporations to pursue profit at the expense of everything else, and many do not do so."[17] Courts and scholars will no doubt continue to ponder the limits of for-profit corporations' ability to diverge from the shareholder value maximization norm. As this open debate stems, at least in part, from the lack of statutory language addressing for-profit corporations' proper objectives, those crafting an MPH prioritization mandate will find few lessons in for-profit corporate law.

For-profit forms do, of course, range beyond corporations. But statutory specifications of objectives for unincorporated entities offer no greater clarity. Some reference business purposes; others use even more generic formulations, allowing unincorporated entities to pursue any lawful purpose, whether it relates to business activity or otherwise.[18] This lack of statutory precision presents even less of an issue than in for-profit corporate law because of the primacy of contract for unincorporated entities. Those advising partnerships and limited liability companies (LLCs) design individualized partnership or operating agreements to govern their entities. Generic statutory defaults exert less influence, and the variety of individual agreements makes them difficult to categorize. Under many state laws, LLC members can even vary fiduciary duties to a considerable degree. Enabling statutes for these forms too, therefore, offer little guidance to those crafting a prioritization mandate for an MPH.

Nonprofit corporate law will prove only slightly more helpful. Nonprofit corporation statutes speak in quite general terms, permitting incorporation for "any lawful purpose."[19] Some do include more specific purpose requirements for charitable nonprofits, typically employing a list and including the objectives one would expect—such as pursuit of religion, education, and the relief of poverty. Statutes going as far back as the English Statute of Charitable Uses of 1601, however, also include a catchall category like "purposes beneficial to the community."[20] As this category has a broad reach and most statutory lists explicitly decline to be exclusive, nonprofit incorporation statutes provide adopters a very large berth for their organization's goals. Fiduciary duty provisions also speak obliquely, if at all, about the purposes nonprofit leaders should pursue, generally invoking care or prudence and the best interests of the corporation. The best interests of a nonprofit logically demand devotion to mission, but statutes do not address this explicitly.

The real work of distinguishing nonprofit entities tends to be done through limitations on their activities. Though stray cases and statutory references can be found prohibiting charitable nonprofit corporations from engaging in business, pecuniary, commercial, or political activities, state law uniformly bars them from distribution of profits to owners.[21] Without the ability to distribute profits to owners, business activity is possible, but accepting equity capital is not. This nondistribution constraint, which does not limit what nonprofits *can do* but only what they *can do with their profits*, is what marks and enforces the boundary between nonprofit and for-profit endeavor.[22]

MPH legislation will break new ground by affirmatively mandating social good prioritization. Legislation enabling existing legal forms addresses organizational objectives only broadly, if at all. Instructions to fiduciaries enjoin them to undertake their jobs with care and loyalty, but do not articulate those duties beyond general invocations to pursue the entity's best interest. Prioritization mandates imposed both in provisions spelling out the proper objectives of an MPH and the duties of its fiduciaries will differentiate it from existing for-profit and nonprofit alternatives. Affirmative prioritization will set MPH apart, a differentiation critical for the MPH to succeed as a brand—another reason to highlight this feature in the legislative text.

Operationalizing the Mandate

Legislation creating the MPH form will first address prioritization in a provision on proper purposes. Adopting entities will be explicitly permitted to earn and distribute profits, but will also be unambiguously required to prioritize their pursuit of social good. In simple, straightforward language the statute would say: "Corporations organized under this chapter will pursue both social good and profit for owners, but pursuit of social good will be prioritized." Requiring social mission to be prioritized, rather than pursued exclusively and at all costs, leaves room for adopting entities to take many profit-maximizing actions. Imposing the mandate as a purpose requirement makes clear that every decision need not demonstrably prioritize social good over profit. Rather, the mandate demands only that a social enterprise organized as an MPH be able to show that it prioritizes social good in the aggregate.

This nonexclusivity echoes the charitable purpose requirements found in nonprofit corporate law. After all, a museum organized as a charitable nonprofit formed to pursue educational goals can certainly choose to discontinue a lecture series when its attendance falls below the number sufficient to justify the costs of hiring the speakers. It may do so even if this decision reduces the education remaining attendees might have received, and even if it increases the entity's revenues, profits, or both. Likewise, an MPH organized to manufacture and distribute low-cost lanterns in the developing world in an effort to combat poverty need not violate the prioritization mandate by choosing a supplier that produces the metal sheeting it needs at the lowest price point. It may do so even if patronizing higher priced suppliers would result in higher pay for some low-income manufacturing workers. As long as the entity's broader constellation of actions prioritizes its antipoverty mission, individual decisions will not run afoul of the relevant purpose requirements.

On its own, the purpose requirement will not adequately protect an MPH's mission. The prioritization mandate must also be incorporated into its fiduciary standards. As in other corporate contexts, MPH fiduciaries will be required to discharge their duties in a manner they reasonably believe to be in the best interests of the MPH. But MPH legislation will define the best interests of the MPH as prioritization of social good. MPH legislation will thereby fold the overarching commitment to prioritization into fiduciary law, while still retaining the valuable work done by the conventional twin duties of care and loyalty.

The duty of care requires organizational leaders to act with the level of diligence and prudence a reasonable person would take under similar circumstances. When a court reviews a claim that a fiduciary has failed to meet that standard, however, it does so with great deference. We all have had the experience of realizing in hindsight that we have made a poor choice. Overzealous review of the quality of fiduciaries' decisions would make them excessively conservative, especially since a violation can result in personal liability. To avoid such an outcome, courts concentrate their review of corporate fiduciaries' decisions on the process by which they are made. Decisions made without sufficient information or while suffering from a conflict of interest come under heavy scrutiny. For decisions made using appropriate procedures, courts instead apply the "business judgment rule."[23] They decline to substitute their after-the-fact business judgment for that of the directors involved at the time, and impose liability based on the poor quality of a decision only when it was essentially irrational.

Courts much more easily find fiduciary violations when an organizational leader breaches the duty of loyalty. This obligation requires a fiduciary to serve her organization's interests rather than her own. It obviously bars stealing from the organization—as would the criminal law—but also limits a fiduciary's ability to compete or transact with her organization. Conflicts of interest, when a fiduciary stands on both sides of a deal, can be perilous for fiduciaries, who risk personal liability if they fail to meet exacting standards of procedural and substantive fairness.[24]

Social enterprises, like all other businesses, need to take risks to succeed and can act only through their leaders. MPH statutes will therefore not displace the deferential, process-focused approach to the duty of care. They will also leave in place a strong loyalty obligation, as the most basic defense against fiduciaries acting to enrich themselves. To this useful pair of duties, MPH legislation will add its express clarification that the best interest of an MPH is defined by prioritization of its social mission.[25]

The prioritization mandate will not only constrain, but will also provide helpful guidance to fiduciaries. When faced with the inevitable trade-offs between enhancing profit for owners and generating greater social good, directors and officers can ask themselves, "If I opt for greater profit in this decision, can I still reasonably argue that the organization prioritizes social mission?" Courts evaluating fiduciary decision-making will also be able to employ this lens. Of course, reviewing courts can be expected to offer some deference to organizational leaders. Still, the potential for prioritization to be reviewed should impel fiduciaries to make an implicit or explicit assessment of the trade-offs between profit and social good as they run their enterprises, and to resolve close cases in favor of social mission. With prioritization plainly provided by the MPH statute, all stake-holders will be put on notice of this important organizational bias.

Anticipating Critiques

Critics of the prioritization standard might decry it as vague, noting in particu-lar its failure to define "social good." But the absence of a definition is a feature of MPH legislation, not a bug. The term, like the legal concept of charity, cannot help but be capacious. Social good under an MPH statute will include the broad range of traditionally charitable activity, as well as pursuing the interests of the great variety of organizational stakeholders by benefiting employees, improving the local economy, conserving environmental resources, and any other lawful vision of creating good for society. MPH status would offer founders no signifi-cant legal benefits beyond its branding value and a more aptly structured organi-zational form with access to limited liability. As limited liability is already widely available under a range of existing legal forms, MPH legislation can afford to be generous. MPH legislation will create a recognizable brand not by circumscrib-ing the type of social good adopting entities can pursue, but by requiring them to prioritize their chosen social goals over profit for investors.

To some, prioritization's emphasis on cumulative social good will also seem nebulous. More clarity for adopting entities and their leaders could come from stripping away one of the two competing goals: profit or purpose. But narrow-ing the obligations of MPHs and their leaders to a single goal would betray the core of the double bottom line. After all, the uncertainty as to how much social good and how much profit an MPH must produce flows from the dual nature of the social enterprise concept itself. If social ends can be well served by an organization engaged in both social good production and profit generation, the legal form developed to house them cannot amputate one. Moreover, the result would merely replicate the single-purpose nonprofit or for-profit forms already available.

Legislatures might attempt to provide guidance by requiring adopting enti-ties to show that a certain percentage of their efforts pursue social good. The right percentage might be a bare majority, or perhaps something greater, and effort would need to be reduced to some measure, such as expenditures or revenues. Despite the appeal of such a reductive approach, we advocate the more open-ended legislative standard. Access to an organizational form is policed lightly at the outset. State officials receiving a request for MPH status could not effectively test the prospective claims applicants would make about meeting these percentage requirements. Instead, as discussed below, MPH leg-islation would utilize a rough preponderance-of-expenditures rule to anchor a mandatory annual review process to safeguard the statutory prioritization mandate.

The Need for Enforcement

A prioritization mandate will be a paper tiger unless MPH legislation also provides some means of enforcement. Building the mutual trust necessary to solve the stag hunt problem preventing social enterprise founders and would-be investors from capitalizing their ventures requires more than aspiration. For adoption of a legal form to function as a strong brand, there must be quality control. People buy Coke because they trust they will be getting a very particular type of fizzy, sweet brown liquid in each can. If consumers learned (the hard way) that some cans instead contained motor oil—or even iced tea—the strength of the brand would dissolve. Likewise, for a legal form to work as a brand, its prioritization requirement must be reliably enforced. The branding work of a legal form begins by recognizing the responsibility adopting entities have to prioritize social good. For the brand to convince investors and entrepreneurs to risk their money and their dreams on each other, however, the form must provide protection rather mere acceptance.

Unfortunately, this task requires far more manpower than formulating and enacting new legal standards for entities and their fiduciaries. The work of enforcement mechanisms will not be done when a legislature approves a statute and a governor signs it. They must be designed not for the showroom, but for the road. They will succeed only when they can be relied upon to use the MPH form to motivate, if not force, entities to be truly different from standard for-profits.

The MPH form will incorporate an array of enforcement mechanisms, aimed at creating confidence in the strength of its brand.[26] Some operate at formation, limiting access to MPH status at the outset. The more potent enforcement tools subject adopting entities to continuing review for compliance with the prioritization mandate, especially at the moment when entities seek to exit the form. This arsenal of overlapping enforcement techniques also draws on a deep pool of enforcers, including government officials, private certifying bodies, investors and other stakeholders, and even potential competitors. Many are adapted from methods used in policing for-profit and nonprofit entities and their leaders, but each is carefully adjusted to take account of the social enterprise context.

Compliance on Entry

The first enforcement window for the MPH's prioritization mandate opens at inception. Other legal forms dispense with preformation review but the MPH's corporate architecture provides an initial screening process. For example, general partnerships arise whenever there is "an association of two or more persons to carry on as co-owners a business for profit."[27] No government regulator need be involved; in fact, a partnership can arise even without the knowledge of the partners involved. Settlors of charitable trusts must create their entities deliberately, but they too can do so without notifying the state or anyone else of their actions. Corporate forms, as well as the limited liability company, require founding documents to be filed with a state official. To ensure at least a cursory gatekeeping role for the state, MPH legislation will follow suit and require filing.

Of course, the secretary of state's office confirms only that applicants have complied with the basic requirements for proper articles of incorporation or organization, such as organizational name and an address for service of process. Those who fail to meet these simple requirements must cure their defaults in order to incorporate or form their LLC. The process is straightforward, and can move fast.[28] Submissions often may be made online; Delaware even offers a "one-hour" process.[29] MPH legislation will require state actors reviewing formative documents to screen them for a statement identifying the MPH's social mission and commitment to prioritizing it. While valuable, this kind of nominal review will not, on its own, build trust between investors and entrepreneurs.

MPH legislation will not attempt to impose more meaningful scrutiny during this initial review process because doing so would be pointless. Governmental bodies or private delegates could be tasked to test applicants' business models and future plans. But deep inquiry into future actions would be wasted effort. The problem facing social enterprises in need of capital is one of building trust between entrepreneur and investor. Investors can already review a company's business model and future plans, and presumably have done so if they plan to invest. Entrepreneurs know their plans; their worry is that investors lack the commitment to maintain the double bottom line if they must sacrifice profits to do so. External endorsement that an entity's plan at formation does, indeed, contemplate pursuit of a dual mission and commit to prioritize social good will not lead MPH status to function as a strong brand. This initial review will do little to convince the two to trust each other beyond this moment. Other, more robust methods must provide each with reassurance that the other will not unilaterally abandon the commitment to social enterprise over a longer time horizon.

Compliance over Time

MPH legislation will include both external and internal enforcement mechanisms to test compliance with the prioritization mandate over time. External enforcement relies on disclosure. The statute will assign a new or existing public agency to receive annual reports, review these disclosures for compliance with the prioritization mandate, and penalize those who fail to conform. MPH legislation will also provide for ongoing enforcement from within adopting entities themselves. By empowering shareholders with informational, voting, and litigation rights, an investor will be able to scrutinize her MPH and its fiduciaries, and challenge their missteps.

Disclosure

Existing nonprofit and for-profit corporate forms rely heavily on disclosure-based methods of enforcement. States require nonprofits holding charitable assets to submit financial information annually to the state attorney general.[30] In addition, those who receive federal tax exemption must file an informational tax return with the federal Internal Revenue Service.[31] These disclosures (often referred to as "Forms 990"), vary in complexity by organizational size and provide up-to-date information on tax-exempt nonprofits' revenue and expenditures, as well as details about their activities and governance. Of course, for-profit entities selling registered securities must also make a variety of reports to the SEC and the public.[32] These reports must be issued at regular intervals and supplemented by special reports in response to significant events. Many state statutes also require corporations to make annual financial reports to shareholders or members. MPH legislation will likewise impose disclosure requirements on adopting entities, and will add to financial data requirements a demand that they document compliance with the prioritization mandate.

Mandatory Reporting

An MPH will confirm compliance by reporting a combination of qualitative and quantitative data annually. Narrative reports on the activities of reporting organizations will give reviewers important details of the MPH's activities, but also tend to paint authoring entities in the best possible light. As the glossy annual reports produced by companies and charities show, it is easy to play up one's strengths in a long-form document. To provide greater insight into whether it continues to prioritize social good, each MPH will also report on the balance of expenditures made in pursuit of profit and those made in pursuit of social good. Reporting an imbalance in favor of social good will support a presumption of compliance; the opposite imbalance will be a red flag.

To mitigate the sharp edges of this expenditure test, MPH legislation will structure it as a "comply or explain" obligation. Each adopting entity will be required to report its expenditures for pursuing social good and those for generating profits every year, with dual-purpose expenditures allocated between the two categories. Compliance with the prioritization mandate may be shown through an imbalance of expenditures, with social good expenditures outpacing those for profit generation. An entity unable to show such an imbalance, however, would also be permitted to provide supplementary data demonstrating that it continues to prioritize social good.

There are, of course, drawbacks to expenditure-based reporting. First, the challenge in designing accurate metrics cannot be understated, and chapter 6 takes up this crucial issue. Even in assessing an entity's dedication to generating value for owners, one might consider revenue generated, profit cleared, dividends distributed, or some combination of these measures. Measuring an entity's dedication to social good is yet more complex, but comparing expenditures will rely on information relatively easily extracted from an organization's financial records. Expenditure reporting can still be manipulated, but it is easier to evaluate documentation of concrete expenditures than platitudes and stories of redemption.

Second, disclosures can be quite costly to produce. For comparison, the cost of completing the standard Form 990, in employee time, accounting expertise, etc., motivated the IRS to issue a new Form 990-N. This extremely brief report can be filed by tax-exempt organizations with annual gross receipts of $50,000 or less. It includes only identifying and address information for the reporting entity and its principal officer, confirmation of its gross receipts below the threshold, and an opportunity to indicate the entity is going out of business. For extremely small and new social enterprises, reporting costs to show continuing compliance with the prioritization mandate could be overwhelming. For MPH status realistically to be available for embryonic social enterprises, exceptions like the Form 990-N would be important. Since the MPH aims to serve entities large enough to attract capital from beyond the range of a founder's family and friends, imposing overhead costs of reasonable reporting obligations should not be fatal.

Third, the expenditure metric could at times create perverse incentives. Consider a green-technology company formed as an MPH and seeking to maintain its ability to report compliance with the prioritization mandate. The intent of the mandate is to push the company to choose social good—in this case environmental protection—over profit as a general matter. But imagine it is faced with a choice of two inputs for its product. The manufacturing processes for both inputs have the same environmental impact, but because of unrelated factors, one input is more expensive. The company could select the higher-cost product to bank extra social good expenditures, ensuring its margin of compliance, but not actually increasing its social good generation and perhaps making a poor business decision. In theory, increasing the sensitivity of the allocation process and the rigor of the scrutiny of disclosures could solve this problem. But no evaluator of MPH reports will be as expert in every area of business as all of the regulated entities. Even with delegation, at some point, this kind of over-counting is unavoidable.

The final problem is the precise opposite. The expenditure metric can also undercount social good generation because not all benefits will be traceable back to specific expenditures. To which expenditures can a social enterprise point when pricing its services below the market-clearing rate to create a market for them among low-income consumers? There also might be multiplier effects, whereby the mere existence of the social enterprise generates social good beyond that which its expenditures would track. Consider the value of educational technology developed by a social enterprise for underperforming low-income school districts that radiates back through the students utilizing it, but also their families and communities. Tracking expenditures alone will miss some of these important benefits. A degree of slippage is inherent in any system of metrics, particularly one deployed to track an issue as complex as social good generation. Even accepting this fact, though, expenditure data would give regulators considerable insight into compliance with the prioritization mandate. By allowing for "comply or explain," those entities suffering an undercount can make a case for compliance in an alternative fashion.

Who Will Review?

Of course, for disclosure-based regulation to reassure investors and entrepreneurs that their commitments will be enforced, someone must review these disclosures and effectively penalize noncompliance. Existing legal forms rely on a mix of government regulators, stakeholders, and market actors to review and act on information gained through disclosures, and so would MPH. Adopting entities would be required to make their reports available to investors and the public, but also would be subjected to regulatory review. Since the MPH is a new legal form established under state law, one obvious regulator candidate is the state attorney general. The AG's experience monitoring charitable nonprofits has some similarity to the task proposed for MPH review, suggesting state AGs might be prepared for the job. In fact, however, AG investigations rarely arise from review of the voluntary disclosures by charities, which unsurprisingly paint their activities in the best possible light. Instead, attorneys general typically respond to whistleblower tips and media investigations.

Moreover, state AGs concentrate their nonprofit enforcement efforts on rooting out lapses in financial accountability like embezzlement, unfair compensation, or charitable solicitation fraud. These types of actions best use their skills as investigators and prosecutors; they are also more politically salient. After all, what makes better news copy for an AG than exposing a charity stealing from its beneficiaries? In contrast, AGs avoid taking on questions of a nonprofit's fidelity to its social mission unless they must. When required to opine on or approve charities' plans to sell a major asset, dissolve, or seek court approval to change their purposes under the cy pres doctrine, the process can generate bitter conflicts. Understandably, they have little appetite for conflagrations like the disputes over moving the Barnes Foundation from its historic home to a new building in downtown Philadelphia[33] and over a decision by trustees to close the Sweet Briar women's college in Virginia.[34] They also require AGs to depart from their professional expertise in prosecuting wrongdoers and use up precious political capital—no matter which side they defend.

Finally, the charity enforcement role of state attorneys general receives little funding. Even AGs in the states with the largest charitable sectors operate with a small team of lawyers and support staff. In many states, only a single assistant attorney general monitors charitable activity, sometimes doing so only part-time. While federal agencies like the IRS or SEC could not take on an enforcement role over purely state entities, state tax or securities authorities could take part, or a new state agency modeled on these federal entities could be contemplated.

Whichever state agency should be assigned to monitor and review MPH disclosures, MPH legislation must identify and fund a regulatory body to do so. Were resources no limitation, the Rolls Royce of regulators would hire a staff with the skills to create perfect metrics, apply them carefully, consistently, and with rare errors. This ideal agency, however, might as well be staffed by fairies wielding magic wands. The realities of diminishing state budgets and the powerful push for limited government dash any hopes for this kind of perfect state regulator. A real-world MPH regulator will require states to make substantial funding commitments, but the perfect need not be the enemy of the good. An adequately staffed and funded new state agency, or a new bureau within an existing agency, could provide accountability gains and useful assurances to investors and founders. This disclosure-based enforcement mechanism would constitute only part of a larger compliance framework imposed by MPH legislation.

State regulators might also leverage their enforcement resources by delegating the tasks of initial and ongoing review of compliance to private certifying bodies. This approach would require an entity to obtain this private certification to access the MPH form. Of course, if they venture beyond the expenditure imbalance review described above, these certifiers will still face the challenge of developing metrics that will reliably evaluate rather than describe. Success will require the right team and sufficient resources, so the problem comes back to funding these certifiers. One cannot solve the state's resource problem by assuming the state will fund the process. Instead, some form of user fees will need to support it. The problems that can arise from requiring payment for certification are well documented. The part supposedly independent rating agencies played in the subprime mortgage implosion is only the latest example of how standards can slip when certifications are needed to pay the bills.

Certification can brand ventures even without being linked to legal form. As chapter 6 explains, harnessing a revealing metric to a robust legal form would allow a social enterprise to make reliable claims about its future as well as its past. For government regulators to rely on private expertise, though, they will need to guard those guardians. Without careful monitoring, private certifiers authorized to grant MPH status will not brand adopting entities as places where investors and entrepreneurs can trust their counterparts. This oversight role will hardly be costless.

Designing a Remedy
Finally, for any disclosure-based enforcement mechanism to ensure those sporting the MPH brand comply, effective remedies must be available. When a state

regulator or its delegated certifying body finds a social enterprise does not prioritize social good, what happens? If the failure manifests at the initial application stage, the applicant will simply be denied access to the form. Founders can use some other legal form and some other mechanism to solve the assurance game that separates them from potential investors. But lapses in prioritization can, and are probably more likely to, occur later—after the social enterprise has adopted the MPH form and even after it has used the form to attract capital. Enforcement will not generate trust if failure means merely striking offending MPHs from the rolls after the fact.

Just like skeptical hunters considering whether to pursue a stag, social entrepreneurs and would-be investors need forward-looking assurances of each other's commitment. They can review each other's background and the organizational documents at the outset for themselves. A legal form serves as a brand to assure each party that its fellows will not be able to unilaterally scrap social good in favor of profit down the line. The MPH designation would function poorly as a brand if it could be effortlessly cast aside when the going gets tough or the dollars start flowing.

Accordingly, MPH legislation will mete out penalties that will hit nonprioritizing entities and their investors in their pocketbook. Government regulators can levy these monetary penalties separately or together with stripping an entity of MPH status. The challenge lies in accurately pricing and timing these penalties. A founder or investor considering abandoning social good in favor of profit will only be given pause by a penalty painful enough to make this profit-earning goal no longer attractive. Penalties must be set high enough that defection will not pay for itself.

That does not mean confiscatory penalties. This nuclear option, perhaps empowering regulators to convert nonprioritizing entities into full-fledged charities, goes too far. The possibility of trapping capital inside adopting entities would loom too large, making MPH status so threatening to investors that they would avoid it entirely. Rather than solving the assurance game faced by investors by creating a strong and enforceable brand, this penalty would be so devastating that it would destroy the category altogether.

Paradoxically, the power of this doomsday penalty could render it impotent. Consider a similar problem in the charitable context that led to the development of sanctions on individuals, rather than organizations. Before 1996, the only remedy the IRS could impose on tax-exempt charities for allowing profits to inure to the benefit of individuals was to remove the victimized charity's designation under section 501(c)(3). Both regulators and regulated entities viewed this remedy as toxic; removing 501(c)(3) status would lead swiftly to a charity's demise. At first blush, one might think this weighty penalty would serve as a strong deterrent to transactions funneling profits away from charitable purposes. However, precisely the opposite was true. Since the removal of 501(c)(3) status amounted to a death penalty for the organization—and its ability to pursue charitable purposes—leaving the individuals who benefited from private inurement unscathed, regulators were loath to impose it. Its actual deterrent effect was negligible, because nobody believed it would be applied. MPH regulators would likewise understand the pall that applying a charity conversion penalty would cast on capital markets that social enterprises seek to access. To avoid undermining the core goal of developing the MPH form, they might unilaterally disarm. If it posed no real threat, it would have no real enforcement effect.

A final lesson emerges from the 501(c)(3) status removal example. Regulators unwilling to apply this penalty still wanted to police conflict-of-interest transactions by tax-exempt entities. To do so, Congress adopted a series of more targeted penalties—imposed on individual parties to these transactions, rather than their organizations.[35] Similarly, transforming a nonprioritizing MPH entity into a charity or imposing a confiscatory fine upon it risks tremendous collateral damage. The problem faced by entrepreneurs and investors is one of coordination. They want assurances of each other's commitment to the dual mission of the organization and to avoid unilateral defection. Replacing the threat of betrayal with the specter of grievous self-inflicted wounds would hardly reassure.

These penalties would also need to be timed with precision. If fines are applied only after it becomes impossible to undo nonprioritizing decisions, the penalty will not right the ship. It will only commandeer or destroy its remaining cargo. Monetary penalties must instead be applied as a corrective before a nonprioritizing course becomes irreversible. Doing so, of course, still risks further straining an entity's balance sheet and heightening the difficulty of prioritizing social good while staying afloat. We recognize that MPH regulators will face a difficult task in identifying the exact moment to impose penalties priced to steer nonprioritizing entities back on course but not sink them. Doing so will require entity-specific information and skill, further raising the costs of enforcement.

To deploy disclosure-based enforcement sufficient to assure founders and investors of each other's commitments over the life of the entity, legislators will need to clear many hurdles. Expenditure reporting will provide a relatively simple metric for evaluating social good prioritization, backstopped by a comply-or-explain option. These disclosures will mean little without review by a skilled regulator, private certifier, or both, and the funds to support such institutions will be elusive. Finally, even able and well-resourced regulators will struggle to launch targeted and precisely timed penalties to nudge entities back toward compliance with the prioritization norm. Rather than simply taxing defection, penalties must bolster the ability of adopting entities to attract capital. States will be unable to construct and pay for such a perfect eye in the sky to police every move of adopting entities. Accordingly, MPH legislation must include additional pathways for complementary enforcement.

Empowering Stakeholders

MPH legislation will also empower stakeholders to police each other. As with government regulation, access to information will be vital. Social enterprise founders and investors with a role in governance will obtain information about the decisions and activities of their firms through their day-to-day responsibilities running their companies. In order for a broader group of stakeholders to take action, they must receive annual reports and any other disclosure documents to be submitted to regulatory bodies. MPH legislation will require such access for passive investors and others, but disclosure alone will be insufficient to allay the mutual suspicion that keeps social enterprise investors and founders apart. Action by stakeholders must be reliable to protect founders and investors against defection.

Those MPH investors with influential roles in governance will be able to pre-empt decisions undermining prioritization of social good. An entrepreneur or investor with a majority position, of course, need not worry about her counterpart's fickleness. Purchasing or maintaining a controlling stake constitutes the most powerful enforcement technique a founder or investor can employ. Majority holders call the shots through direct management decisions or by voting in a set of managers to their liking. For every majority (but not sole) owner, however, there is a minority. Protections can attract capital willing to fill this minority role, and even convince a founder to reduce her stake and share power. In these situations, investors' formal management and voting power may not be sufficient to protect a dual-mission orientation, even though offering a seat at the table and a voice in decision-making may help build goodwill.

For-profit corporate law provides a useful model for enforcement by shareholders without a controlling interest. Shareholders typically must authorize major corporate decisions: mergers, sales of all or substantially all assets, or dissolution. Like the first-generation hybrids considered in chapter 3, MPH legislation will follow suit, assigning shareholders voting rights in each of these instances, as well as in any transaction that would eliminate MPH status. Shareholders also exercise indirect control, electing the directors who manage a corporation's day-to-day affairs. In small and closely held corporations, shareholders and directors may be the same individuals, and rights may be secured through contracts between investors. These shareholder agreements cannot compel specific corporate actions, but can ensure investor input and indirect control through assigned board seats. In small, closely held MPHs, shareholder agreements will be powerful tools. But they are necessarily negotiated between individual shareholders and offer no help to a social entrepreneur seeking dispersed or passive investors. In this setting, the power of voting rights will be limited by a shareholder's membership in an uncoordinated group.

An isolated investor's voting power can be easily overcome by colleagues who prefer a shift to prioritize profit. Such an outcome need not indicate that other investors were disingenuous from the start. Preferences are dynamic. Committed founders and devoted subsequent capital contributors alike can change their minds. Whether these changes result from disillusionment or the possibility of a windfall profit, shareholders content with a deviation from social good prioritization will line up to approve nonprioritizing transactions or fiduciaries who will undertake them. Voting rights will be little comfort to minorities if a new majority coalesces around prioritizing profit.

Litigation rights, the mainstay of most discussion of investor power in for-profit corporate law, do offer a path for enforcement by minority, and even individual, shareholders. Corporate law grants standing for shareholders to challenge the conduct of corporate fiduciaries for failures of care and loyalty. MPH legislation will expand standing to include shareholder challenges that fiduciaries have breached their duty by allowing the entity to overemphasize profit.

This enforcement route is strewn with obstacles. For investors and entrepreneurs to rely on shareholder litigation to enforce their counterparts' commitments, they must have faith that courts will recognize and punish failures to prioritize social good. Courts long reluctant to review the quality of directors' decisions would need to cast aside the business judgment rule's emphasis on process and evaluate substance. In doing so, courts will take on the roles of both a regulator and a certifier. Making their task at once easier and more challenging, they will be asked to conduct this review not over an annual period but with respect to a single decision.

Litigation will also saddle the courts with the problem of remedies. Corporate law imposes personal liability on fiduciaries who violate their duties. How should this liability be set? Consider One World Play Project, a social enterprise selling ultradurable soccer balls on a buy-one, give-one basis, and collaborating with sponsors and nonprofits to distribute the balls to needy children worldwide.[36] Imagine One World Play Project was formed as an MPH, took on investors, and began to grow in popularity and profit. Down the line, several World Cup–level soccer players praise the company's balls as better quality than others on the market. Soccer enthusiasts and leagues begin buying the balls in droves, but do so based on their quality for elite and recreational play, rather than their interest in the social mission of the company.

Seeing this as an opportunity, the board votes to change its business model radically. Messages about the power of play in distressed communities are removed from its marketing materials and replaced with testimonials about the performance of the company's unique balls. Further, the company discontinues its practice of providing a ball to a needy community every time a consumer purchases a ball, retaining a commitment only to make a ball donation for every hundred balls sold. The new approach works, in the sense that it vastly increases profits, but it also significantly reduces the social good the company generates.[37] Disgruntled investors sue directors, alleging a violation of the duty to prioritize social mission, and win on the merits.

Now the court must decide on a remedy. Courts can enjoin the company to return to social good prioritization, if it is possible to do so after the fact. They can also strip it of its MPH status, but that would not help the disappointed social investors who already sank their investment into a company that failed to make good on its promise to generate a social return. Like the IRS under the intermediate sanctions regime policing transactions in which charity fiduciaries suffer conflicts of interest, MPH legislation will authorize courts to impose personal liability on MPH directors and managers.[38]

Unfortunately, pricing liability for MPH fiduciaries will be much more difficult than assigning penalties for self-dealing by tax managers and fiduciaries. Courts cannot simply rely on the diminution in value of investors' stake in the company because this stake may well increase as a result of abandoning prioritization. MPH legislation will authorize courts to levy a punitive damage award, intended to penalize defendant fiduciaries and deter other MPH leaders from following their example. But making this assessment places courts in the shoes of regulators constructing an ex post penalty for nonprioritizing firms identified through disclosure. Unless the remedy imposed on fiduciaries deters others from similar actions, the threat of litigation will ring hollow. Convincing investors and entrepreneurs that courts will accurately assess fiduciaries' compliance with the prioritization mandate and will punish them effectively will be difficult.

Even if courts overcome these problems, procedural difficulties will also bedevil efforts to enforce prioritization through claims of fiduciary breach. Fiduciary claims are derivative in nature, meaning the shareholders who bring them act in the place of the corporation. It is to the corporation that fiduciaries owe their duties, and it is the corporation that suffers harm as a result of the breach, to only the indirect detriment of investors. The nature of the action as one truly on behalf of the corporation means that the corporation's board has the right to halt it. Before the action may begin, shareholders must demand that the board bring the action instead, unless such a demand is excused as futile. Moreover, even after shareholder-initiated litigation has begun, the board can settle and end the case. Although in both situations the board is generally required to act through an independent committee, these fundamental limitations on derivative actions may stop many MPH claims in their tracks. MPH legislation will need to address this and other complexities of derivative claims, like bond requirements, to avoid further muting the enforcement power of investor litigation.

Finally, as highlighted in chapter 1, shareholder enforcement suffers from serious incentive problems. Even an investor who remains deeply committed to prioritizing social good may not be committed enough to bring a costly and time-consuming lawsuit on his own. Why not instead simply sell one's shares, especially if the dissatisfied investor can liquidate her position and find a new destination for her social capital. Disappointed investors may even find remaining invested in a nonprioritizing MPH more attractive than absorbing the costly court and attorneys' fees litigation will produce. They can simply change their expectations for the combination of financial and social returns this investment will generate, and use the greater profits they earn to contribute to other producers of social good.

For shareholder litigation rights to persuade investors and entrepreneurs to trust each other, they must believe that shareholders will bring enforcement actions, despite their expense and difficulty. Spreading the costs of litigation across a group of shareholders makes this enforcement avenue more viable. But finding like-minded colleagues and pooling efforts takes coordination. Investors who attempt to free-ride on the enforcement efforts of others will further undermine this weak tool. In the for-profit corporate context, this problem is partially overcome by attorney coordination of plaintiff suits, in return for payment of fees out of damage awards. To incentivize such a role for lawyers in MPH litigation, legislation will provide for payment of shareholder legal fees in successful cases even if they do not produce monetary damage awards.

Litigation rights could, of course, also be bestowed on stakeholders other than shareholders. MPH legislation could grant standing to enforce fiduciaries' prioritization obligations to an entity's employees, customers, beneficiaries, or even the public at large. Broad grants of standing to police the activities of private entities are unheard of in current for-profit and even nonprofit law out of concern that noninvestor stakeholders would bring wasteful and frivolous nuisance suits. Opening MPH fiduciaries to personal liability in actions from broad swaths of the public would make it hard to recruit qualified board talent and could frighten away potential adopters.

Of course, the fear of strike suits may well be overblown, since noninvestor stakeholders would also face serious incentive problems impeding enforcement. Employees and customers may stand to gain financially from higher wages and reduced prices if they ignore an MPH's failures to prioritize social good, and employees may risk their livelihoods by suing. Consumers, beneficiaries, and the individual citizens would have to be both highly altruistic and well-off to take on litigation, conditions that are very unlikely to exist on a consistent basis, if at all. To solve these incentive problems with group effort requires surmounting difficult collective action problems as well. The twin concerns that noninvestor stakeholders would bring so much litigation that it would undermine adoption of the MPH form and that they would be so inactive as to provide little added enforcement convince us MPH legislation should forgo granting standing to these groups.

MPH legislation would, however, empower state regulators to bring actions against fiduciaries. A single state agency would avoid the coordination problems that figure prominently in stakeholder enforcement. But regulators would bring such claims to courts unaccustomed to evaluating prioritization and would themselves face the funding gaps that compromise disclosure-based enforcement. No matter who sets the wheels in motion, enforcement via litigation alone will be too unpredictable to convince entrepreneurs and investors to trust one another. When paired with disclosure requirements, these techniques will go a long way toward providing the certainty that could bring investors and entrepreneurs together, but would leave one glaring vulnerability in place.

Compliance on Exit

Enforcement mechanisms that operate on exit will provide a crucial third leg to the enforcement stool for MPH legislation. The disclosure regime discussed above will require an MPH planning to dissolve or undertake another transaction that will forsake its dual-mission orientation to notify state regulators. Assuming notice occurs, regulators can use this moment to review compliance with the prioritization mandate to that point, and may assign penalties or bring fiduciary actions seeking redress for past failures. In addition, erstwhile MPHs will be barred from using the MPH brand going forward. Notably, though, these regulatory reactions depend on self-reporting by exiting MPHs, who will have little incentive to invite scrutiny. Money and administrative complexity remain just as relevant here as in the context of disclosure and litigation.

Shareholders, too, will play a role on exit. MPH legislation will require shareholder approval for dissolution and other actions that will end an adopting entity's commitment to pursue social good. Moreover, approval will require a two-thirds majority, rather than the bare majority or plurality rules that generally apply to shareholder decision-making and director elections. Imposing a supermajority rule increases the confidence that founders and investors can have in each other by making it more difficult for an MPH to change course over their disapproval. A unanimous consent rule would provide complete protection, but we do not recommend it. Once there are more than a handful of shareholders, unanimity becomes extremely impractical. As much as investors and entrepreneurs might like to hold a veto even if all other investors disagreed with them, they would also bristle at granting that level of holdout power to each other. The supermajority rule is a workable middle ground, offering some uptick in assurances without making the MPH form too unwieldy. First-generation hybrid corporations impose comparably heightened shareholder approval thresholds on exit.

MPH legislation would add another, more powerful tool to enforce social good prioritization on exit. Its approach takes a page from the nonprofit corporate form and its nondistribution constraint. Recall that this prohibition bars the distribution of profits of a nonprofit corporation to its members, directors, officers, or others in control. This means when a nonprofit charity plans to merge, sell its assets, or otherwise go out of business, it cannot pay out its remaining resources to its founders or leaders. It also cannot repatriate the funds to original donors, even if they can be located. Instead, the assets must be transferred to some other charity. Assets devoted to charitable purposes must remain in the charitable stream. Removing the possibility of taking the entity's value for oneself blunts the incentive for those with authority to pursue their own interests. It also encourages donors to invest in the charity's mission, knowing this goal will be continued perpetually even if another entity will be the one pursuing it.

Clearly, the nonprofit nondistribution constraint will not work for the MPH. In fact, this very feature makes nonprofit forms inhospitable to social enterprise. Social enterprises pursue social mission as well as profit generation and distribution to owners. The nondistribution constraint thus cannot be simply transplanted. Nevertheless, the core concept of constraint on distribution could provide social enterprises with the same stability it has long offered to charities.

Rather than banning distribution completely, MPH legislation will instead only limit it. Such a partial constraint could apply prior to exit, limiting the amount of permissible midstream profit distributions to owners. But enforcing an ongoing partial constraint would require someone to monitor each midstream distribution and related transaction, a burdensome process that would erode the advantage of employing such a structural solution. MPH legislation will instead impose its partial constraint only on transfer of assets on exit from the MPH form. An entity formed as an MPH may dissolve or transition to a fully profit-pursuing entity at any time, but a percentage of its assets would not be permitted to be repaid to investors. Neither shareholders nor directors will have the power to weaken this commitment.

Making the MPH form inhospitable to those desiring to quickly siphon out its profits should make it unappealing to those interested only in a pretense of commitment to social mission. In designing this constraint, it is important to set a limit high enough to assure investors and entrepreneurs of each other's dedication. But it must not be so high that it will repel those seeking a level of potential profit realization easily accommodated alongside a commitment to prioritize social good.

We propose that MPH legislation impose a limit of 60 percent at the outset. The 60 percent figure corresponds nicely with MPH's mission prioritization. A 60 percent constraint should also screen out investors and founders without a strong commitment to social good. Investors seeking profit alone, or even primarily, would not invest in an entity today knowing they could recoup only 40 cents on the dollar if it were sold tomorrow. Likewise, entrepreneurs intent on turning as quick and handsome a profit as possible would be fools to adopt the

MPH structure when it commits them to leave the lion's share of the proceeds behind if their wish should happen to be granted. This partial constraint allows investors and entrepreneurs to solve their assurance game by forcing both parties to make a real and enduring commitment to social good.

Even devoted entrepreneurs and investors might balk at a promise to leave the majority of the assets behind no matter how long an MPH remains faithful to the double bottom line. Accordingly, MPH legislation would draw down the limit annually, bottoming out at 10 percent after ten years. The promise of an eventual exit leaving only 10 percent of assets in the social mission stream will appeal to investors who value social good highly, but are also interested in a long-term financial return. The drawdown feature will also entice entrepreneurs that need trustworthy, patient capital. It will also allow most of the assets to be taken both out of an entity and out of the social good stream over time, discouraging MPHs and their leaders from throwing good money after bad by postponing dissolution indefinitely, sparing MPHs the indignity of charities' bad habit of failing at a snail's pace.

The partial constraint on distributions embodies both enforcement and remedy. But charity scandals reported in local papers every day prove that such measures will not enforce themselves. Someone must be authorized to challenge failures to comply. A partial constraint could easily be paired with the external regulatory or stakeholder approaches discussed above, and the MPH statute should enable any of these potential enforcers to challenge noncompliance with it. Their lack of resources, poor incentives, and coordination problems will, however, check regulators' and stakeholders' ability to pursue this remedy too.

The partial constraint fashions the value of the assets involved into a potent incentive. Legislation will require that, at formation, each MPH identify a charity that will have standing to enforce the partial constraint.[39] The identified charity will also be authorized to receive the percentage of assets that cannot be distributed if and when the identifying MPH exits the form. The assets would only be available for carrying out the social mission of the dissolving MPH, but access to this reward would incentivize the identified charity to monitor the MPH and to take action. The amount of assets remaining in the MPH will vary. So, too, will the costs of enforcing the partial constraint, depending on the issues in dispute. Regardless, access to these resources will defray the costs, and increase the feasibility, of enforcement activity. Finally, identifying a recipient charity committed to using the constrained assets to pursue the MPH's social mission sends a strong signal of commitment to investors and entrepreneurs.

The asset reward could also be made available to prompt other enforcers to action. Unfortunately, allowing government agencies, fellow investors, or even individual beneficiaries to take an MPH's constrained assets for themselves does not represent a viable option. A social enterprise should be founded and capitalized by individuals willing to see some of the entity's assets remain dedicated to social good. But watching assets transferred to fellow investors or into government coffers raises fundamentally different concerns. Imposing an exit fee payable to the state or creating a class of individual bounty hunters will drive investors and entrepreneurs away from the MPH form, rather than toward it.

Some dissolving or transforming MPHs might initiate the transfer process, contacting the identified entity and voluntarily shift to it any remaining assets subject to the constraint. The process, of course, will not always be this easy. Leaders of an MPH exiting the status will have every incentive to put off the moment of transfer, and even to spend down existing assets. Such behavior will not always be obvious. Legislation will entitle the identified charity to receive required disclosures, and make reasonable inspections of the MPH's books and records. Even with this access, not every misstep will be transparent.

An MPH and its leaders would also have incentives to refuse to transfer constrained assets, or to attempt to spirit them away to their own pockets or those of a new venture. MPH legislation will authorize the identified charity, as well as state regulators and shareholders, to challenge such actions in court. Since the transfer obligation will be triggered only on formal exit from MPH status, courts will be better able to identify such breaches than the moment when fiduciaries cease prioritizing in their ongoing management of the company. The percentage limit represents a bright line, even though courts must identify and trace the assets to which this percentage will apply. Courts' experience policing the assets of corporations, partnerships, and nonprofits make them uniquely qualified to carry out this task.

Conclusion

Creating a specialized form for social enterprises represents more than an interesting experiment in institutional design. Social entrepreneurs seeking capital and investors interested in generating a combination of profit and social good with their dollars need a way to telegraph their commitments. Solving the assurance game they face with a brand would accomplish just that. This chapter fashions a brand out of corporate law. Unlike the first-generation hybrids considered in the next chapter—entities that may harbor unwelcome surprises—the MPH offers a brand investors and entrepreneurs can trust.

The MPH maps one trail legislatures could blaze to bring impact investors and social entrepreneurs together. Make no mistake, this journey will be arduous. Only state governments that invest significant time and resources will be able to negotiate its daunting obstacles. States must first draft and pass a comprehensive new enabling statute granting access to a specialized form. The statute must include a mandate that adopting entities and their fiduciaries prioritize social good. These statutory provisions will differentiate the new form from its first-generation predecessors by affirmatively safeguarding mission, rather than merely posing no threat. They will also set the speed limit necessary to evaluate adopting entities' performance.

The statute must further authorize a series of interlocking enforcement tools, sufficient to convince founders and investors that the form will protect their commitment to social good. We recommend activating a triad of state officials, stakeholders, and the community of organizations dedicated to social good to reinforce each other's enforcement efforts.

Enacting legislation marks only a beginning. Next, states must identify and responsibly fund the state regulator identified to monitor and enforce the prioritization mandate. They must also recognize the role that state courts will play in enforcement and the time, money, and energy that role will demand. States must be willing and able to take on these legislative and resource commitments to develop a legal form that will brand social enterprises effectively.

The next chapter provides a tour of jurisdictions in the United States and abroad that have attempted to design legal forms for social enterprise. As one might expect, none yet meet all of the requirements we set forth for the MPH. To date, few jurisdictions have even enacted a prioritization mandate. None has provided the suite of enforcement mechanisms needed to provide meaningful assurances to entrepreneurs and investors. Still, these legislative attempts are worth unpacking. Identifying what legislatures have been able to accomplish thus far will help us to evaluate the likelihood that they will be able to push further—toward the MPH ideal. That said, the potential for legislatures to brand social enterprises using legal forms of organization is dishearteningly small. For this reason, chapters 4 and 5 develop alternative paths to solving the stag hunt faced by social entrepreneurs and investors.

3

Evaluating the Current Menu of Legal Forms for Social Enterprise

In less than a decade, a majority of US states have adopted specialized social enterprise forms, and most others appear poised to follow suit. This chapter breaks that legislative handiwork into discrete models, contrasting the results with the framework developed in chapter 2 to highlight why none is likely to bridge the trust gap between social entrepreneurs and investors. Of course, the question boils down to empirics. The first-generation hybrid forms remain too novel for empirical study of their uptake to be reliable, but the wide gap between the MPH's assurances and the first generation's aspirations makes success appear unlikely.

A Dynamic Menu of Choices

The benefit corporation, the current front runner in terms of legislative adoptions with benefit corporation statutes on the books of over 30 states and the District of Columbia,[1] has spawned a number of variations. Perhaps most significantly, Delaware entered this space in 2014 with its "public benefit corporation" (or PBC), creating a potential rival to the benefit corporation. Just a few years ago, the benefit corporation gained momentum as legislative adoptions of the first specialized form developed for social enterprise in the United States—the low-profit limited liability company (or L3C)—slowed dramatically. A handful of other first-generation forms, such as the social purpose corporation, also dot the landscape.

The Current Front Runner: Benefit Corporations

The benefit corporation repurposes the traditional for-profit corporate form for social enterprises by altering statutory language relating to four aspects of corporations: corporate purpose, fiduciary conduct, shareholder voting, and disclosure. Dozens of states have now adopted benefit corporation statutes. A legal form's availability in a single US jurisdiction would make it available for adoption by firms throughout the country, suggesting that legislative enthusiasm for the form is being driven by more than just demand from social enterprises. Each iteration offers its own variations, but all benefit corporation statutes shape these four components to transform standard for-profits into dual-mission entities.[2]

Corporate Purpose

A typical for-profit corporate statute permits incorporation for a broad range of purposes, so long as they are lawful.[3] Benefit corporation statutes add to these provisions a required "purpose of creating general public benefit"[4] and permit individual adopting entities to enumerate "specific public benefit" purposes as well.[5] The statutes' definition of a general public benefit introduces another hallmark of benefit corporation legislation—the invocation of third-party standards. A general public benefit means "[a] material positive impact on society and the environment, taken as a whole, *assessed against a third-party standard,* from the business and operations of a benefit corporation."[6]

To qualify, a standard must be comprehensive and credible, and articulated by a transparent and independent entity.[7] Comprehensive standards address the impact of the business on a broad range of constituencies, from employees to the community and even the global environment.[8] Experts develop credible standards, providing for input on each standard's development. To be transparent, the criteria the standard applies must be publicly available, along with the process for developing and revising the standard. To be independent, a standard must be developed by an entity that the enterprise to be assessed does not control.

These rigorous tests for qualification as a third-party standard can be misread as imposing third-party certification as a prerequisite for benefit corporation status. In fact, the statutes operate quite differently. No third-party standard-setting agency need pass on the bona fides of an aspiring benefit corporation for it to access the form. Founders need not produce their certification by such an outside expert to incorporate under the statutes. Third-party standard setters play a far more modest role. A social entrepreneur desiring to form a benefit corporation may seek external approval from a third-party standard setter if it suits her. But she need not. Access to the benefit corporation form requires only that she seek out the content of a qualifying third-party standard and use that external standard to assess her enterprise herself. (Naturally, those so inclined will find they clear the hurdle.)

In addition to requiring a general public benefit purpose, benefit corporation statutes also expressly deem adopting entities' creation of such public benefits to be "in the best interests of the benefit corporation."[9] Taken together, these altered purpose provisions inoculate the dual-mission concept against any *Dodge v. Ford* challenge. Adopting entities must pursue a general public benefit, and this and any specific public benefits they articulate in their charter will conclusively be regarded as in the corporation's best interest. Just as decisively, albeit less helpfully, these provisions command that adopting social enterprises "do both" profit-making and social good. They advance no prioritization of social goals whatsoever.

Fiduciary Conduct

Benefit corporation statutes' provisions regarding fiduciary conduct grant similarly wide discretion. Standard corporate statutes' instructions on fiduciary conduct require directors and officers to act with care and skill, good faith and loyalty to the corporation and its shareholders. To these requirements, benefit corporation statutes instruct directors to consider the effects of their decisions on a wide array of groups and interests. These include

> (i) the shareholders of the benefit corporation; (ii) the employees and work force of the benefit corporation, its subsidiaries, and its suppliers; (iii) the interests of customers as beneficiaries of the general public benefit or specific public benefit purposes of the benefit corporation; (iv) community and societal factors, including those of each community in which offices or facilities of the benefit corporation, its subsidiaries, or its suppliers are located; (v) the local and global environment; (vi) the short-term and long-term interests of the benefit corporation, including benefits that may accrue to the benefit corporation from its long-term plans and the possibility that these interests may be best served by the continued independence of the benefit corporation; and (vii) the ability of the benefit corporation to accomplish its general public benefit purpose and any specific public benefit purpose.[10]

Moreover, the statutes often give directors discretion to also consider any "other pertinent factors or the interests of any other group that they deem appropriate."[11] The range of interests these statutes expect directors to consider presents these fiduciaries with a Herculean task. At the very least, benefit corporation board meetings will need to be much longer than traditional ones. These provisions, of course, aim to accomplish much more than forcing directors to put in longer hours.

First, directors face affirmative pressure to consider nonshareholder interests when making corporate decisions. Forcing directors to confront these groups and interests means they will regularly grapple with the impact of corporate actions beyond share price and the company's valuation. Perhaps then directors will act to further nonshareholder interests; perhaps not. Benefit corporation statutes explicitly reject the idea that directors would be required to prioritize any interest on this long list over any other one.[12] But they do have to consider all of these interests. They need to talk about them. They must engage with them.

Having urged directors to broaden their vision, these provisions then offer them a safe place in which to do so. Ordinarily, directors who take actions that benefit nonshareholder interests fear liability, especially when such actions result in reduced value for shareholders. The debate in chapter 2 over the extent to which directors must maximize shareholder value remains lively, with strong advocates for a variety of positions. But even the staunchest supporter of directors' ability to trade off shareholder value for other goals in a particular transaction or decision will admit that traditional for-profit corporations should see promoting shareholder value as their primary goal. Benefit corporation statutes allow directors greater discretion—though, again, they do not require directors to act on it. The statutes give directors room to make the decisions they see as best, shielding them from liability even should decisions cause shareholders to consistently lose out to interests of employees, communities, or the global environment.

Benefit corporation statutes often represent something of a second bite at a legislative apple to offer directors this kind of comfort. More than 30 states have so-called constituency statutes, which contain lists of nonshareholder interests and factors very similar to those found in legislation addressing conduct by the directors of benefit corporations.[13] Constituency statutes originally developed as a response to jurisprudence about directorial responses to takeover threats.

As takeover activity heated up in the 1980s, anxious directors (and their lawyers) fashioned new techniques to defend their companies from potential acquirers. These defensive tactics make a company less attractive to would-be acquirers or make it more difficult and expensive for them to mount a successful takeover. Or both. When corporations adopt defensive measures, takeover attempts in progress may be stalled or abandoned. If sufficiently onerous, such tactics can stave off bids in the first place. Not surprisingly, investors challenged these defenses in court, alleging that defensive tactics were merely attempts to safeguard executives' and directors' jobs—at shareholders' expense.

After all, two very different pictures of a takeover emerge. In the rosy image of a takeover, a would-be acquirer sees a takeover target company for the undervalued asset it is—perhaps due to poor management by the incumbent board and executive team. Accordingly, the acquirer is willing to pay shareholders a premium above the market price for their shares, as long as that price (and the costs of completing the deal) is less than the underlying real value the acquirer sees and is willing to unlock for himself after the deal. Shareholders make a profit, the company is run more efficiently, and everybody—except an incompetent or indolent management—wins. If this is an accurate picture of takeovers, courts *should* impede directors' attempts to implement structures and transactions that prevent them.

But one can paint a darker picture of takeovers, surely accurate in some cases. Here, an acquirer pays shareholders a premium over the market price not because the target is poorly managed, but because it is ripe for a raid. Such an acquirer does not envision running a more efficient and valuable company over the long term. She instead seeks to purchase the company from its shareholders in order to break it up, sell its parts, or siphon its assets, perhaps in a highly leveraged transaction. Shareholders will receive a premium over the market price for the sale of their shares, which will motivate them to take the deal. But the company may not survive the transaction. Employees will lose jobs, communities will be hurt, and the broader economy will suffer long term. Directors should frustrate these nefarious takeovers, but it will be hard to differentiate them from the benign variety.

Courts faced with shareholder suits seeking to tear down director-enacted defenses faced just this quandary. In its seminal *Unocal* decision, Delaware law opted for an intermediate level of scrutiny.[14] Directors' obvious self-interest in the takeover context meant a strongly deferential standard like the business judgment rule would be a poor fit. On the other hand, takeovers seeking to exploit or destroy corporations represented compelling threats that directors needed authority to combat. So Delaware courts allow directors responding to a reasonably perceived threat posed by a takeover or the possibility of a takeover to erect defenses, as long as those defenses are reasonable in proportion to the threat posed.[15] Importantly, the *Unocal* court accepted that the threat involved could extend beyond the harm to shareholders to include the takeover's impact on "creditors, customers, employees, and perhaps even the community generally."[16]

The following year, however, the Delaware Supreme Court announced an important caveat in the *Revlon* case.[17] When directors' defensive maneuvers devolve into acceptance that the company will be broken up or shareholders' investment will be otherwise irreversibly transformed, they must narrowly focus on obtaining the best value for shareholders. Other constituencies must be forsaken in order to achieve the best price for shareholders in such endgame transactions. Defensive tactics that undermine this role of "auctioneer" will be neutralized.

Although many states' courts apply more deferential review to takeover defenses than Delaware's, state legislatures soon got into the business of limiting hostile takeover transactions too. Some enactments validate particular defenses, heighten voting requirements to approve business combinations necessary to complete takeover transactions, or impose onerous waiting periods on transactions that fail to achieve board approval. Constituency statutes

proceed less directly. They reduce takeover activity by statutorily empowering directors to act defensively to protect against the risks takeovers pose to
nonshareholder constituencies as well as any dangers to shareholders.[18] Some
constituency statutes even apply beyond the context of the takeover, to all
directorial action.

Importantly, constituency statutes permit rather than require. They allow
directors to rely on nonshareholder interests to anchor their decisions. In
contrast, benefit corporation statutes utilize a similar list of nonshareholder
constituencies but impose mandatory obligations on directors. Certainly, constituency statutes foreshadowed benefit corporation legislation. Indeed, the
terms of benefit corporation statutes often address takeovers directly.

Despite the formal distinction between requiring directors to consider these
other interests and factors rather than merely permitting them to do so, benefit
corporation statutes share an important vulnerability with constituency statutes. By expanding the range of factors upon which directors may safely rely in
making decisions, both types of legislation expand the already broad grant of
discretion directors enjoy. Directors make decisions for a corporation capitalized with the investments of others, creating an obvious principal-agent problem. Some, if not most, of the losses generated by poor directorial decisions will
fall on others—especially investors. Fiduciary duty law is one tool available to
discipline directors and keep them focused on making careful, reasoned, and
loyal decisions. A statute that offers directors the ability to justify their actions
by the desire to further nonshareholder interests can be used to cover for mismanagement or worse. Furthermore, expanding directors' freedom to unleash
defenses limits the ability of takeover activity to discipline directors as it might
in a robust market for corporate control.

Benefit corporation statutes' sheltering of directors from personal liability
if they fail to pursue general public benefit compounds this prodirector bias.[19]
Directors must consider nonshareholder interests, but need not pursue them.
Once they have given the interests of employers, the environment, and so on
their due consideration, they need not fear for their bank accounts if they prioritize value for shareholders.

The statutes do frequently establish a new "benefit enforcement proceeding"
in which claims can be brought alleging that an adopting entity has failed to pursue public benefit.[20] These proceedings do not create a free-for-all to debate and
disparage the social good claims of benefit corporations. Only directors, shareholders (often only if meeting certain ownership thresholds), and stakeholders
identified by an individual benefit corporation in its charter are granted standing to bring a benefit enforcement proceeding. Furthermore, even if successful,
such a proceeding will result at most in a trenchant court order to toe the line.
Benefit corporation statutes preclude imposition of monetary liability on defendant corporations and fiduciaries alike.[21]

Shareholder Voting

If litigation will not discipline a wayward benefit corporation or its directors, there is always the ballot box. As chapter 2 noted, shareholders in traditional corporations elect boards of directors, and shareholder approval serves a gate-keeping function for certain fundamental corporate transactions. Director elections can proceed by plurality, and ordinary matters for shareholder decision require a bare majority of shares represented at a meeting with a quorum. Fundamental transactions like dissolution and merger statutes mandate greater consensus: a majority or even a supermajority of outstanding shares. Benefit corporation statutes add to the fundamental transaction list any charter amendments or transactions that will result in the creation or termination of benefit corporation status. Shareholders must approve them by a two-thirds supermajority.[22] MPH legislation likewise imposes a supermajority vote requirement for an adopting entity to shed its special status.

Shareholder voting's potency depends on the identity, sophistication, and distribution of shareholders. In a corporation with a large pool of widely dispersed shareholders each holding a small stake, shareholders' information, collective action, and incentive problems will impede their ability to mete out effective discipline. Rationally apathetic individual shareholders will either fail to monitor at all or will respond to dissatisfaction by selling their shares rather than engaging in costly attempts to spur change through voting or litigation. It is hard to imagine an individual investor with a small stake in a benefit corporation with a widely dispersed shareholdership making much use of the voting rights the statute allocates to her. Even if she did, she would have significant difficulty convincing other investors to follow her lead.

In contrast, shareholder voting rights can be powerful tools in the hands of investors in a corporation with a modest number of owners. Such closely held corporations tend to be characterized by substantial overlap between ownership and management and by lack of a robust market for their shares. Under those conditions, voting rights often interact with shareholders' broader arsenal of governance-related enforcement mechanisms. Shareholders in closely held for-profit corporations may have the power to elect themselves directors and may also hold officer positions, affording them a direct role in management. Additionally, they will often be employed by the corporation, further improving access to information. Given their manageable numbers, they can also negotiate shareholder agreements. These contracts further bolster their ability to maintain a desired power balance.

Shareholders with a substantial stake in the corporation, or those whose own business model requires monitoring of investees' corporate governance, will also operate differently than the proverbial "mom" or "pop" investor for whom voting offers little comfort. As recent successful efforts by private equity firms and pension funds to remove staggered boards, obtain proxy access, and shift from plurality to majority voting for directors vividly demonstrate, shareholders with a reason to care about governance can use voting rights to make real changes. The complexion of a benefit corporation's shareholdership will likewise determine whether shareholder voting provisions—particularly on the special category of fundamental changes that will shift the entity away from social mission—will endow its investors with powerful rights or only illusory ones.

Disclosure

Of course, even a sophisticated investor with strong incentives to act cannot do so without information. Benefit corporation statutes respond to this information imperative through an elaborate set of disclosure requirements. Legislation obligates each adopting company to prepare a "benefit report."[23] It must be distributed to shareholders and made available to the public either through posting on the benefit corporation's website or provision of free copies upon request.[24] The model legislation cited in the notes to this chapter and many statutes— though by no means all of them—require benefit reports to be filed with the secretary of state.[25] But almost none of them penalize failure to produce, distribute, or file it.[26]

Benefit corporation statutes struggle to ensure these reports will contain more than glossy photos and self-congratulatory fluff. Unsurprisingly, benefit reports must include a description of the social good (technically, the "general public benefit") the corporation has achieved during the past year. But it must also describe any circumstances that have hindered the benefit corporation's ability to produce these valuable benefits. Forcing benefit corporations to identify and speak to the challenges they face aims to make disclosures more hard-hitting and insightful.

Beyond this narrative of achievements and obstacles, the statutes primarily rely on their invocation of third-party standards to foster fair and fulsome disclosure. As noted, to form as a benefit corporation, an entity must identify a comprehensive, credible, transparent standard developed by an independent third party, against which it will evaluate its achievements. In their annual benefit reports, benefit corporations must again identify their chosen third-party standard, assess their achievement with reference to it, and explain their "process and rationale for selecting" the standard they choose.[27] Benefit reports must apply the standard they adopt consistently from year to year, or explain the reason for any changes in approach.

Finally, benefit corporation statutes offer a ready-made internal structure to incentivize valuable and effective disclosure. Adopting entities may designate a "benefit director" to prepare a statement of his opinion on the benefit corporation's compliance with its public benefit purpose, and that of its directors and officers.[28] If a benefit director is named, this opinion must be included in the benefit report. The statute also describes a "benefit officer"; if one is named, he or she is obligated to produce the organization's benefit report.[29] Notably, other than for publicly-held benefit corporations (thus far a category occupied only by the newly public Laureate Education),[30] the benefit director position remains optional, and no benefit corporation is required to name a benefit officer. Benefit directors also enjoys statutory immunity from liability for falling down on this important job, unless their failures can be characterized as "self-dealing, willful misconduct, or a knowing violation of law."[31] The statutes, therefore, provide a useful road map for benefit corporations that wish to create a structure for ownership and responsibility for creating valuable disclosures. Whether to follow this course, however, represents a choice for each individual benefit corporation.

B Lab's Role

The critical role of standard setters in benefit corporation statutes has much to do with the form's origins. The benefit corporation form was developed, in large part, by B Lab: a nonprofit, tax-exempt organization "that serves a global movement of people using business as a force for good."[32] B Lab was founded by two successful apparel entrepreneurs and a private equity investor, who developed a three-part strategy for pursuing this ambitious mission.[33]

The first of these interrelated parts is the group's signature B Corp certification process. Despite the similarity of the "benefit corporation" and "B Corp" monikers, they fill very different niches in the social enterprise ecosystem. As explained above, a benefit corporation is a legal form of organization available under state law on terms defined by state statute. B Corp is a private designation, licensed by B Lab to companies that make changes to their governance documents to require board consideration of nonshareholder constituencies and score highly on its internally created B Impact Assessment of social and environmental commitment.[34] The B Impact Assessment consists of questions addressing governance, treatment of workers, the environment, and the local community, as well as many other topics, the answers to which accumulate to a possible total of 200 points. Companies that earn at least 80 points may license the "B Corp" mark and display it to signal their social impact to potential customers, suppliers, employees, and investors.

The second leg of B Lab's strategy nurtures the efforts to develop benefit corporation legislation and roll it out for adoption by state legislatures.[35] B Lab worked with Maryland state senator Jamie Raskin on the nation's first benefit corporation statute, adopted in April 2010.[36] It also worked with a team of lawyers and advisers to develop and continually update the Model Benefit Corporation Legislation that many states have used as a blueprint for their own statutes.[37]

Through these efforts and an extensive website devoted to the explanation and promotion of the benefit corporation concept, B Lab encourages jurisdictions and individual entities to embrace the form. In fact, certified B Corps incorporated in states without constituency statutes are required to elect benefit corporation status within two to four years of this status becoming available to them.[38]

B Lab's third and newest component, B Analytics, now offers customizable benchmarking products to measure social impact.[39] These products serve impact investors and others seeking metrics to evaluate, compare, and track the often intangible and sometimes contested impact of social enterprises. They will be discussed in more detail in chapter 6.

Both the certification and analytics products dovetail with B Lab's support for benefit corporation legislation. The certification's B Impact Assessment tool offers a framework for conducting the self-evaluation statutorily required of benefit corporations, and B Lab encourages benefit corporations to use its assessment free for this purpose.[40] Using the B Impact Assessment in this context, of course, only means a benefit corporation has judged itself to create a general public benefit. Aspiring benefit corporations need not obtain B Corp certification to obtain and keep their special status under state law. If a benefit corporation wants the ability to claim certified B Corp status or to obtain more extensive benchmarking, however, it can do so by using one of B Lab's other products. Although benefit corporation form and B Corp certification represent à la carte options that entrepreneurs can, but need not, combine, benefit corporation legislation's triumph in state capitols would not have been possible without the focused support and dedication of B Lab.

Alternatives to Benefit Corporations

Despite the concerted efforts of B Lab and the runaway success of its favored organizational form with state legislatures, the benefit corporation has not been the only game in town. Before benefit corporation statutes reached critical mass, the L3C form made impressive gains in state legislatures. During the ramp-up of benefit corporation statutes across the country, a few states also adopted alternative incorporated forms. Ultimately, the Delaware legislature—corporate law's 800-pound gorilla—launched its own unique offering. Delaware law's primacy gave B Lab little choice but to claim the Delaware public benefit corporation as part of the benefit corporation movement, despite the statute's important differences from the model legislation B Lab promotes.

An Unincorporated Approach (L3C)

A year before Maryland adopted the first benefit corporation statute, Vermont adopted legislation enabling its "low-profit limited liability company," or L3C.[41]

Just as the benefit corporation form tweaks the standard for-profit corporation, the L3C offers a twist on the popular limited liability company. The unincorporated LLC arrived on a prior wave of statutory innovation, which swept the nation decades ago.[42] The LLC combines the advantage of limited investor liability typically offered by incorporation with friendlier tax treatment usually attendant to partnerships. As a creature primarily of contract, few mandatory rules limit LLCs' governance practices.[43]

Legislation adopting the L3C form engrafts special purpose requirements onto this existing LLC legislation. Adopting entities must "significantly further the accomplishment of one or more charitable or educational purposes," and "would not have been formed but for the company's relationship to the accomplishment of charitable or educational purposes." [44] In addition,

> No significant purpose of the company is the production of income or the appreciation of property; provided, however, that the fact that a person produces significant income or capital appreciation shall not, in the absence of other factors, be conclusive evidence of a significant purpose involving the production of income or the appreciation of property.[45]

L3C legislation makes only two other changes to underlying LLC law. One further limits proper L3Cs purposes, forbidding their formation to support political candidates or influence legislation.[46] The other provides a special termination provision. If an L3C "at any time ceases to satisfy any one of the [statute's purpose] requirements, it shall immediately cease to be a low-profit limited liability company, but . . . will continue to exist as a limited liability company."[47] Only the name of the company must be changed. Exactly how anyone will know when such a transformation has occurred remains a bit mysterious. It happens by operation of law, without notice to or involvement by investors, entrepreneurs, regulators, or anyone else.

Like benefit corporation legislation, L3C statutes were not developed within state legislatures, but by a nonprofit organization on a mission. Robert Lang, CEO of the Mary Elizabeth and Gordon B. Mannweiler Foundation, likes to call the L3C the "for-profit with a nonprofit soul,"[48] and he and others originally conceived it to facilitate "program-related investments" (or PRIs).[49] PRIs constitute a special category of private foundation investments made primarily to accomplish the foundation's charitable purposes, rather than to earn financial returns. The language L3C statutes use to limit the purposes of adopting entities draws directly from Treasury regulations defining the PRI category.

Private foundations differ from other nonprofit organizations in that they receive support from a relatively small number of donors and primarily make grants to operating charities. The tax law imposes a variety of special regulatory obligations on private foundations, including scrutiny of their expenditures and investments. Private foundations must make "qualifying distributions" equal to 5 percent of the fair market value of their net assets each year.[50] Most qualifying distributions are grants to nonprofit, tax-exempt public charities. But foundations may also count PRIs as qualifying distributions, even though these are investments, such as debt or equity of for-profit entities, which could result in a financial return to the foundation, rather than grants.[51] Further, although the tax law imposes penalties on private foundations that make imprudent investments that "jeopardize the carrying out of any of its exempt purposes," even very high-risk PRIs pass muster.[52]

Despite this favorable treatment, private foundations seem to make few PRIs.[53] The PRI regulations, which even with recent amendments leave crucial questions unanswered, make such investments risky. As the penalties for mischaracterizing an expenditure as a PRI can be severe, some advisers recommend that foundations secure a costly and time-consuming regulatory preapproval before making a PRI. The L3C's originators set out to change this by creating a new vehicle to encourage PRI use. With the requirements for PRI status embedded in a state organizational form, they hoped that one-off approvals would not be needed.

The L3C, like its LLC forbears, takes its form from the individualized bargains struck between investors and entrepreneurs. As an added bonus, the flexibility that comes naturally to this LLC-derived form made it suitable for tranched investing by a heterogeneous group of equity investors. Tax-exempt private foundations, individual investors, for-profit corporations or partnerships, and virtually any other kind of entity can be an LLC investor, called a "member" in legal terms. Moreover, members can be assigned differing sets of rights—both rights in governing the LLC and rights to share in its financial returns. Different sets or "tranches" of investors may also receive stakes with different risk-return profiles. For example, an L3C could offer investors in an equity tranche a below-market rate of return combined with governing rights to ensure the entity would not stray from its social mission. L3C advocates suggested private foundations would be willing to invest in this tranche because of their motivations to achieve charitable goals rather than financial returns. After all, for foundations PRIs replace grants, which offer a negative financial return.

The willingness of one equity tranche to forgo financial returns would allow most of any such return to be shared instead between "mezzanine" and "senior" tranches. Mezzanine tranche securities would be attractive to investors seeking investments that combined social returns with financial returns above the equity tranche rate of return, but below comparable returns from market-rate investments. There are clearly some investors with an appetite for combining financial and social goals in their investments; over $6 trillion was invested in socially responsible mutual funds by the beginning of 2014.[54] The more concessions mezzanine and equity tranche investors make, the more gains can be transferred to senior tranche buyers. Investors in the senior tranche could, in theory, even receive a rate of return indistinguishable from non-socially oriented firms in the marketplace. Advocates believed that, by easing the use of tranched investment, the L3C form could unlock significant capital for social enterprises.

Tranching, and the other governance and operational elements of an L3C, exist for any given L3C only to the extent that its underlying contractual terms specify them. L3C statutes do not address fiduciary conduct and impose neither investor voting nor disclosure requirements. The underlying LLC statutes give members of such firms substantial freedom to design management processes to suit their particular needs, which will be memorialized in each firm's particular operating agreement.[55] To ease the transaction costs of negotiating terms in every case, Americans for Community Development (another organization Mr. Lang leads), offers a series of model L3C operating agreements on its website.[56]

At the end of the day, the L3C has little to recommend it over the LLC and has languished. Between 2008 and 2011, nine states adopted L3C legislation, with most following a pattern very similar to the initial Vermont statute.[57] Bills seeking to establish a PRI safe harbor for investments in L3Cs were introduced in Congress during this period,[58] but none succeeded. Unsurprisingly, given the absence of any enforcement apparatus to ensure that L3Cs comply with the PRI requirements, the IRS also never offered any blanket preapproval or other assurance that investments in L3Cs would meet the PRI standards. Legislative interest in the L3C form waned as interest in the benefit corporation increased. Maryland and Oregon adapted benefit corporation legislation to the LLC context, creating a benefit LLC form.[59] But no new states have adopted the L3C since 2011, and one actually repealed its enabling statute.[60]

Single-Jurisdiction Alternatives

A few states have developed jurisdiction-specific forms. Unfortunately, they tend to bear sound-alike names, only compounding the confusion over B Corps and benefit corporations. At the same time that it passed benefit corporation legislation, California adopted a statute enabling "flexible purpose corporations."[61] The form was renamed "social purpose corporation" (or SPC) in 2014.[62] Washington adopted its own SPC legislation in 2013.

As the name suggests, an SPC leverages existing corporate law frameworks. Like the benefit corporation, it tweaks purpose provisions, fiduciary standards, shareholder rights, and disclosure obligations. Yet there are notable differences. Perhaps because B Lab has not been involved in drafting SPC legislation,[63] these regimes do not invoke third-party standards. Nor do they require directors to consider a laundry list of constituencies. Instead, they demand that each SPC select a specific non-shareholder-focused purpose or purposes to pursue,[64] and require directors of each SPC to consider only those special purposes identified in its own charter.[65]

The SPC statutes also include innovations. Washington's statute requires an adopting entity to include the following notice provision in its articles of incorporation:

> The mission of this social purpose corporation is not necessarily compatible with and may be contrary to maximizing profits and earnings for shareholders, or maximizing shareholder value in any sale, merger, acquisition, or other similar actions of the corporation.[66]

Both SPC statutes impose public and shareholder disclosure requirements that dwarf their benefit corporation counterparts—particularly those under the California statute.[67] They also bolster shareholders' role in approving any shift to pure for-profit status[68] by granting dissenters the right to be bought out.[69] The SPC form has yet not attracted as many adherents as the L3C and benefit corporation have, but these remain the early innings for social enterprise form legislation, and the possibility of a come-from-behind victory remains distinct.[70]

Delaware Dives In

A betting person, though, would wager on Delaware's public benefit corporation. Small businesses intending to remain closely held and local typically form in their home jurisdictions. But companies hoping to attract capital from angel investors, venture capital, private equity firms, or an eventual public offering choose Delaware incorporation, which these investors generally prefer, and sometimes demand. These factors, themselves driven by a fastidiously updated corporate law, a dedicated and sophisticated judiciary, an expert and energetic bar, and a swift and accommodating filing office, make Delaware incorporation the gold standard. Delaware's dominance in the market for for-profit incorporations may not spill over into the hybrid form space, but one should certainly not underestimate its influence. After all, its leadership role in corporate legal innovation gave Delaware the ability to break from the pack by creating its own sui generis form in 2013.[71]

The Delaware public benefit corporation follows the now familiar pattern of adjusting the standard for-profit corporate framework to create a form more suited to double-bottom-line enterprises. Delaware PBCs are expressly for-profit entities, but are "intended to produce a public benefit or public benefits and to operate in a responsible and sustainable manner."[72] Each adopting entity must identify itself as a public benefit corporation in its charter, and indicate one or more specific public benefits it will pursue. The statute defines public benefits as positive effects on persons, entities, communities, or interests other than stockholders and offers a long but nonexclusive list of examples running from charitable to environmental to technological effects.

The Delaware statute also gives a unique tripartite instruction to public benefit corporation directors. As they manage their corporations, they must "balance" the financial interests of shareholders, the interests of other stakeholders impacted by the firm's conduct, and the public benefit the firm identifies in its charter.[73] As in typical benefit corporation legislation, two-thirds of outstanding shares must approve any charter amendment or transaction that would change or remove a PBC's public benefit commitments.[74] But the new Delaware form provides no special enforcement proceedings, and its disclosure requirements mandate reports on the company's public benefit be shared only with shareholders, and only every two years.[75] These reports need not assess the entity's progress using a third-party standard, though individual adopting entities may choose to apply one.

Despite these glaring differences from the Model Benefit Corporation Legislation advocated by B Lab, its leaders were quick to claim the Delaware statute as a victory.[76] Although arguably a win for B Lab in its role as a champion of social enterprise, the emergence of the Delaware public benefit corporation creates a potent rival for its Model Benefit Corporation Legislation. Colorado swiftly adopted its own public benefit corporation legislation modeled on the Delaware form, and other states may well follow suit.

Potential Unrealized

While almost all of these forms have proved popular with state legislatures, adoption by social enterprises has been slow. Many secretary of state offices do not keep detailed records of these formations, so the uptake question is difficult to pin down. Still, the numbers available offer little reason for optimism. A 2016 study reports that only about 4,500 organizations had assumed any of these specialized forms since the inception of first L3C statute in 2008.[77] These low figures could be explained as the very gradual acceptance of a new and untested legal concept, and time will tell. At least part of the explanation lies instead with shortcomings in the adopted forms themselves. These organizational forms have obvious curb appeal, promising social impact to progressive state legislators and a market approach to conservative ones. Creating these legal forms offers legislators an opportunity to please the entire political spectrum without spending a dime. But getting behind the wheel of a benefit corporation or an L3C presents far greater risk with only speculative rewards. They certainly will not solve the trust problems separating the indispensable parties to capitalizing a social enterprise, as they neither untangle the prioritization dilemma nor create reliable methods for enforcement.

Muddy Messages Instead of Prioritization Mandates

As chapter 2 explained, specialized legal forms for social enterprise cannot resolve the assurance game faced by entrepreneurs and investors if enabling statutes provide no guidance as to what adopting entities must do when mission and profit conflict. A legislative command that social good must be prioritized over profit makes adoption of the form the strong, clear signal of commitment necessary for it to function as a brand. This clarity also makes enforcement of such commitments possible. Unfortunately, first-generation US legal forms typically include no prioritization mandate. Neither adopting organizations nor their leaders must prioritize social good. The vague exhortations these statutes contain deliver a muddy message at best.

Organizational Imperatives: Do Both

Of the three basic categories of specialized forms detailed above, L3C statutes come closest to imposing a prioritization mandate on adopting organizations. Recall that these statutes adapt language from the PRI regime to (1) command that an adopting entity "significantly further the accomplishment of one or more charitable or educational purposes," (2) require that it "would not have been formed but for the company's relationship to the accomplishment of charitable or educational purposes," and (3) warn that "[n]o significant purpose of the entity is the production of income or the appreciation of property." This warning comes with the proviso "that the fact that an entity produces significant income or capital appreciation shall not, in the absence of other factors, be conclusive evidence of a significant purpose involving the production of income or the appreciation of property." This wishy-washy language falls well short of a strident prioritization mandate. Yet it does require a founder to have a social mission priority at the organization's founding; and it does communicate disfavor for a profit-focused agenda.

Delaware's public benefit corporation and Washington's social purpose corporation fall next in line. A Delaware PBC must be "intended to produce a public benefit or public benefits and to operate in a responsible and sustainable manner."[78] A Washington SPC "must be organized to carry out its business purpose . . . in a manner intended to promote positive short-term or long-term effects of, or minimize adverse short-term or long-term effects of, the corporation's activities upon any or all of (1) the corporation's employees, suppliers, or customers; (2) the local, state, national, or world community; or (3) the environment."[79] Both statutes express concern for the motivations driving the adoption of these forms. Their identification of social goals as defining characteristics of the forms underscores that social good generation represents a proper goal of Delaware PBCs and Washington SPCs. Washington buttresses this support for social mission with a requirement that an SPC's articles of incorporation state that "[t]he mission of this social purpose corporation is not necessarily compatible with and may be contrary to maximizing profits and earnings for shareholders, or maximizing shareholder value in any sale, merger, acquisition, or other similar actions of the corporation."[80] Unfortunately, even this stern warning falls short of a clear statutory mandate to prioritize social mission.

Benefit corporations statutes patently reject social good prioritization; a benefit corporation's social purposes merely supplement their business purposes.[81] Some state enactments do grant individual adopting entities the option of prioritizing their public benefit purposes.[82] But this means that whether prioritization is in effect can be determined only by reviewing the formative documents of a particular entity. Such an opt-in approach cannot create a benefit or social purpose corporation brand strongly signaling social good prioritization to entrepreneurs and investors.

Fiduciary Directives: Do Both, Do Everything, Balance

Enabling statutes' requirements for fiduciaries could effectively impose a prioritization mandate even if organizational purpose provisions fail to do so. Unfortunately, current statutes do not seize this opportunity. L3C statutes do not contain any provisions on fiduciary conduct at all. Benefit corporation statutes require directors to consider the impact of their decisions on long lists of constituencies. These lists include shareholders and many other groups and interests, but the statute expressly provides that directors "need not give priority" to any of them.[83] As discussed earlier, requiring consideration of such a lengthy catalog of interests may, perversely, undermine rather than bolster director discipline.

When acting as a member of its board, an SPC director must have a narrower focus than her benefit corporation counterparts. These statutes layer concern for the specific social purpose expressed in an SPC's articles of incorporation over the typical set of considerations driving for-profit directors.[84] The two SPC statutes vary as to whether directors may or must consider an entity's specific social purpose, but both differ from benefit corporations by eliminating the laundry list approach. Whether an SPC statute's instruction boils down to "you may do both" or "you must do both," it compares favorably with benefit corporation statutes' instruction that "you must do everything." Even so, no SPC statute demands that their leaders prioritize social good.

Delaware's public benefit corporation statute embraces a new idea: balance. Directors are instructed to act "in a manner that balances the pecuniary interests of the stockholders, the best interests of those materially affected by the corporation's conduct, and the specific public benefit or public benefits identified in its certificate of incorporation."[85] The notion of balance suggests that public benefit must be an ever-present factor in directors' decision-making—one they could not forsake at every turn. But so too with shareholders' pecuniary interests and the mysterious "interests of those materially affected by the corporation's conduct." The statute plainly does not give public benefit precedence.

Hope for Change

Benefit corporation legislation in a few individual states parts ways with the chorus of "do both," "consider everything," and "balance competing interests." New York's statute contains what appears to be a prioritization mandate at the organizational level, stating that an adopting entity's "purpose to create general public benefit shall be a limitation on the other purposes of the benefit corporation, and shall control over any inconsistent purpose of the benefit corporation."[86] This seemingly clear command clashes, however, with the statute's familiar rejection of prioritization in its directive to fiduciaries.[87] Minnesota's version of benefit corporation legislation (actually using the term "public benefit corporation") imposes a kind of deprioritization mandate on fiduciaries. Directors under this statute "may not give regular, presumptive, or permanent priority to (i) the pecuniary interests of the shareholders; or (ii) any other interest or consideration unless the articles identify the interest or consideration as having priority."[88] Although it does not affirmatively embrace prioritization, the Minnesota statute provides hope that state legislatures might one day do just that.[89]

Legislative amendment does not represent the only way that social good prioritization could be injected into existing specialized form legislation. The judiciary has long played an influential role in interpreting and elaborating upon the obligations of fiduciaries. If and when cases arise under these various statutes, state judiciaries can deploy a number of approaches to mandate prioritization of social good. While spare L3C statutes do not address fiduciary conduct directly, some scholars have argued the purpose requirements in these statutes would compel judges to require L3C fiduciaries to prioritize their organizations' charitable or educational purposes.[90] Judges themselves may disagree, but such interpretation certainly would be helpful.

Judges would need to stretch further to impose a prioritization mandate on fiduciaries of benefit, social purpose, and Delaware public benefit corporations, but it is certainly within their reach. The duty of care imposes largely procedural limitations, but judges could opine that careful action equates with erring on the side of social good. The duty of loyalty cabins fiduciary self-interest, but judges could expand it to spur fiduciaries to prioritize social good in the context of organizations created to generate public benefit or operate in a sustainable manner. Fiduciaries' obligations to act in good faith in this context could be interpreted to require social good prioritization. Or the nonprofit corporate concept of a duty of obedience to organizational mission[91] could be imported to achieve this goal. None of these interpretations leaps from the statutory language; none of them neutralizes the statutory bars on monetary liability for fiduciary breach; and courts can only act if shareholders (the only constituency with standing) mount a case. Yet courts inclined to take any of these positions could introduce social good prioritization into any of these systems without legislative action. Doing so would be well within the long tradition of common-law fiduciary duty interpretation, but could take many years.

Questionable Enforcement

First-generation hybrid forms cannot be refashioned into a strong brand engendering trust between social entrepreneurs and investors just by including a clear prioritization mandate in enabling legislation. For a legal form to unlock capital to scale social ventures, entrepreneurs and investors must actually believe that adopting entities will comply with this mandate. To develop into effective brands, a specialized form must provide reliable means to enforce the meaningful difference the social good prioritization standard signifies. This is no easy task. As chapter 2 detailed, the potential enforcers of a prioritization mandate face information asymmetries, resource shortfalls, and coordination problems. Thus far, American legal forms designed for social enterprise have done little to address these challenges, and leave enforcement very much in question.

Unilateral Opt-Out

Perhaps most troubling on this score are pervasive unilateral opt-out rights. They allow either entrepreneurs or investors to abandon their entity's social goal without the consent of the other. In this sense, the L3C form appears the most potentially ephemeral. If an L3C entrepreneur and her management team simply stop running the entity in accord with the charitable and educational purposes the statute lays out, it automatically and immediately transforms into an ordinary LLC. The organization's dual-mission commitment can be cast off in an instant, with no warning, announcement, or fanfare. Adopting such a fragile form will provide little confidence to investors fearing that an entity's founder and managers might stray from social mission—even if the statute were amended to clarify a strict social good prioritization mandate while the L3C lasts.

Benefit, social purpose, and public benefit corporations provide greater protection and staying power for dual-mission commitments than the L3C, yet they too contain unilateral opt-out rights. To amend its articles of incorporation to abandon its social mission or undertake a transaction that will remove it, a benefit, social purpose, or Delaware public benefit corporation's board of directors must approve and its shareholders must consent, generally by a supermajority. Board approval and shareholder voting requirements make the dual missions of benefit, social purpose, and public benefit corporations considerably more resilient than would a standard for-profit form. Yet—flipping the problem identified with the L3C on its head—these board approval and voting requirements allow investors to cast off the organization's social mission over a founder's objection. It simply comes down to numbers. If investors control enough shares to shift the board to their viewpoint and win a supermajority in the shareholder voting process, they can remove the organization's dual mission. An entrepreneur can protect his vision from being displaced only by maintaining a stake sufficient to retain control over these governance processes—forgoing access to capital that would be gained by selling more equity.

Social entrepreneurs and investors face an assurance game. Each would prefer a course blending social benefit and profit-making, but each lacks confidence in her colleague's commitment to this dual mission. For a legal form to navigate this impasse and draw capital into adopting entities, use of the form must communicate to each party her counterparts' resolve. The ability each of these forms grants to entrepreneurs or investors to shake off a commitment to social mission undermines, rather than reinforces, the necessary trust between these indispensable parties.

Reasons to Doubt Disclosure

To varying degrees, the benefit, social purpose, and public benefit corporate forms also rely on disclosure. Each provides investors with periodic reports on their social enterprise's achievements, including descriptions of the (otherwise opaque) decision-making processes used to work toward those goals. Of course, enforcement would be impossible without access to such information. Regrettably, while mandating production of information may be necessary for enforcement, it seems unlikely to be sufficient to ensure it.

These regimes hinge on the dubious assumption that disclosures' shareholder recipients will be engaged and responsive. But shareholders may pay little attention to these reports and have difficulty parsing their metrics. Studies have shown many donors do not use accountability information available regarding charities to which they are considering making a donation.[92] To the extent that social enterprise investors view their investments as akin to charitable contributions, these studies suggest they may pay disclosures little heed.[93]

On the other hand, if social enterprise investors treat their investments in social enterprises as they do those in purely for-profit endeavors, the information they contain might be closely reviewed and scrutinized. In the for-profit context, though, a whole industry of analysts and middlemen help investors decipher those disclosures. The same is not yet true for social enterprises, and may never be. Whether such an industry will develop will depend in part on whether money can be earned by providing this comparative information and in part on the power of available metrics for social impact. Both reporting and assessing performance in a dual-mission enterprise pose challenges. Many organizations diligently work to develop better social performance measures, as chapter 6 details, but the metrics available today leave much to be desired.

Even assuming that useful disclosures can be developed and shareholders will ably assess their content, they still may not respond to them with attempts to enforce social good prioritization. Shareholders' preferences can change. Investors once willing to give up some financial returns for social ones may change their minds, want greater profit for themselves, or be willing to sell to those who would. When faced with a disclosure suggesting a social enterprise veering off the rails, even shareholders who remain committed to prioritizing social good may not attempt enforcement through intervention in management, voting activity, or litigation.

Consider a solar energy social enterprise formed as a benefit corporation. Initially, it manufactures components for solar energy production in a 75 percent solar-powered manufacturing plant. Over time, however, demand for its components exceeds the quantity it can supply with a primarily solar-powered production process. The managers might respond by increasing production to meet this new demand with a plant using nonsustainable energy sources, turning greater profit and enabling growth. This decision would be reported in the company's annual benefit report. Although the value of the company increases, as does the value of its shares, a shareholder committed to solar-powered production might disapprove of the decision. Would she attempt enforcement? Perhaps, but perhaps not. She might instead try to sell her shares, using the proceeds to replace the disappointing social investment with a new more reliable one or with a charitable contribution. Even without a ready market for her shares, she still may not engage in enforcement activity. Instead, she may simply change her attitude toward the investment—mentally reassigning it within her portfolio from the impact category to the conventional one. Neither of these actions would spur directors to return to social good prioritization.

Finally, disclosure requirements impose costs on adopting entities. Legislators have not acknowledged the potentially prohibitive costs of compliance for small social enterprises. The original California social purpose corporation legislation (at that time, using the term "flexible purpose corporation") exempted adopting entities with fewer than 100 shareholders from its disclosure requirements.[94] But amendments to the legislation repealed the exemption.

Many early adopters of benefit corporation status appear to be dealing with the costs of producing reports in a more straightforward fashion—they simply do not produce them. A recent study found just 8 percent of benefit corporations produced the statutorily required benefit report.[95] This may be unsurprising given the nearly universal lack of penalties for failure to comply with reporting mandates. Whatever one thinks of the value of disclosure, it cannot do much good if it does not exist.

Reliance on Enforcement from Within

Current US forms for social enterprise all place unwarranted faith in enforcement from within. Only fiduciaries and shareholders have standing to challenge a shift away from social mission, either by using rights to govern the organization, to manage it, or to litigate organizational or leadership failures. These first-generation forms and, in particular, their lack of a clear mandate to prioritize social good will challenge even the most circumspect fiduciary to impose discipline on herself and her colleagues. A plain statement requiring fiduciaries to prioritize social good would improve the prospects of fiduciary self-policing, but only to a degree. Boardroom reminders to colleagues about the obligation to elevate social good over profit can only go so far, and it is hard to imagine leaders intrepid enough to sue their colleagues for fiduciary breach if their advice goes unheeded. Even in the for-profit context, where obligations have sharper edges, directors rarely take the uncomfortable course of suing each other.

Investors, on the other hand, should feel no awkwardness about raising such challenges. But in benefit, social purpose, and public benefit corporations, management lies well out of investors' reach, and litigation is a costly exercise with limited remedial utility. Directors make everyday decisions and initiate extraordinary transactions, with shareholder participation limited to director elections and approving fundamental changes. Centralized management allows social enterprises to be managed efficiently by experts, leaving investors free to concentrate on other matters. It also means investors have little ability to influence the everyday trade-offs their companies make between pursuing profit and social good.

Investors in particular social enterprises may hold directorial or management roles that grant them access to these decision-making processes and enable them to give teeth to a mandate to prioritize social mission. When social enterprises remain small or closely held, shareholders will frequently serve in such multiple, overlapping roles. Limited liability company statutes underlying the L3C form set investor management as a default, though one would need to consult individual operating agreements to understand the management of any given adopting entity. These idiosyncratic, entity-level choices can give entrepreneurs and investors in a particular social enterprise the confidence needed to overcome their initial distrust. But, like soda cans filled with a diverse assortment of liquids, they do nothing to establish these first-generation forms as a brand, signaling to the market a set of reliable counterparties.

The statutes do grant shareholders standing to sue, but investors facing the time and monetary outlays required to litigate failures to prioritize mission will rarely take up the fight. Under benefit, social purpose, and public benefit corporation law, statutory elimination of liability for such lapses makes injunctive relief the only possible vision of success, further limiting the appeal of shareholder litigation as a remedy. Moreover, as the discussions of enforcement through voting and disclosure make clear, serious collective action problems and changing preferences will stymie shareholder enforcement. Too often, and especially in litigation where costs of enforcement are high, shareholders will instead simply capitulate—and make a quick buck for their trouble.

The UK Community Interest Company: A Very Different Model

The UK's community interest company (CIC) proves that legislatures can adopt a specialized form with the features necessary to function as an effective brand. The CIC form first became available in the UK in 2005, and to date over 12,000 have been created.[96] CICs are companies, analogous to US corporations, and those formed as limited by shares may take on investors and distribute profits to them. Yet CIC legislation differs from standard UK company law by requiring adopting entities to comply with a broadly drawn "community interest test." The test asks "if a reasonable person might consider that its activities (or proposed activities) are carried on for the benefit of the community."[97] Rather than merely instructing adopting entities to pursue community benefit while making profits, and in any combination, community benefit serves as the CIC's primary purpose.[98]

This firm embrace of social good prioritization anchors robust enforcement architecture. Like other UK companies, CICs are governed by a board of directors who must exercise their management and supervisory duties with "reasonable care, skill and diligence," and avoid conflicts of interest or other situations of potential disloyalty.[99] CIC directors must also preserve the CIC's ability to meet the community interest test.[100] Every year, each CIC must report on its community interest achievements and its attempts to bring nonshareholder stakeholders into its governance process.[101] CICs must make these reports to Companies House—the UK's public collector of business disclosures. This filing makes the reports available to a dedicated government agency, the CIC Regulator, for review. The CIC Regulator, established to provide oversight with a "light touch,"[102] manages the formation process, offers guidance and advice, and conducts investigations. It has explicit authority to bring claims challenging directors' fiduciary compliance, to appoint and remove CIC directors, to act to protect a CIC's assets, or even to dissolve a CIC. This public regulatory presence bolsters an enforcement-from-within regime similar to that found in US first-generation forms.

Perhaps the most potent weapons in the CIC enforcement arsenal relate to financing. CICs' assets are subject to an "asset lock," which prohibits a CIC from disposing of assets for less than fair market value consideration, except in pursuit of the community benefits or in a transfer to a charity or another CIC.[103] The asset lock ensures that, even after dissolution, a CIC's assets are perpetually devoted to community benefit. This asset lock is a supercharged commitment to social good, applying to all organizational assets at dissolution, rather than allowing distribution of assets on a sliding scale over time as the MPH would prescribe.

A CIC may, however, make limited midstream distributions to owners. The statute authorized CICs to pay dividends to investors, but empowered the CIC Regulator to cap such distributions[104]—and cap them it has. The Regulator issued a series of CIC dividend limitations, each of which increased the ability of investors to share in a CIC's midstream profits. The current (and, thus far, highest) cap requires the total dividend declared for all shares not to exceed 35 percent of distributable profits in any given year.[105] The Regulator's continued increase in dividend levels demonstrates its desire to incentivize investments in CICs, as does the recent passage of tax relief designed to stimulate investment in them.[106] These moves can be read to suggest that the statute's forceful asset lock and prior, lower caps made CIC status insufficiently attractive to investors. Another fact that might be read in the same light is that as of March 2015, while 10,639 CICs were on the UK's public registry, only 2,317 were operated as for-profits. The roughly three-quarters remaining consist of CICs limited by guarantee, analogous to a US nonprofit rather than for-profit corporation.[107]

Conclusion

The first generation of social enterprise law embraced the notion of a double bottom line. Neutralizing the perceived threat to social enterprise posed by legal institutions represents a critical expressive victory, a watershed moment for dual-mission ventures.[108] To flourish, though, social enterprises need capital along with that newfound acceptance. As the MPH and the CIC demonstrate, the law can serve as a catalyst by providing social entrepreneurs and impact investors with trust.

This potential, however, has not yet been realized in the United States. L3Cs convert into LLCs by operation of law the minute they cease "significantly further[ing] the accomplishment of one or more charitable or educational purposes." The L3C form tolerates a dual mission, but does nothing to impose it on a wayward entrepreneur. The benefit, social purpose, and Delaware public benefit corporation forms give shareholders a similar power, allowing them to convert enterprises into ordinary for-profit corporations, sacrificing whatever protections for social mission these specialized forms offer. Shareholders determined to abandon a social mission may do so over any objections raised by entrepreneurs. These escape hatches, combined with tepid protections for adopting entities' missions, cannot create a reliable brand for social entrepreneurs and impact investors to trust.

The CIC model predated all of the US forms, but none took a page from its prioritization and enforcement playbooks. Virtually none of today's specialized organizational forms call for adopting firms to prioritize social mission over financial return. Few even articulate precisely how fiduciaries and managers should balance their enterprises' dual commitments. Although the failure of these forms to adopt a social good prioritization standard could be ameliorated through relatively simple legislative amendment or gradual judicial interpretation, they offer no realistic prospects for enforcement. Like the MPH, the CIC shows that enforcement techniques are possible, but a US political climate hostile to government expansion and the current era of budget constraints make the costly infrastructure needed to create real enforcement seem impossibly out of reach. Moreover, the CIC's curbs on profit distribution may well go too far to create a truly hospitable home for dual-mission investors.

Instead of holding out hope that any of these forms (or further remixes of them) will focus a steady stream of funding on social enterprise, chapters 4 and 5 chart two radically different paths forward. The first draws on the power law grants private parties, while the second highlights how nimble government actors could respond to the needs of the social enterprise sector. Like the MPH, but unlike the first generation of social enterprise law, either would allow entrepreneurs and investors to solve the assurance game they face. Each would create a trusted social enterprise brand, capable of supplying dual-mission ventures with the capital they need.

4

From Form to Finance

The first-generation hybrid forms neither provide protection for the missions of social enterprises nor solve their capital access problem. Each accommodates a double bottom line, but that is not enough. Absent a robust second-generation hybrid like the MPH that can shield mission, social entrepreneurs and investors must look elsewhere for help. Fortunately, a survey of the legal landscape reveals a wide variety of tools that can be refashioned to broach the trust deficit separating social entrepreneurs and impact investors. Perhaps the least likely, a federal tax regime designed to subsidize social enterprises that emphasize mission and paid for by social enterprises that elevate the pursuit of investor profit, takes the stage in chapter 5.

This chapter explores an entirely different mechanism: a financial instrument. Relying on the tools of private law—here agreements among individuals and institutions—obviates the need for a new state or federal legal regime.[1] Just as it employs business methods in furtherance of mission, social enterprise can turn the technology of business to its own ends. Although finance rather than governance is their primary function, the financial instruments conventional capitalism relies on to fuel ventures allow private actors to formalize their commitments to one another across a number of dimensions. By designing an instrument that draws an explicit link between financial support and mission preservation, our flexible low-yield (FLY) paper proposal represents just such a mechanism.

Simple financial instruments create plain vanilla equity or debt. Equity ownership grants a degree of affirmative control over a venture's course. Debt ownership generally arms an investor with veto power over a range of actions that would otherwise fall within the discretion of its owners or managers. Hybridizing these two options makes it possible to develop one-of-a-kind creations that blend features of both to satisfy idiosyncratic concerns. Sophisticated investors and entrepreneurs have the resources to craft bespoke agreements, and traditional entrepreneurs and investors often do. The handful of fully profit-oriented instruments described below suggest not only the degree of freedom private actors enjoy in designing them but also the surprisingly favorable regulatory results they can deliver.

Unlike the first generation of social enterprise legal forms, a hybrid financial instrument such as FLY paper could succeed in striking a sustainable balance between profit and social mission. Like chapter 2's MPH, FLY paper would connect and reassure investors and entrepreneurs committed to pursuing a double bottom line. Given the resource constraints faced by government actors, turning to the legal architecture of finance to provide a reliable signal of commitment could offer a distinct advantage by preserving the missions of double-bottom-line enterprises without any need for public intervention. Such an approach empowers investors and entrepreneurs by harnessing the creativity of the financial sector, substituting a bottom-up citizen solution to the capital access problem for top-down remedies from state or federal governments.

Hybrid Financial Instruments

For many, the for-profit corporation serves as an avatar of global capitalism, embodying its disruptive potential and conjuring all the ills attributed to multinational businesses. In the wake of the recent global financial crisis, complex financial instruments would certainly hold their own alongside the corporation in any unpopularity contest. Years before the financial crisis, Warren Buffet famously opined that "derivatives are financial weapons of mass destruction, carrying dangers that, while now latent, are potentially lethal."[2] Today, although the risks posed by complex financial instruments have never been more apparent, they continue to play a key role in the world's economy.

The Role of Hybrid Financial Instruments

There may be no better proof of the extraordinary flexibility of the law than the diversity that prevails among financial instruments. One branch, often referred to as hybrids, incorporates both debt and equity characteristics.[3] By blending the basic recipes for secure debt and volatile equity, hybrid financial instruments can present a wide range of risk profiles. Different hybrids likewise offer investors varying degrees of control over the recipient of an investment and potential to share in the funded venture's prosperity. High-yield debt, or junk bonds, arguably the most widely known hybrid financial instrument, took root through the efforts of financiers such as "junk bond king" Michael Milken during the 1980s.[4] They offer investors no ownership stake and carry very high risk of loss, but also pay well above market rates of interest—while the issuing company lasts. Like newer variations such as leveraged loans,[5] junk bonds allow an investor to make a bet on a company that promises neither the security of a traditional loan nor the unlimited growth potential of stock, instead offering a surprisingly appealing mix of the two.

While it cannot match the rewards or security that traditional equity or debt purchasers enjoy, high-yield debt fills a niche that can help businesses secure investment capital when they otherwise could not. By offering a financial return significantly higher than traditional debt, a borrower can compensate investors for the higher likelihood of losses. Moreover, as a lender, the investor enjoys priority over both preferred and common shareholders. Frequently, variations provide additional concessions to the borrower such as an option to defer cash payments.[6] Traditional lenders would benefit from—and likely insist on—a freeze on all cash payments on the relatively risky high-yield debt until after their loans are fully repaid. Junk bond lenders accept this risk of subordination in return for the chance of extraordinary returns from successful ventures.

Although this potential to share the upside sounds much like equity, in key ways high-yield debt differs significantly from stock. Some of those differences, such as voting power, favor shareholders. Not all stock offers owners the right to vote, but as a group, a corporation's shareholders elect its directors. A high-yield lender can, of course, negotiate for an array of commitments from a borrower, but lenders do not elect directors. In some respects, the differences leave shareholders at a disadvantage compared to high-yield lenders. As with any loan, if the principal and the considerable interest burdens are not satisfied, the specter of insolvency threatens equity holders with disproportionate economic losses and the prospect of yielding control to lenders.

The details of what high-yield debt makes possible for private parties that employ it mean far less than the precision with which it serves their needs. Whatever its idiosyncrasies, high-yield debt and its analogs play an important role in bringing together those that supply capital with those that put it to use. Put simply, these arcane instruments can make capital available to an enterprise when simple debt or equity might not. Of course, high-yield debt represents only one of many tools investors and businesses have at their disposal. Convertible debt, discussed below, offers a second popular example.[7] They, along with countless others, fill unique niches by offering a distinct combination of features. Although they contain elements of debt and equity, hybrid financial instruments represent more than the sum of their parts.

More Than the Sum of Their Parts

The power of financial instruments derives partly from their diversity. They allow private parties to order features a la carte from a broad menu of choices. As a result, counterparties get just what they need, nothing more nor less. Beyond that made-to-measure perfection, financial instruments have a surprising capacity to transcend their source material. Hybrid instruments offer advantages that extend beyond their ability to combine features of debt and equity into a single convenient package. Convertible debt, for example, empowers its holders to convert debt into equity on specific terms. The end result offers investors protection in lean times and the ability to share in the prosperity when a venture succeeds.

Of course, an investor could accomplish that by purchasing a combination of stock and debt. As the hybrid label suggests, convertible debt represents something other than a simple amalgam of equity and debt. The economics of a convertible note, for example, would be mirrored by a combination of debt with an option to purchase shares of the debt's issuer. There, though, the result is not one but two distinct pieces of property bundled together, collectively bearing the somewhat unwieldy label "investment unit."[8]

In purely financial terms, the difference between a single instrument and bundled pair may be negligible. From a regulatory perspective though, the contrast between investment units and convertible debt emerges in stark terms. Simply put, convertible debt receives considerably more favorable tax treatment. For reasons that have less to do with policy than with history, convertible notes benefit from an exemption from a complex and potentially costly set of tax rules.[9] Those tax rules look beyond the nominal terms of debt instruments in order to reveal—and to tax—hidden interest. While investment units trigger this burdensome system of valuation, allocation, and yield calculations, convertible debt does not.

The alchemical principles that underlie financial engineering produce these nonlinear results. The same pattern can be seen in the treatment of financial instruments known as trust-preferred securities. These instruments gained prominence in the 1990s as issuers such as Enron capitalized on their ability to provide tax benefits in the form of interest deductions by being classified as debt while avoiding the debt label for accounting and other regulatory purposes.[10] That very appealing combination of a reduction in income for tax purposes without suffering the other costs of debt treatment has made this variety of hybrids popular with everyone but the fisc.

As this very brief discussion suggests, financial instruments have proven to be flexible tools with the power to do the unexpected. The remainder of this chapter shows how social enterprise could harness them to address its capital access problem, offering another example of the capacity of the law to create common ground where social entrepreneurs and investors can come together. Like financial instruments designed to serve the needs of for-profit ventures, the FLY paper instrument we propose plays a highly specialized role. Explicitly tying such an investment to carefully crafted protections for mission creates the transparency and trust that serve as the hallmarks of the second generation of social enterprise law.

A Targeted Solution to the Capital Access Problem

Reframing the challenge social enterprise faces from one of designing an ideal form to the less daunting task of channeling the flow of capital from committed investors to promising social enterprises suggests a number of possible solutions to the capital access problem. In this chapter, the focus rests, appropriately enough, on finance. There may have been good reason to emphasize form when social enterprise struggled to gain acceptance. As the critical obstacle to the growth of individual social enterprises—as well as the sector as a whole—shifts to the task of matching investors and entrepreneurs, a new emphasis on capital structure is overdue.

One reason finance offers more promise than form turns on the simple fact that it matches up well with the sector's needs. Simply put, creating a social enterprise no longer poses a challenge, but supplying it with capital remains difficult. Financial engineering cannot, of course, address every facet of a social enterprise's operation in the way that form must. But that need not be a weakness. Unburdened by the need to address each aspect of a venture's birth, operation, and death, the design of a financial instrument can nevertheless provide a comprehensive account of an investor's relationship with a venture. In other words, hybrid financial instruments can serve as a direct, targeted solution to social enterprise's capital access problem.

Form and the Capital Access Problem

An ideal form such as the MPH would create common ground between investors and entrepreneurs. Establishing clear expectations regarding the relationship between profit and mission would enable like-minded individuals to identify one another. Rather than devoting resources to filtering out insincere potential partners, they could plow their energy into the more important task of finding others that share their particular vision of a dual-mission venture and bringing that idea to life.

Form leaves much to be desired as a fix for social enterprise's capital access problem. It aims for perfection and, perhaps inevitably, falls short. Even our idealized MPH social enterprise form might offer investors and entrepreneurs more reassurance than they need or even want. An investor with a five- or 10-year time horizon for a given investment might prefer that a venture's commitment extend beyond the term of his investment, but he also might not. It could be sufficient for this investor to be assured that whatever balance between profit and mission he strikes with his counterparts will be maintained while his financial relationship with the venture endures. A permanent balance would suit some investors, but will discourage others.

As the MPH warily recognizes, some might actually view future profits—earned after a social enterprise's mission has run a predetermined course—as a desirable aim. While a potential source of discord, such a life-cycle approach to social enterprise may provide a relatively long-fused incentive to maintain a double bottom line. Providing capital for a specified period at concessionary rates coupled with terms designed to secure a social enterprise's mission for that fixed length of time could fully satisfy many investors' aims. Social entrepreneurs needing patient capital to bring their dual-mission visions to life could also be satisfied with this kind of stable, though not perpetual, investor commitment. A financial instrument can easily achieve this end. Legal forms aim to establish a comprehensive, lasting set of relationships among investors, entrepreneurs, managers, and, in some cases, other constituencies. In some cases, that may be essential. In others, permanence may be unnecessary or even anathema.

Capital and the Capital Access Problem

The first generation of social enterprise law's focus on form highlights the danger of letting the perfect be the enemy of the good. Creating an ideal form for an idealized social enterprise would inevitably fail to serve the needs of real ventures. Using financial instruments to formalize imperfect but potentially fruitful bargains struck directly between entrepreneurs and investors as an alternative to more comprehensive arrangements would serve both. Financial instruments offer potential suppliers of capital a means both of communicating the precise terms on which they will provide that capital to double-bottom-line ventures and perhaps even of enforcing those terms.

A fully realized form to house social enterprise would allow mission and profit-seeking to coexist free from disruptive threats to the venture's mission in perpetuity. Such a positive outcome turns on enforceability. In the corporate context, shareholders exercise the ultimate control over a corporation's fate. Preserving mission means curbing their autonomy. That loss of authority necessarily means an increase in authority for those charged with the task of preserving the venture's mission.

Relying on hybrid financial instruments to preserve a social enterprise's mission limits shareholders' freedom by empowering other investors. Form does much the same, although perhaps distributing that mission-shielding authority to a third-party regulator rather than to other investors. In either case, power would be allocated along predetermined lines specified by statute. Financial instruments offer a more tailored form of protection.

In one sense, the financial instruments we advance would play the same role an ordinary loan might. Such loans, for example, often impose limits on the ability of a corporate borrower to distribute profits to shareholders in the form of dividends and curb shareholders' power to merge or dispose of corporate assets.

Those loan terms wrest power from shareholders for the benefit of lenders in order to preserve a corporate borrower's capacity to satisfy its obligations to repay the loan's interest and principal.

Social enterprise investors could, and undoubtedly do, embrace such conventional measures to safeguard their interests.[11] The same loan covenants that prevent shareholders from drawing dividends that might imperil the lender's repayment could also be deployed to shield a venture's mission. Hybrid instruments offer investors a broader menu of options to pursue similar ends. As with high-yield and convertible debt and trust-preferred securities, a blend of debt and equity characteristics can produce a result uniquely suited to a particular context.

The Limits of Hybrid Finance

No hybrid instrument can replace an ideal form like the MPH. Focused entirely on the stake of one or more investors, a hybrid instrument cannot match form's potential to offer a comprehensive resolution to the tension between mission and profit. Moreover, an instrument's potency will generally parallel its duration and size. No matter how cleverly it may be designed, a small investment with a short duration may have little power to influence its recipient's development.

Form can directly address the relative priority of mission and profit, embedding instructions directly into an entity's DNA. Hybrid financial instruments must take an indirect route to the same end. Limiting dividend payouts will discourage greenwashing but will not prevent it as effectively as a well-enforced statutory mandate to prioritize mission over profit. Their unique combination of strengths and weaknesses may or may not represent the best alternative to form as a solution to the capital access problem, but they do demonstrate that form need not represent social enterprise's only hope.

Characteristics of a Social Enterprise Hybrid Financial Instrument

The remainder of this chapter imagines how a hybrid financial instrument designed for social enterprise might function. It considers how far finance might go toward closing the trust deficit to allow investors and entrepreneurs to find one another. At the same time, it uses the notion of a social enterprise hybrid instrument as a thought exercise to explore the challenges posed by capitalizing dual-mission businesses. Understanding precisely what role finance plays in inhibiting—and what role it could play in fueling—the growth of social enterprise yields valuable insights into the nature of the trust deficit.

A Tailored Solution to the Capital Access Problem

Imagining deep-pocketed investors and well-advised entrepreneurs collaborating to create a robust financial instrument that would simultaneously provide capital and mission security to a social enterprise does not require a great leap of faith. The increasing prominence of impact investing[12] and the willingness of those investors to integrate impact directly into deals[13] suggest that innovative approaches to financing social enterprise have already begun to take root among those with sufficient resources. The following discussion identifies the key elements in one version of such an instrument: FLY paper.

FLY paper is a debt product with a modest financial yield supplemented by a contingent conversion feature. The conversion feature would be triggered if control of the issuer changed hands or if other specified transactions took place that could be used by shareholders to extract profits. For example, the declaration of big dividend payments to shareholders would enable FLY paper holders to trade their social enterprise hybrid financial instruments for stock (and an outsize share of those dividends).

Issuing a financial instrument like the FLY paper sketched out here represents a lasting—but not permanent—commitment to a double bottom line. During its limited lifespan, a significant issuance of FLY paper by a social enterprise would profoundly reduce the likelihood that the owners of that venture's shares would abandon its social mission. It does so simply by stripping away an important source of temptation. In other words, FLY paper helps to make social mission sticky.

High-yield debt brings investors and entrepreneurs together not by offering a perfect financial instrument, but by crafting one that serves a specific set of needs. High-yield purchasers find returns to match their risk. Senior lenders take comfort in knowing that they receive their relatively modest yield before payments can be made to the holders of the high-yield debt. Equity holders embrace the fact that they retain both their financial upside and decision-making authority. Cataloging the very different combination of characteristics that would appeal to social enterprises and their investors is not only essential to designing a successful hybrid but also perhaps key to understanding social enterprise itself.

Subsidizing Mission

For some, concessionary returns represent a central characteristic of an investment in social enterprise.[14] These impact-first investors expect to trade financial gains for the enhanced social return their investment generates. Other investors see no trade-off between social mission and profitability and expect market rate returns, perhaps because consumers implicitly support that mission by paying higher prices for goods or services. Although they may not be an essential feature of social enterprise investments, to some, concessionary returns represent a defining trait. To allow for this characteristic, FLY paper would feature either a slightly or significantly below-market yield.

Like its high-yield analog, FLY paper would fall between traditional debt and equity in terms of priority. Given sufficient profits, priority would not be particularly important. Since for some social enterprises financial profits will be moderated by mission, priority may take on a greater importance than it otherwise might. Banks and other creditors would be paid before their flexible low-yield counterparts. But FLY paper lenders would be repaid before any distribution of earnings to equity holders. As is always true, shareholders would be most at risk if profits proved inadequate to satisfy both the social enterprise's creditors and its other investors, while traditional creditors would be the last to suffer. Investors in FLY paper would sit somewhere in the middle.

Patient Capital

FLY paper would be issued for a relatively long term, perhaps five to 10 years, to provide social enterprises with the patient capital their double-bottom-line ventures require. Although the yield would also be low rather than high, other FLY paper features mimic those of high-yield debt to extend this patient capital feature further. High-yield debt often offers a borrower what amounts to a payment holiday.[15] Even though the instrument nominally calls for the payment of interest on a regular basis over its life, the borrower has the right to defer all or some of that interest. Any borrower might benefit from the extra breathing room offered by such an option. For a social enterprise, the possibility of deferral could help to shield its commitment to mission. At a minimum, it would allow the enterprise to focus on a time horizon longer than the instrument's quarterly or semiannual accrual period.

That implicit link between the right to defer interest payments and mission could, of course, be made explicit. A borrower could be required to meet mission-related benchmarks, like those discussed in chapter 6, in order to qualify for deferral. Unlike a concessionary return, the deferral of interest need not subsidize a venture's mission. Deferred payments could be added to the loan's principal, accruing interest at the same rates as the original borrowing. The ability to defer would simply offer borrowers temporal flexibility as they work to balance a pair of bottom lines.

Allocating Control

A low yield and the payment deferral option would allow mission to take priority over profit at any given moment. Together, those features would adapt for-profit tools and techniques to create a space for double-bottom-line enterprises. As the discussion of hybrid organizational forms above demonstrated, accommodating a social enterprise's mission serves only as a first step. Securing that mission requires more. Fortunately, the great flexibility of hybrid financial instruments offers opportunities for doing precisely that.

The purchasers of low-yield instruments with an interest deferral feature might be doing nothing more than subsidizing the returns of other investors.[16] Presumably, the motivation for their purchase of low-yield hybrids lies in bolstering the venture's mission rather than the returns of other investors. To ensure that social investors are not simply subsidizing market rate counterparts, FLY paper is also designed to help secure a social enterprise's mission.

This protection is provided by a conversion feature, making FLY paper's low-yield, deferrable debt convertible into the borrower's common stock. Such a conversion feature could provide a lender an opportunity to acquire a voting stake in the borrower in exchange for his relatively secure—but nonvoting—interest. If the loan were large enough, or the conversion terms generous enough, conversion could hand control of the enterprise to the erstwhile owner of the social enterprise hybrid financial instrument. Even without an actual conversion, the power to convert and to exert some measure of control over a venture would give the owners a voice in the affairs of a social enterprise that they otherwise would lack.

As with other convertible debt instruments, the conversion feature would compensate an investor for some amount of forgone yield. Here, it would counterbalance a concession, in part by ensuring that it represents an exchange rather than a gift. If a FLY paper purchaser were disappointed with respect to the social return yielded by his investment, he could work to affect the venture's course whether or not he actually converts. For ordinary convertible debt instruments, the financial quid pro quo of yield for a conversion feature can be weighed with precision. The low-yield and convertible hybrid we propose would present a more complex picture, but one that gives an investor an opportunity both to quietly support a venture's mission and to speak up loudly if his expectations are not met.

Protecting Mission

The conversion feature would also give FLY paper purchasers a mechanism through which they could gain control of a wayward social enterprise. That, of course, opens the door to questions about what would constitute a wayward venture and who makes such a determination. The need to explicitly describe the circumstances under which conversion could occur encapsulates both the central challenge and opportunity represented by a social enterprise hybrid financial instrument. Requiring a majority of its purchasers to vote in favor of conversion might dampen the risk of mischief. Building specific triggers for conversion into the terms of the instrument itself would provide precisely the sort of transparency the second generation of social enterprise law targets. Contingent convertible debt instruments have been a notable feature of the financial landscape for more than a decade, serving a variety of specialized ends. Some provide favorable tax treatment for issuers.[17] Others offer comfort to bank regulators.[18]

The risk that shareholders will sell a social enterprise to a buyer intent on maximizing financial returns by eliminating its mission has been given a prominent place in the minds of social entrepreneurs and impact investors. FLY paper uses this particularly salient event to trigger conversion. Doing so helps deter such acquisitions by reducing the incentive for entrepreneurs to pursue them, and thereby assuages fears surrounding the possibility of a sellout. The conversion effectively reassigns the gains a sellout produces to the owners of the social enterprise hybrid financial instrument. How potent a protection such an instrument would offer would depend on its particular terms. Regardless of the details, sufficiently favorable conversion terms would inhibit a sale.

For a closely held social enterprise, perhaps owned largely by one or more founding entrepreneurs, a change of control would result from the sale of this majority stake, triggering the conversion feature. The sellers would not suffer directly from the conversion, particularly if they received cash in exchange for their shares, but the purchasers could find their stake in their newly acquired venture significantly diluted. With the conversion feature triggered by the sale, FLY paper holders would have the right to buy stock at rock-bottom prices. Knowing this, buyers willing to pay a high price for identical shares would be few and far between.

A widely held social enterprise might rely on a different sort of trigger for its FLY paper. Rather than an outright change of control, an appropriate trigger might be the acquisition of a significant stake by any one shareholder. The purchase of shares constituting a 10 percent stake in a social enterprise might, for example, suggest an unwelcome attempt to seize control and change the direction of the venture. In this scenario the pain suffered by the would-be acquirer will be shared by all shareholders. The holders of the remaining 90 percent of the corporation's widely held shares would, in theory, have their stake proportionately reduced just as the purchaser of the 10 percent would when the hybrids convert. In practice, the holders of the hybrids may never have an opportunity to convert.

Just as with the change of control trigger for the closely held venture, the tripwire transaction will either not occur at all or will be preceded by a negotiated truce between shareholders and FLY paper holders to defuse the mechanism. If holders of both the stock and the hybrids agree that the contemplated transaction would not threaten the social enterprise's mission (or both agree that the mission should not be preserved) FLY paper holders could forgo their pound of flesh. If the mission were safe, they might merely reset the FLY paper to guard against future threats. If the mission were set aside, all investors would receive a negotiated share of cash or equity compensation.

In this way, FLY paper functions as an antitakeover advice—not dissimilar to the poison pill.[19] When a corporation adopts a poison pill, it provides in its bylaws for shareholders to receive the right to purchase additional shares at bargain prices at the occurrence of one or more triggering events suggesting a takeover bid is in the offing. These dormant rights to dilute an acquirer make takeovers more difficult and more expensive, and thus create a defense without ever being implemented. Their very existence can deter would-be acquisitions; thus many jurisdictions subject directors who adopt them to heightened review for fiduciary compliance. For example, under Delaware's *Unocal* standard, fiduciaries meet their obligations when adopting a poison pill only if they do so in response to a reasonably perceived threat and when the pill is one of the range of reasonable responses.[20] But poison pills have easily cleared these hurdles when undertaken with careful consideration and documentation. Despite its defensive potential, when issued with similar care, FLY paper can be just as resilient.

Were FLY paper to exist, this low-yield, deferrable, contingent convertible financial instrument tailor-made for social enterprise would hardly be the most improbable one on the market. Against the backdrop of bundled derivatives with names like "iron butterfly,"[21] it can be hard to stand out. An instrument with the characteristics described here would only appear exotic to those familiar only with plain-vanilla debt and equity.

FLY Paper's Reach

At the risk of understatement, a social enterprise hybrid financial instrument with such terms would be more elaborate than most retail financial products. Although not suited for purchase by mom-and-pop investors, FLY paper could nevertheless provide a significant boost to the capacity of social enterprises to raise capital. In part, that effect would be direct. Sophisticated impact investors could evaluate its terms and decide that the particular blend of financial yield and social return they offer presents an appealing package.

Impact investors are a diverse group. Wealthy individuals interested in marrying social impact and financial return take the approach of angel investors in mission-driven businesses, sometimes drawing on experience as angels in traditional ventures.[22] The Ford Foundation has dedicated $1 billion of its endowment to social investments, but along with it and other giants like Rockefeller and Kresge, small family foundations are also showing interest in impact investing.[23] Some invest for impact using the PRI technique discussed in connection with the L3C, and therefore count their investments toward their required annual distributions under federal tax law. Others instead situate their impact investment work on the endowment—rather than the grantmaking—side of their organizations, harmonizing advancement of social mission along with achieving their financial goals. The IRS recently made this latter path easier by blessing the use of private foundation assets to make so-called mission-related investments, even if their "expected rate of return . . . is less than the foundation might obtain from an investment that is unrelated to its charitable purpose."[24] Funds made up of such investors and government and other development finance institutions can pool impact investment capital and package it for impact deals.[25] FLY paper's unique mix of terms is designed to meet the blended financial and social goals of these investors, and lines up well with their capacities and experience.

The complexity of a FLY paper deal should be neither so foreign nor so costly as to turn off these seasoned investors. Estimates of the size of the impact investment market vary substantially, from tens of billions of dollars today to hundreds of billions or nearly a trillion in the next decade.[26] Even the most modest of these projections indicates a substantial pool of capital available to put FLY paper to use. This large and growing impact investment community presently utilizes a broad range of asset classes and instruments.[27] FLY paper adds another, particularly well-matched device to this already powerful toolbox.

Beyond that immediate inflow of capital, the mission security provided by the issuance of FLY paper in and of itself could also attract other investors, even those with neither the appetite nor the experience to purchase such a complex investment themselves. For example, a relatively large, but privately-held social enterprise needing capital to scale its successful double-bottom-line model might issue a combination of FLY paper and stock. The sale might leave two-thirds of the corporation's stock in the hands of the founder (or founders) and shift the remaining one-third into the hands of the public.[28] FLY paper with a modest yield might be sold for the same aggregate price as the newly issued shares. The contingent conversion feature would be triggered by a change in control and would, in the aggregate, give FLY paper holders the right to exchange their interest for shares equal to the total number of shares then outstanding.[29]

In the unlikely event that the controlling shareholder or group of shareholders decided to sell their shares shortly after this initial public offering of stock and the accompanying sale of FLY paper, control would quickly change hands once more. The purchaser that briefly controlled the corporation would find itself holding one-third—down from two-thirds—of the venture's shares. The shareholders who acquired their stake in the initial public offering would find themselves collectively holding one-sixth of the shares rather than one-third. For the same price that purchased a one-third stake the day before (now amounting to just a one-sixth stake) the FLY paper holders would take half of the social enterprise's equity.

Ignoring such details as the elimination of the issuer's FLY paper obligations as the result of conversion, the former FLY paper holders would have purchased considerably more shares with each dollar than the participants in the initial public offering. That benefit would be paid for in part by the shareholders that acquired their shares in the initial public offering. As a result of the conversion, their stake would be reduced by half. In this decidedly hypothetical scenario, the acquisition and conversion of FLY paper would confer a three-to-one advantage in purchasing power over those buying shares in the public offering.

More important is the impact on the purchaser in the precipitating sale. Not only would it suffer the financial impact of a stark reduction in the value of its new investment, but it would yield control at almost the same moment it acquires it. Were such a purchase to take place, the price paid would undoubtedly plummet to reflect both types of harm. Realistically, such a transaction would simply not take place.

Issuing FLY paper together with common stock would send a powerful signal about the durability of a social enterprise's mission commitments. Each shareholder knows that this focus on mission might last only as long as the FLY paper does. For that period, though, even small shareholders unable to exercise control can be confident that the social enterprise will not be bought without the permission of FLY paper holders. With that assurance, even retail investors with neither the appetite for complex financial instruments nor the resources to acquire control over the social enterprise themselves could purchase its stock with an expectation—rather than a hope—that they are investing in a double-bottom-line venture. The issuance of FLY paper would, in effect, function to brand a social enterprise as trustworthy.

Catalyzing Growth

Social enterprise hybrid financial instruments serve a different end than specialized legal forms. Rather than addressing the general nature of social enterprise, these instruments focus narrowly on social enterprise's capital access problem. The FLY paper described above does that by offering a degree of clarity regarding a venture's path that hybrid forms—appropriately focusing on preserving the freedom of social enterprises to pursue their unique visions—do not.

The linked issuance of FLY paper and stock would attract different types of investors. Depending on the extent of the trade-off between mission protection and financial return, FLY paper could be purchased by charities or by impact investors. Their FLY paper investment might be heavily tilted toward mission at the price of deeply concessionary financial returns or might strike a more moderate balance. Particularly in the former case, with mission relatively secure over the FLY paper's term, a path would be cleared for ordinary investors to purchase its shares.

While not an investment for everyone, the stock of a FLY paper issuer would appeal to those interested in balancing social mission and financial return. FLY paper holders would earn their chosen blend of social and financial return concurrently. Shareholders would have their returns distributed across time, with, for example, the opportunity for the significant financial returns associated with an acquisition deferred until after the FLY paper's maturity. There would be no express prohibition against selling shares, but purchasers might heavily discount the future profit potential of the venture. Particularly while FLY paper has a significant portion of its term to run, opportunities for lucrative sales of stock might be relatively few and far between.

Precision and Transparency

FLY paper, like any social enterprise hybrid financial instrument, falls short of the MPH in terms of protecting mission. In all the ways that affirmative oversight ensures a healthy balance of financial and social returns, FLY paper's passive protection does not. It makes no effort to prioritize social mission. More pointedly, it imposes no penalty on a purported social enterprise that chooses to focus entirely on generating, albeit deferring, financial gains.

For all its limits, FLY paper holds at least one clear advantage over the MPH. It does not promise much, but the rights and obligations it details have clear lines and sharp edges. If the MPH offers an appealing standard—in the contest between mission and profit, mission must prevail—FLY paper offers a bright-line rule.[30] Like any rule, including the 55-miles-per-hour speed limit, it represents a compromise. Under some conditions, 55 miles per hour would be dangerous. At other times, it would be needlessly restrictive. Simply put, a rule provides an answer to an important question that is almost certain to be wrong much of the time. Nevertheless, it offers clear guidance to drivers and law enforcement officials that no admonition to drive at reasonable speeds could.

FLY paper targets greed rather than speed. While not a perfect substitute for the close oversight offered by the MPH, like the nondistribution constraint imposed on charities, FLY paper curbs the influence of self-interest. The appeal of the nondistribution constraint derives in part from the fact that it makes no effort to gauge the commitment of a charity to its stated aims. The term *nonprofit* suggests that charitable status precludes profitability. As described in chapter 1, it does not. Profits earned by a charity must simply be plowed into its mission and cannot be distributed to insiders. Like FLY paper, the nondistribution constraint dampens the incentive to sacrifice mission for profits. Unlike FLY paper, of course, the nondistribution constraint eliminates all opportunities for insiders to extract profits. FLY paper targets only a limited set of transactions and those only for a specified period.

Tax Benefits

As is true of the other hybrids discussed above, FLY paper would also offer tax advantages that a simple combination of stock and debt features could not. Convertible debt provides a tax result that investment units do not. Trust-preferred securities manage to secure the heads-I-win, tails-you-lose result of debt treatment from a tax perspective and equity treatment for accounting purposes. FLY paper manages to do a little of both.

Perhaps surprisingly given the stark difference in their tax treatment, the law offers little clarity on the question of how to classify financial instruments beyond prototypical debt and equity. Even setting aside the types of complex derivatives that acquired notoriety in the wake of the 2008 financial crisis, a surprising degree of uncertainty can attach to apparent debt.[31] Frequently, the resulting questions cloud the issuer's entitlement to benefits such as the deductions that accompany interest payments.

Nominal debt that exposes lenders to sufficient risk, either implicitly or explicitly linking an investor's return to the would-be borrower's future profitability, might be viewed as equity for tax purposes. High-yield debt, for example, could promise payments so large that the instruments take on a speculative character. In other words, the lender may only expect to be paid according to an instrument's terms if the borrower prospers. Under those circumstances, although both the borrower and lender agree to treat the investment as a loan, tax authorities could well strip the borrower of valuable interest deductions.[32]

A sufficiently large issuance of FLY paper by a fledgling social enterprise would represent just such a bet on the venture's future and would be treated as equity despite the presence of debt characteristics. Fortunately, for an early-stage social enterprise running on a blend of enthusiasm and optimism, equity tax treatment would be a blessing rather than a curse. A seed stage venture with its sights set on breaking even would, of course, place little current value on interest deductions. For their part, investors in a not-yet-profitable social enterprise would undoubtedly frown at the prospect of being taxed today—as debt treatment would require—on payments they may or may not receive in the future.

At the other end of the spectrum, a profitable social enterprise could issue a moderate amount of FLY paper with confidence in its debt classification. As long as the borrower had ample resources to satisfy its obligations, FLY paper would not have the speculative character it has when the same instruments represent the lion's share of a start-up's capital. Counterintuitively, the conversion feature would not weigh against debt treatment. Although it is always true that an investor's capacity to transform debt into equity should weigh strongly in favor of treating a convertible note as equity, in a typical case it does not. A conversion feature—on its own—is so thoroughly ignored for tax purposes that it does not even trigger the special rules that apply to debt instruments with unconventional or uncertain payment structures. As it is designed *not* to be triggered, the contingent nature of the conversion feature would not change that result.[33]

The result would be interest deductions for the borrower and interest income for the lender. Impact investors might plausibly see this as a means of promoting mission by shouldering a portion of the social enterprise's tax burden. Tax-exempt investors such as charities would not pay tax on that income. As a result, they could use FLY paper as a means of sharing their privileged tax status with a double-bottom-line venture.

Remarkably, without changing any of its terms, FLY paper would seamlessly adapt to suit both a seed stage *and* a mature social enterprise. Less extreme cases would produce less obvious results, but tax advisers routinely make such judgments. Since a conclusion need only be reached once—at the time of issuance—the burden on issuers would be modest.

The different needs of social enterprises as they mature suggest that a constellation of hybrids might better serve needs of a diverse pool of ventures. Investors and entrepreneurs might look to tools ranging from loan guarantees to revenue-sharing arrangements[34] to the simple agreement for future equity (SAFE) devised by Y Combinator[35] for models for creatively structuring the finance of social enterprises. But such tailoring may not be necessary or even desirable. The appeal of specialization must be weighed against the benefits of standardization. A single hybrid instrument like FLY paper[36] could become a known quantity. Ventures bound by the terms of a sufficient quantum of that social enterprise hybrid financial instrument could be readily identified by potential investors or consumers.

Conclusion

Simply put, a standardized social enterprise hybrid financial instrument like FLY paper not only could serve as an off-the-shelf tool for bringing investors and entrepreneurs together, but could become a reliable brand with broad appeal. Like the MPH proposed in chapter 2 and the SE(c)(3) regime the next chapter describes, FLY paper could serve as a reliable signal of commitment to mission. Third-party certifiers such as B Lab and other metrics considered in chapter 6 have the potential to do the same, but the state of the art currently bases these judgments in large part on information that may be dated or unverified.

Bringing the MPH or SE(c)(3) to life would demand legislative intervention and, perhaps, public resources. A social enterprise hybrid financial instrument like FLY paper could provide reliable, forward-looking mission protection without the need for any government action. This chapter offers no answer to the question of which route seems most promising, but does demonstrate that government inaction need not hobble the growth of the social enterprise sector.

Overall, financial instruments offer investors and entrepreneurs the benefit of greater autonomy, but they also place greater responsibility on private shoulders. Those with sufficient resources making substantial investments can turn to professionals skilled in their design to achieve the goals they desire. Despite its longevity and relative popularity, though, even high-yield debt remains a tool used primarily by sophisticated investors. While its design follows established patterns, the terms of any given high-yield bond emerge from careful negotiations.

Financial instruments designed to address social enterprise's capital access problem likewise seem unlikely to ever become a retail product. Even if it never evolves beyond the rarified context occupied by high-yield debt, FLY paper could still have a significant impact. Bespoke financial instruments could still catalyze the growth of social enterprise, serving both as a lifeline for ventures hungry for capital and proof that the leap from the first to the second generation of social enterprise law does not hinge on the success of hybrid forms or any other government action.

The Holy Grail of Retail Investment

FLY paper could take flight tomorrow. By contrast, the MPH will remain stuck in neutral without an unthinkable public sector infrastructure expansion. Nevertheless, as this chapter shows, the second generation of social enterprise law does not simply reject the public in favor of the private. To the contrary, in some contexts, government intervention will play a critical role. Social enterprises and sophisticated impact investors can use creative financing arrangements like FLY paper to signal and enforce their mutual commitments to a dual-mission venture—and perhaps bring some other investors along for the ride. But these innovations will not help entrepreneurs searching for the holy grail of offering equity to retail investors. Given their urgent need for capital, social enterprises have good reason to desire access to this immense market. According to the Federal Reserve's most recent study in 2013, 48.8 percent of US families owned publicly traded stock, either directly or through pooled investment vehicles like mutual funds.[1] This number was down from over 53 percent in the prior survey in 2007, but half of all US families remains a staggeringly large pool of possible investors.[2]

Firms seeking to reach the potentially vast pool of retail investment capital face a number of significant obstacles. One, persuading small investors to entrust them with a meaningful part of their modest savings, rises above all others. For the better part of a century, the federal government has played a central role in helping build trust between investors and entrepreneurs. Over the past few years, Congress has renewed its focus on that task, paying particular attention to democratizing investor access. Traditionally, the price tag associated with the government's investment-screening process has been extraordinarily high. The government heavily regulates the issuance and sale of securities. Small and start-up social enterprises, like other businesses of such modest size, simply cannot absorb the costs of complying with this sea of regulation.

Recent federal legislation has attempted to tame these costs in order to provide small and start-up firms with greater access to capital. These efforts have engendered significant criticism, and many are justifiably skeptical that the regulations implementing these changes will enhance small business capital formation. Even if these are effective in providing traditional entrepreneurs with access to retail investment, social entrepreneurs face additional challenges. The same assurance game that complicates matching social entrepreneurs and sophisticated impact investors will bedevil social enterprises seeking investors at the retail level. Unfortunately, do-it-yourself financial creativity will not bridge this trust gap. Strategies like FLY paper require investors to shoulder transaction costs much higher than those individual investors can typically bear. Retail investors lack the coffers, the know-how, and the influence to develop their own complex financial vehicles. Social enterprises intent on tapping this deep pool of shallow pockets will require a fundamentally different approach.

In the retail environment, a third party will need to supply signals of trustworthiness social enterprises can afford. The Internal Revenue Service may not be the obvious choice to provide such reassurance on a vast scale, but its access to the corporate purse strings gives it the leverage to do just that. Equally important, the corporate tax it oversees gives it the power to fairly allocate the mechanisms' costs among participating social enterprises.

The SE(c)(3) tax regime we propose would offer social enterprises a carefully balanced mixture of benefits and burdens. Companies that opt into the system would qualify for an annual exclusion from the corporate income tax, to shelter mission-driven income of up to $500,000. SE(c)(3)s would receive this current tax benefit, but only in exchange for also accepting a future tax burden. Any profits they distribute and any gains on sales of their shares would be taxed at higher rates than nonelecting firms. This mix of carrots and sticks will be attractive to truly mission-focused businesses, but distasteful to greenwashers.

The embrace of SE(c)(3) status would also function as a signal of trustworthiness for social enterprises and retail investors, as powerful, in its way, as the transparency the Securities and Exchange Commission provides to the investing public. Few entrepreneurs and investors will initially think of the IRS as a likely solution to any problem, but existing tax law and the expertise of the IRS in administering it can be turned to this improbable task without requiring a government subsidy. Paired with the targeted disclosure requirements Congress has carved out for fledgling ventures seeking to raise capital, SE(c)(3) could connect start-up social enterprises directly with small investors eager to support them.

Big Pool of Small Investors

Social entrepreneurs, like other entrepreneurs, need to look for money in the hands of those who have it. This group is not limited to only the well-heeled, sophisticated venture capitalists, angel investors, and institutional and other impact investors best able to deploy FLY paper and other complex investment products. Millions of everyday Americans also have savings to invest. Each of these individual investors standing alone has little capital to offer a social entre-preneur. As noted above, though, taken together their resources are formidable.

The next obvious question, of course, is whether everyday investors will be interested in investing in social enterprises. There is reason to believe the answer is yes. First of all, retail investors are also consumers, and consumers bundle their purchases in a variety of areas with contributions to achieving social goals. One need look no further than the sea of pink products that line grocery stores each October in connection with Breast Cancer Awareness Month. But there is also Gap apparel, Apple gadgets, and many other products supporting anti-AIDS efforts through the Product (RED) campaign[3] and AmazonSmile, which offers shoppers the

> exact same low prices, vast selection and convenient shopping experi-ence as Amazon.com, with the added bonus that Amazon will donate a portion of the purchase price to [their] favorite charitable organization.[4]

There have been many challenges to the effectiveness—and even legitimacy—of cause-related marketing in general and some particular campaigns, reacting to their opacity, the misconceptions they can create, and their potential to crowd out direct charitable contributions.[5] Whether one is a booster or a critic of efforts to link purchases with donations, one cannot deny their appeal to consumers.

The mere fact that some consumers prefer a pink yogurt cup or donate a dol-lar with their drugstore purchases at holiday time does not mean they will be willing to take a haircut on their investments to pursue social good. Fortunately, inferences from consumer spending are not the only indication that individual investors would be interested. Many already invest in products that combine financial return with the "warm glow" of doing good (or at least avoiding evil). Millions of investors place their retirement and other investments in socially responsible mutual funds each year. This category is significant and mounting. The Forum for Sustainable and Responsible Investing found in its 2014 trends report that

> total US-domiciled assets under management using SRI strategies expanded from $3.74 trillion at the start of 2012 to $6.57 trillion at the start of 2014, an increase of 76 percent. These assets now account for more than one out of every six dollars under professional manage-ment in the United States.[6]

The Forum explains this rise as driven in part by the "continued . . . trajectory of dramatic growth" in funds using environmental, sustainability, and governance factors in investment decisions, including mutual funds as well as other pooled investment products.[7]

The recent success of crowdfunding sites like Kickstarter, GoFundMe, and Indiegogo reinforces the notion that retail investors would be willing to invest capital in social enterprise. Sites like these have attracted millions of individuals to contribute to ventures with no chance of financial return. They share the broad goal of funding projects for which traditional financing is unavailable or priced out of reach, using the power—and many small wallets—of the crowd. This phenomenon—small, private companies wishing to combine a positive impact with profits successfully raising modest amounts of capital directly from far-flung kindred spirits—offers an appealing template for social enterprise start-ups.

Much of crowdfunding's appeal lies in enabling everyday individuals to nurture early-stage ventures. Crowdfunding success occurs when a project stirs the interests, and often the heartstrings, of a large pool of potential investors reached online. Social enterprises fit that mold precisely. They embrace a community ethic, and their double-bottom-line vision fits with crowdfunding platforms' commitments to balancing financial rewards with creative productivity. Social enterprise founders, employees, and customers already rub elbows with the hipster, millennial crowd of retail investors involved in crowdfunding. It seems almost inevitable that crowdfunding would also be used to build capital for these dual-mission businesses. Indeed, commentators have argued that direct finance tools like crowdfunding are more plausible when investors seek more than just financial gains.[8]

Legal and Practical Challenges in Reaching Retail Investors

Despite social entrepreneurs' desire to reach retail investors and investors' likely interest in investing in social enterprises, a number of roadblocks will limit their ability to work together. Firms seeking retail investment can proceed by various routes, but none of them will be entirely smooth paths for the small, privately-held firms typical of social enterprise.

Indirect Investment

Of course, one major way that retail investors invest is through mutual funds, and the socially responsible mutual funds just addressed might sound like the perfect intermediary for social enterprises and retail investors seeking blended value. Unfortunately, regulatory and practical concerns will limit mutual funds' investments in these firms. Mutual funds are open-end vehicles, meaning that investors can withdraw their capital at any time—today via a quick click on a smartphone app. Mutual funds set the daily prices at which investors can redeem their interests, and funds' profitability depends upon setting these prices at appropriate levels. To ensure they can price investor redemptions accurately, mutual funds prefer portfolio investments that are both liquid and transparent. Even if they did not, under SEC guidance, an open-end mutual fund cannot invest more than 15 percent of its assets in private companies.[9] These prudential and regulatory considerations constrain even socially responsible mutual funds seeking investee firms achieving social good from investments in small and lightly traded social enterprises. Their dual social and profit missions will complicate the process of assessing these companies and their prospects in order to mark a fund to market, discouraging participation by these heavily regulated investment vehicles.

Pension funds also act as a major intermediary between retail investors' capital and the marketplace. Billions of dollars in retirement assets are managed by public and private pension funds in the United States today.[10] These dollars are likewise an improbable source of capital for social enterprise. Pension fund managers operate under fiduciary duties, and also frequently under the additional obligations of the federal Employee Retirement Income Security Act (ERISA). Both of these authorities require pension fund managers investing pooled assets for future retirees to do so in the best interests of the funds' future claimants. Recent Department of Labor guidance has clarified that ERISA fund managers may consider environmental, social, and governance issues as a component of determining an investment's long-term value, and can invest for social return when all other facets of an investment are equivalent to one without the accompanying social benefit.[11] Even with this latitude, however, explicitly forgoing financial gain to achieve social benefit remains forbidden. Managers subject to these rules will thus often be unable to countenance social enterprises' acceptance of a trade-off of financial return for social good.

The retail investment market represents a deep pool of capital that could be used to start and scale social enterprises, and much evidence suggests that many retail investors desire to invest for a blend of financial and social return. Mutual and pension funds bundle individual contributions into substantial streams of capital, making them obvious candidates for the task of connecting retail investors and social enterprises. Unfortunately, the legal and practical realities of managing mutual and pension funds will prevent these intermediaries from providing ready vehicles for matching investor capital and small-scale social enterprise.[12]

Direct Retail Investment

It is also difficult for social enterprises to bypass these go-betweens and reach retail investors directly. Even the most casual observer of business affairs will be familiar with the splashiest way to proffer shares to the retail investors: the IPO.

An IPO, or initial public offering, occurs when a company first sells its shares to the general public. To sell securities to the public beyond the borders of a single state, however, a company (also called an "issuer") must register its securities with the federal Securities and Exchange Commission (SEC) or qualify for an exemption from the registration requirement. The registration process requires the SEC to pre-vet materials investors will receive, and also makes an issuing company subject to ongoing and onerous requirements to report on its operations to the SEC and the public.

Investors value the ability to sell their securities on a secondary market; so firms planning an IPO usually also apply to list their new securities on an exchange. Each exchange sets its own listing standards—requirements to offer a security for trading on that exchange. For example, the fabled Big Board at the New York Stock Exchange will only list companies with over $10 million in pretax earnings over the past three years or a global market capitalization of over $200 million.[13] To meet the listing requirements for Nasdaq's Global Select Market through earnings, one must show at least $11 million in pretax earnings in the last three years, and none of these years can show a loss.[14] Alternative markets with lower thresholds also exist, and these are the only realistic possibility for most start-up businesses seeking capital.

Even if a firm plans to list on a smaller exchange, however, the highly regulated process of launching an IPO will often remain cost-prohibitive. IPOs are incredibly expensive. At the very least, the issuer will need to retain attorneys and accountants to prepare the necessary documents and guide it through the complex process, and investment bankers to put the deal together and help in pricing the securities. Issuers also may need to hire a variety of other costly professionals, like media relations firms to generate the type of buzz the company seeks. The costs associated with an IPO will continue to generate benefits after the initial capital infusion it permits, as public companies then have great flexibility to access public equity and debt markets in the future. Even considering these longer-term benefits, however, only companies that have truly hit the big time will be able to spend the fortune it costs to jump through the hoops required to go public.

Most enterprises never reach this level of success, but there are firms that tout their social missions and have grown successful enough to take this path. Google (now through Alphabet) is perhaps the most notable high-flying company that styles itself a prosocial force and has tapped the public markets. But even the most successful social enterprises cannot emulate Google—it is just too big, too successful, and too singular.

Etsy provides a more earthbound comparison.[15] When it launched an IPO in April 2015,[16] Etsy embraced a number of social goals along with its profit-generating mission and had obtained B Corp certification. Financial results from this effort so far are mixed. The stock generated significant interest on its debut, when shares rose to $30 from the initial offering price of $16. Since then, though, the trend has been downward, with the stock dipping below its offering price over the summer and not yet recovering. It also remains too soon to tell what effect retail investment will have on Etsy's commitment to its social mission, but its aggressive tax planning accompanying the 2015 IPO suggest there may be reason to be wary.[17]

Etsy's experience did not dim the enthusiasm of Laureate Education, another certified B Corp, for an IPO.[18] Laureate runs for-profit colleges around the globe, and touts its adoption of the Delaware public benefit corporation form as proof of its commitment to its social mission.[19] Some have expressed skepticism about the social benefit generated by Laureate (skepticism we share), considering that the for-profit education industry has been dogged by legal and regulatory concerns for years and that one of Laureate's colleges has the second-highest student debt burden in the nation.[20] But the company remains steadfast in its claims that it will balance its social and profit-making goals after an IPO, and when the launch went forward in early 2017, it became the first Delaware PBC to go public.[21] In contrast, the company behind crowdfunding giant Kickstarter has publicly rejected the possibility of an IPO. It has undertaken commitments in its charter to support "arts and culture, mak[e its] values core to . . . operations, fight[] inequality, and help[] creative projects come to life."[22] Cofounder and chief executive Yancey Strickler cited fears that an IPO "would push the company to make choices that we don't think are in the best interest of the company."[23] Responding to concerns like these, of course, is precisely what the second generation of social enterprise law aims to accomplish.

Rather than quarrel over which companies qualify as social enterprises or engage in existential objections, there is a simpler and more fundamental explanation for the absence of social enterprise IPOs: size. Most social enterprises, like most businesses, simply won't ever be large enough to qualify for an IPO, or to have the wherewithal to pay its price of admission. Fortunately, there are a number of alternative routes for small and growing companies to raise capital from the public—or at least slices of the public. Companies wishing to issue securities can do so outside of the traditional IPO by utilizing one of the ever-growing list of exemptions from the SEC's registration requirements or by avoiding the SEC's jurisdiction altogether by selling their securities only in their home state.

Legal Changes Designed to Ease Access to Retail Market

Part of the fuel for the 2012 Jumpstart Our Business Startups (JOBS) Act was the desire to reduce the regulatory hurdles companies must clear in order to access the capital markets. At the signing ceremony, President Obama lauded it as a "game changer," celebrating that "[s]tartups and small businesses will now have access to a big new pool of potential investors, namely the American people."[24] SEC action in 2016 also enabled greater use of single-state securities offerings. These changes are addressed to small businesses in general, not social enterprises in particular. Nevertheless, by dramatically reducing the costs of issuing securities, these changes create new opportunities for social enterprises.

Private Placements: Investments for the (Affluent) Masses

The first major change worked by the JOBS Act relates to what has been the most popular exemption used to avoid the SEC's registration requirements: Rule 506 of the SEC's Regulation D.[25] The rule has long created a safe harbor, providing issuers a blueprint for selling unregistered securities with minimal regulatory cost and little fear of running afoul of federal securities law. This exemption also removes any concerns that might arise under state securities law. Although every state has a securities regulator, Congress made federal regulation the exclusive authority for these offerings in 1996—an action called "preemption." Rule 506 issuers must file a very brief public notice with the SEC after the securities have been sold. These steps, tiny when compared to the Herculean effort required to launch an IPO, suffice to make a legally acceptable offering of securities under Rule 506—provided the securities are sold to "accredited" investors.[26]

US securities law segments investors into accredited and nonaccredited groups, and limits the sale of many unregistered securities to accredited investors only. As a default, every investor is deemed nonaccredited. To be accredited, an investor must meet one of a number of criteria demonstrating the investor's likely sophistication and ability tolerate risk and loss. For natural persons— living, breathing, human beings—these criteria are based on either earnings or assets. An individual with earned income greater than $200,000 (or $300,000 together with a spouse) for two prior years, along with the reasonable expectation of earnings over that threshold in the current year, qualifies as an accredited investor. Alternatively, net worth excluding one's primary residence of over $1 million (again alone or together with a spouse) will do.[27] We assume that investors with enough money to cushion a substantial loss can tolerate the additional risks involved in investing in securities with lesser disclosure and poorer liquidity.

These criteria reduce the pool of potential accredited investors, but not as much as one might think. According to the Government Accountability Office, approximately 8.5 million US households could have qualified as accredited investors in 2013.[28] The thresholds for income and net worth have not been adjusted for some time, and there have been calls for the SEC to do so,[29] as well as to impose additional requirements to demonstrate investor sophistication. Even if this happens, the number of accredited investors will remain high. For example, after adjusting the current requirements for inflation, an SEC staff report found there would still have been over 4 million US households eligible in 2013.[30] An SEC report measured the market for unregistered securities offerings at over two trillion dollars the following year.[31] Offerings limited to accredited investors offer social enterprises access to a very large pool of capital, and with quite low levels of regulation.

Importantly, though, securities under the Rule 506 exemption have always been "restricted," meaning they cannot be sold freely after purchase. Waiting periods of up to a year are typical, and issuer consent is generally required for sale. These restrictions make securities sold under the Rule 506 exemption less liquid, and thus less attractive to investors. That said, private marketplaces for trading restricted securities have recently been launched to ease this process, and appear poised to facilitate greater liquidity for sufficiently affluent and sophisticated investors.[32]

Until the enactment of the JOBS Act, one additional limit applied to Rule 506 offerings: a proscription on advertising. The JOBS Act and its accompanying regulations repealed this so-called general solicitation ban, which had formerly prohibited issuers under Rule 506 from advertising their offerings to the general public through the mass media. Issuers that claim exemption from registration under new Rule 506(c) need not rely only on word of mouth, personal referrals, or brokers' client lists to find those who qualify. They can use radio and television ads and the Internet as well. Issuers must take reasonable steps to verify that those to whom they sell in fact meet the accreditor investor criteria, but the repeal of the ban will increase issuers' access to investors and investors' access to offerings made under it.[33]

Reinvigorating the "Mini-IPO" Process

In its second innovation clearing the path between small businesses and retail investors, the JOBS Act aimed to increase the attractiveness of a little-used alternative to the traditional IPO. This alternative appears in another of the SEC's alphabet soup of regulations, Regulation A, first promulgated in 1936. Shares issued pursuant to this regulatory framework may be purchased by all investors, accredited and nonaccredited alike, but until recently issuers using it remained subject to state securities regulation. The federal disclosure obligations applied to these issues were less onerous than those applicable to a standard IPO, but issuers using this "mini-IPO" option were also limited to raising at most $5 million in a year. This relatively low cap on raises generally did not justify the cost of potentially 50-state regulatory compliance, so few issuers made use of it.[34]

The JOBS Act directed the SEC to issue revised regulations allowing these public offerings to raise up to $50 million in a 12-month period,[35] and the SEC complied in March 2015 with what has been dubbed "Regulation A+."[36] As public offerings, issuers qualifying under Regulation A+ may advertise to the public and sell to all takers. Issuers are also given a choice of two regulatory options—one offering them a $20 million raise cap and the other $50 million.[37] In exchange for the higher raise limit, issuers must contend with greater federal regulation of their offerings. Nonaccredited investors may only invest up to 10 percent of their income or net worth in the securities offered, though issuers need not verify investors' claims they meet accredited investor criteria. These issuers are also subject to greater federal disclosure, though in return they receive preemption of state securities law. Offerings subject to the smaller cap remain exposed to state securities regulators' authority. States are coordinating their regulation of offerings more than ever before, in an attempt to make multistate compliance more practical, but it remains a complex process.[38]

Regulation A+ has met with some real excitement, as the vastly increased caps on capital raising represent a sea change, and it addressed major factors that caused issuers to avoid this route in the past.[39] As revised, it may function as true mini-IPO, giving smaller companies access to participation by a wide pool of accredited and nonaccredited investors. Yet these beneficial attributes come combined with disclosure and reporting obligations still closer to those for a traditional IPO than those for private placements—with significant costs. It remains to be seen whether this combination is sufficiently attractive to generate widespread use of Regulation A+.

Investing for the Crowd

The third, and much ballyhooed, innovation of the JOBS Act was its direction to the SEC to create a regulatory system for crowdfunded securities. If a traditional IPO were a luxurious French-cuffed dress shirt at home only in gleaming office towers on Wall Street, the Regulation A and D exemptions might represent the sort of Oxford shirt worn by well-heeled professionals everywhere. Crowdfunding represents something fundamentally different. If a button-down shirt at all, it would be flannel.

Crowdfunding is the aggregation of small amounts of money from a very large group of participants—the crowd—to capitalize a project. Online platforms make this aggregation economically and practically feasible. It is easy to see how crowdfunding might help fill the gap in financing faced by projects and companies with prospects too uncertain to qualify for bank loans and business plans too unconventional to attract angel investors or venture capital funding. Crowdfunding successes, albeit in the noninvestment context—ranging from Kickstarter darlings like the Veronica Mars movie to political upstarts like Howard Dean—have demonstrated its incredible power and potential.

It should come as no surprise then that online platforms have proliferated to entice a crowd of funders to capitalize an incredible range of ideas. These platforms use a great variety of models. The simplest are pure donation sites like GoFundMe.com.[40] Individuals post a description of why they need money. Others (often friends and family) click through donations that the person in need can claim and use. Funders receive nothing beyond the gratitude of the recipient and the satisfaction of furthering a person or cause they support. Political crowdfunding follows a similar logic, and it can also describe the fund-raising efforts of many traditional charities. Indeed, state charity regulators may consider appeals on these platforms to fall within their registration and report-ing requirements for charitable solicitation.[41] But this donation-based crowd-funding, which offers funders only psychic returns, does not implicate securities law. So long as funders do not make "investment[s] of money in a common enterprise with profits to come solely from the efforts of others,"[42] no securities under the federal definition are involved, and the SEC will remain at bay.

Of course, not every cause will stir enough passion to generate strings-free donations. Reward-based crowdfunding sweetens the deal for contributors, but does so by offering nonmonetary returns that likewise steer clear of the govern-ment regulation of securities. Online platforms like Kickstarter and Indiegogo offer funders a set of tiered, but nonmonetary, incentives for their participation. These rewards often include receiving the product or playing a part in the project being funded. So the creator of Jelly Belly candy sought funding on Kickstarter to start a new candy line. Modest contributors could earn rights to be among the first to try his new flavors, and substantial ones could qualify to tour his factory.[43] Highly publicized runaway crowdfunding hits like smart-watch man-ufacturer Pebble have raised millions of dollars through reward crowdfunding sites.[44] But it is more modest success stories like bands campaigning to record new albums that fill the pages of these sites. Contributing fans might receive the album and, if their contribution is large enough, special extras like a ride-along on the band's tour bus or a chance to sing backup vocals.[45]

There are also two quite different types of crowdfunding that use a lending model. The non-interest-bearing type pioneered by Kiva.org again avoids cre-ating federally regulated securities.[46] Kiva, a nonprofit organization, functions primarily to aggregate funds to be used by other NGOs around the world. These local entities screen borrowers for inclusion on Kiva's website, and funds are often disbursed to them for use in loans even before a visitor to the site selects a particular borrower. Otherwise, funders visiting Kiva have the recognizable experience of choosing among a large number of funding requests. The site fea-tures a diverse, global group of aspiring borrowers seeking funds to pay for edu-cation, business development, and many other needs. When a funder selects one or more borrowers, she sends her money to Kiva and will receive updates on the borrower's progress. If the borrower defaults, the funder loses her money. If a loan is ultimately repaid, however, the most a funder may receive is return of her principal. Funders earn no interest or any other financial return on their contribution, so for federal securities law purposes no securities are at play.

Indeed, Kiva encourages funders to think of funds allocated to its site much more like a donation than an investment. It recommends lending the returned principal to another borrower, and even suggests contributing it to Kiva itself (tax-deductibly).

Interest-bearing lending platforms like Lending Club and Prosper differ dramatically. These sites offer lenders the possibility of financial returns, by way of interest payments in addition to the return of their principal. Predictably, this aspect of their business models attracted the attention of the SEC. In 2008, it ordered Prosper to cease and desist in selling securities without proper registration. Both sites swiftly accepted that they were involved in the sale of securities and changed their business models to conform with registration requirements. Today, "lenders" on these platforms are not really lenders, but purchasers of notes issued by the platforms themselves.[47] Repayment of these notes is dependent on borrowers' repayments of the underlying loans—and lenders do lose if borrowers fail to repay—but Lending Club and Prosper issue these debt securities, which are registered with the SEC.

Like interest-bearing lending model sites, equity crowdfunding falls squarely within the jurisdiction of the SEC. In this kind of crowdfunding, an entrepreneur posts information on her business to an online site and seeks funds from microinvestors. If she is successful, the investors receive ownership stakes (albeit tiny ones) in exchange for their contributions. This clearly represents a sale of securities to the public. Unless the entrepreneur registers with the SEC or meets one of the exemptions from the registration requirement, such an offering would patently violate securities law. Formerly, no exemption to the SEC's burdensome registration requirements suited equity crowdfunding. Even after the JOBS Act changes discussed above, a Rule 506(c) offering only caters to the more limited crowd of accredited investors, and it remains to be seen whether the new Regulation A+ will make the mini-IPO path realistic for issuers.

Even assuming these changes would prove sufficient to accommodate crowdfunded offerings within existing registration exemptions, daunting regulatory obstacles remained for online platforms desiring to host them. Such a platform would likely be a "broker," as it would function to effect the securities transactions of others for compensation.[48] Under another part of federal securities law, brokers must register with the SEC and become members of a self-regulatory organization (SRO).[49] Registration and SRO membership would subject platforms to a raft of rules regulating these middlemen.[50] In this regulatory environment, the vision of equity crowdfunding for the masses through simple, private online marketplaces could not be realized—at least not legally.

The JOBS Act sought to change all that. Its Title III was separately—and impressively acronymously—named the Capital Raising Online While Deterring Fraud and Unethical Non-Disclosure (or CROWDFUND) Act. The CROWDFUND Act laid the basic groundwork for a crowdfunding exemption from securities registration requirements as well as for preemption of state securities law, and created a new category of intermediaries empowered to host crowdfunded offerings. It directed the SEC to issue implementing regulations within 270 days, but the regulatory process dragged on for over three years.[51] It is too soon to tell precisely how entrepreneurs, investors, and intermediaries will react to the new system the regulations erect, but the JOBS Act and final regulations establish basic ground rules.

First, offerings may raise a maximum of $1 million in any 12-month period. Compared with the unlimited capital that can be raised through private placements and the $20 million or $50 million caps under new Regulation A+, the $1 million cap for crowdfunded offerings is exceedingly modest. This limitation means that only very small and early-stage start-ups could use the crowdfunding exemption alone to meet their funding needs, though crowdfunding issues can be used to supplement private placements or other issues. Those issuers who opt to raise capital through crowdfunding are subject to scaled financial disclosure obligations, which vary based on the size of the offering.

The system was also designed to attract small investors, while simultaneously limiting their exposure. There are no income or asset requirements to be eligible to participate, but all investors are subject to limits on how much crowdfunded investing they can do. In each 12-month period, the most any investor with either annual income or net worth under $100,000 may invest in crowdfunded securities is $5,000. Many will be limited to an even lower total investment. Above these income and asset levels, investment limits increase, but not by terribly much, and there is an overall cap of $100,000 per investor—regardless of how high-earning or wealthy she may be.

The core of these investment limitations can be found in the JOBS Act itself,[52] and serve as a check on risk for the smaller, unsophisticated investors crowdfunded offerings reach. Small businesses like those that would use crowdfunding simply have a very high failure rate. Investors in this space will likely lose money, but the crowdfunding regime tries to ensure they will not lose all that much. These offerings also present a higher risk profile than more traditional retail investments for a variety of reasons. Their limited disclosure obligations may make it more difficult for the SEC or others to root out and combat fraud effectively. Less sophisticated individual investors may be unable to spot fraudulent or poor investments for themselves.

Crowdfunded offerings also must occur through a registered broker-dealer or through one of a new type of intermediary the JOBS Act created called a "funding portal."[53] Like broker-dealers, funding portals must register with the SEC and join an SRO, though the requirements for funding portals are somewhat less onerous. Still, many critics argue they are too burdensome to be feasible considering the relatively limited opportunities funding portals have to profit from a crowdfunded offering.[54] Funding portals may not offer investment advice, hold investor funds, or offer commission-based compensation.[55] Yet they must perform due diligence on the offerings they list on their platforms and help ensure investor compliance with investment limits.

Funding portals also cannot create a secondary market for crowdfunded securities,[56] the sale of which is restricted for one year. Investors may sell their shares thereafter, but they may have difficulty identifying interested buyers. It is uncertain whether and how secondary markets for crowdfunded securities will develop, and how this liquidity problem will impact investor interest in crowdfunded securities.

Finally, while the JOBS Act cleared the way for issuers under new Rule 506(c) to engage in general solicitation of accredited investors, crowdfunded offerings can be advertised in only a bare-bones "advertising notice."[57] Proper notices can include little more than the name of the issuing company and a link to the intermediary hosting the offering. Again, investor protection is the obvious motivation. The SEC did not want to start seeing pop-up Internet videos and late-night television infomercials touting crowdfunded investment opportunities to unsophisticated retail investors. Limiting advertising reduces the likelihood of drawing in uninitiated or foolhardy investors prone to lose their money in crowdfunding's risky waters. Of course, permitting only what are colloquially known as "tombstone ads" likewise decreases crowdfunding's reach—a linguistic irony not likely lost on an SEC skeptical of this new capital-raising route.

Like the repeal of the general solicitation ban for Rule 506(c) private placements and the changes to the mini-IPO option under Regulation A+, the move to allow crowdfunding lines up with the SEC's twin missions of encouraging capital formation while protecting investors.[58] Designing a regime to enable securities crowdfunding embraces a third important goal: democratizing small and start-up business investment.

While individual investors can bankroll their own start-ups, or those of their friends and family, it is difficult for them to access more formal investment opportunities in this space. The accredited investor limitation on most private placements restricts participation to the wealthy and other very high earners—by design. Investments in IPO securities are, in theory, available to the general public. Realistically, though, investment banks manage admission to these investments, and can allocate them to their wealthy and powerful clients.[59] Once the initial offering is made, ordinary investors can purchase IPO stocks on the secondary market, though sometimes this will mean missing out on the greatest gains. Crowdfunding models not only generate capital for small and start-up firms, but also provide a mechanism for everyday investors to participate in, and perhaps to profit from, these early-stage investment opportunities.[60]

Detractors worry these unsophisticated investors will make foolish choices and fall prey to fraudsters, condemning crowdfunding as little more than "an alluring trap."[61] After all, if successful, crowdfunding aggregates many investments into an enticing pot for both true innovators and those intent on fraud. Each investment is so small that it justifies little investigation, and one of the goals of crowdfunding is to enable investors ill-equipped to engage in such investigation to participate. Further, investments in small and start-up businesses are simply riskier than those in larger, more established businesses with longer track records and reserves to fall back on.

Legislators and regulators drafting the new crowdfunding scheme were very much aware of the need to protect crowdfunding investors from fraud and failure—even, to a degree, from themselves. In the end, although the JOBS Act was trumpeted as a path to unlock capital for small and start-up businesses and democratize access to these investment opportunities, the regime ultimately placed greater emphasis on investor protection. The combination of low overall raise limits and still high compliance costs for issuers and funding portals may create a bind for potential crowdfunded offerings, and one wonders if, perhaps, this was the dubious agency's intent.[62]

Intrastate Offerings

The JOBS Act did not affect the final means by which small and start-up businesses can reach retail investors without running afoul of federal securities law—by simply doing all of their securities business within a single state. Crossing state lines to solicit investors is what brings that action within the ambit of federal securities law in the first place. A California firm can avoid this regulatory thicket if it seeks and sells to only California investors. California, like every other state, has its own securities law and securities regulator. A purely intrastate offering need only contend with state requirements.

A number of states have amended their securities laws to make themselves attractive homes for intrastate offerings, and for crowdfunding in particular.[63] These changes allow in-state issuers to make limited offerings to in-state residents with reduced registration, reporting, and investment requirements. The particulars of these state regimes differ widely, but historically the biggest problem for getting intrastate crowdfunding off the ground was, counterintuitively, federal law.

It turns out that limiting one's solicitation activity to a single state is more difficult than it sounds. Until recently, listing an offering on an online platform destroyed the issuer's ability to proceed as a purely intrastate offering—even if the issuer actually sold securities to in-state investors only. Essentially prohibiting use of the Internet meant the most viable and cost-effective way to reach the greatest possible pool of investors was completely out of the question, and greatly diminished the appeal of intrastate offerings.[64]

This barrier too, though, has now fallen. Together with its final crowdfunding regulations, the SEC issued a proposal to remove the bar on Internet advertising of intrastate offerings.[65] In October 2016, the agency promulgated final regulations permitting intrastate issuers to remain outside federal jurisdiction despite posting their offerings on the Internet—provided they sell their securities only to in-state residents.[66] Removing this obstacle provides small and start-up businesses an important additional route by which to reach retail investors.

New Opportunities

The changes worked by the JOBS Act and the SEC's regulatory efforts thereunder have created new paths for small and start-up social enterprises to access the retail investment market. Private placements already allow sophisticated investors to purchase securities issued by social enterprises, and new Rule 506(c)'s permission to engage in general solicitation will allow social enterprise issuers to court the entire accredited investor market. The lower regulatory costs of Regulation A+ may put a mini-IPO within reach of dual-mission firms capable of raising up to $20 million or even $50 million. Depending on how intrastate offerings develop, that route may be open to the wide field of much smaller social enterprises as well.

Crowdfunded securities offer the possibility of an entirely new paradigm for social enterprise, potentially combining the curb appeal of platforms like Kickstarter and Kiva with the power of capital markets. Its strengths—in particular its proven capacity to connect those with a shared vision, no matter what that vision may be—dovetail with the needs of social enterprises. More remarkably, social enterprise's expansive conception of success makes it organically forgiving of the weaknesses of crowdfunded security offerings. With the stubbornly significant burdens imposed on issues limited to raising $1 million per year and substantial regulation it imposes on issuers and funding portals, many wonder if the crowdfunding game will be worth the proverbial candle. In fact, those small raise limits may be attractive to social entrepreneurs eager to access funding while retaining a controlling stake in order to safeguard mission.[67] Social enterprises aim for profit and growth, but other objectives—such as identifying investors with a robust commitment to its mission—will sometimes trump both. Neither going the extra mile to ensure investors pose no threat to mission nor accepting annual investment and asset size limitations necessarily clashes with social enterprise's double bottom line. Early evidence provides tentative support for the notion that social enteprises will find this mode of raising capital particularly appealing. Of the 169 companies that commenced securities offerings under the new crowdfunding regulations in their first year, "[a]pproximately 16 percent were benefit corporations, certified B Corps, or operate within traditional corporate forms with strong social and/or environmental missions."[68]

The regulatory costs compared to the size of a social entrepreneur's planned raise, as well as her interest in seeking investors outside the accredited population, will also surely drive choices among these regulatory routes. But we leave predictions about the wisdom and appeal of these regulations to securities law experts, and return now to our focus on the special needs of social enterprises seeking retail investment. After all, even if these changes prove ideal for traditional for-profit firms, social enterprises face unique and serious challenges in accessing capital—and retail investment will only magnify them. The now-familiar assurance game plaguing social entrepreneurs and impact investors will further complicate dual-mission firms' prospects of attracting individual investors. Crowdfunding may make it possible for like-minded investors and entrepreneurs to find one another, but it does not offer any mechanism for these far-flung collaborators to broadcast their resolve across cyberspace. The balance of this chapter considers a tax regime that does precisely that.

The Assurance Game for Retail Investors

Social enterprise founders and their potential investors find themselves in the same quandary. Neither can succeed in their aims without the other; but both fear entrusting their ideas and resources to someone whose motivations they suspect. Social entrepreneurs seek investors' capital to scale up their mission-driven businesses—or perhaps just to keep the lights on. But, having committed significant amounts of their own time, energy, and often financial resources to their enterprises, they worry about the power of investors to steer their companies away from their vision. Investors seeking to marry financial returns from their investments with social good fear being played the fool by a fraudulent or fickle social entrepreneur—and retail investors have reason to be especially skittish. It will take strong signals and reliable enforcement to bring these two sides together.

Clearly there are good reasons to try. Social entrepreneurs will find the huge sums of capital the retail market appears to dangle in front of them enticing. Still, they have reason to hesitate at the thought of a "crowd" of investors, especially equity investors empowered to overthrow social mission if the price proves right. As noted in chapter 3, adopting one of the corporate hybrid forms springing up across the country provides limited protection against this risk. They permit unilateral termination of an enterprise's social mission—so long as a supermajority of shareholders agree. Whereas an entrepreneur might be able to suss out the bona fides of one or a few large investors, and craft individualized commitment devices to limit this risk, retail investors will be too small and too numerous for such artisanal arrangements. Founders willing and able to maintain a control position can blunt the force of other investors' preferences, assuming they can find investors willing to accept a permanent position in the minority. Social entrepreneurs who cannot maintain a controlling stake, though, will be wary to dive into the retail market without some other means to quell their worries about being forced to sell out.

Investors devoted to achieving a blend of financial and social returns will be equally anxious about entrepreneurs' commitment to social mission—perhaps even more so. Again, when large individual investors are involved, these suspicions can be overcome through carefully negotiated creative deals. Specialized financing structures like FLY paper can lock entrepreneurs and investors into their commitments, or at least create credible signals and reliable enforcement. For small-fry retail investors, arcane financial instruments are a nonstarter. Even the sophisticated accredited investors the broadened reach of new Rule 506(c) contemplates will not want to negotiate individualized investment vehicles. These deals will need to offer standardized products to appeal to a mass market. Adopting one of the available incorporated hybrid forms will give investors some comfort, by requiring supermajority shareholder approval to permanently shift an adopting entity to pure for-profit status. This comfort may turn cold, however, as the only tools for enforcement are commands that fiduciaries "consider" or "balance" profit and social goals, weak and costly claims of fiduciary duty breach, and disclosure. With or without the use of specialized forms, small investors have little recourse against an entrepreneur who casts aside an enterprise's social mission.

Retail investors face the further risk that their fellow investors may come to prefer a purely profit-driven firm. A social enterprise with one or a handful of nonfounder investors could once again negotiate and structure a deal to provide assurances. Retail investors with no control, or indeed knowledge, of their compatriots will have greater need for assurances from their peers and no ability to contract for them. The current corporate hybrids' supermajority rules leave individual investors at the mercy of large players, or a large group of small players. If enough of the crowd decides to cash in, the stalwart social investor will be left out in the cold. Even formerly committed dual-mission investors may join a sellout, rather than engage in a costly fight to halt a seemingly inevitable result.

The opportunity to reach millions of small retail investors, especially via cheap and simple online platforms, is an exciting one for social enterprises in need of capital. Legalizing and optimally regulating new paths for small businesses to access retail investors, however, will not alone suffice to enable social enterprises to access this new funding stream. Capitalizing a social enterprise with retail investment exacerbates the need for assurances and makes them harder to provide. The large numbers of investors—and the modest size of each investment—makes the communication essential to building the necessary trust far more challenging. Social entrepreneurs will need a reliable mechanism

to differentiate committed impact investors in the retail market. Investors likewise will need a strong signal to reassure them their investment is not a foolhardy leap of faith. First-generation hybrid forms will not be up to the task, and
investors cannot be counted upon to build solutions for themselves. Different
approaches, and the engagement of outside entities, will be required.

Creating Trust with a Tax Regime: SE(c)(3)

As neither social enterprises nor retail investors will be able to produce the
assurances they need on their own, we propose an unlikely, but powerful, help-
mate: the US corporate tax. We recognize that few would propose the IRS as a
purveyor of trust, but the mechanism we recommend enables it to play this role
powerfully and relatively seamlessly, adapting tools and competencies it already
possesses. Our proposal combines tax benefits for mission-focused social enterprises and penalties for greenwashed ventures into a potent regime to signal
committed social enterprises. We call our tax regime SE(c)(3): a spin on the
widely known 501(c)(3) label signifying tax-exempt charitable entities.

Like social enterprise itself, the SE(c)(3) regime places mission at its center, shielding a limited amount of mission-driven income from the corporate
income tax. An enterprise opting into it will be able to exclude up to $250,000
of income attributable to its social mission from its taxable income. In addition,
for each dollar of income qualifying for the SE(c)(3) exclusion, electing companies will receive an additional "one for one" exclusion. The SE(c)(3) system
is not all carrot, however. To avoid gaming by firms seeking tax gains rather
than social ones, it also deploys a heavy stick. Distributions of profit and gains
from sales of shares of corporations opting into the regime will be taxed at
the steeper rates applicable to ordinary income, rather than lower ones usually applied to dividends and capital gains. Pairing a contingent benefit with
a relatively high tax on distributions produces a tax regime uniquely suited to
social enterprise—one only a truly mission-driven entrepreneur or investor
could love.

The SE(c)(3) regime upends the existing, dichotomous approach tax law takes
with respect to charitable and profitable activities. Current law accepts that
charities may seek profits and that profit-seeking firms may act charitably, but in
each case the applicable regime treats the secondary mission as an aberration.[69]
Obviously, social enterprises will struggle to fit within either the charitable or
profit-making silos. To the extent that a social enterprise treats social mission
and investor profit as interrelated core objectives, a tax regime that marginalizes
one or the other makes a poor fit. SE(c)(3) creates a more hospitable place for
social enterprises within the tax law. More importantly, though, its combination
of rewards and drawbacks will allow entrepreneurs and investors to telegraph
their commitment to balancing mission and profit.

The Carrot

The SE(c)(3) regime's appeal derives from its ability to increase after-tax profits. But for profits to exist at all, a business must earn income over expenses. For a social enterprise, this task is made all the more difficult by the unorthodox combination of profits and social good. But profitability for such a double-bottom-line enterprise is not impossible. Customers appear willing to pay an altruism premium for the satisfaction of knowing that by purchasing a good or service, they will provide a significant benefit to a hard-working employee or do less damage to the environment. A sufficiently high premium could more than offset the negative profit impact of hewing to the venture's social mission. In such a case, a social enterprise's economic return—like that of any other venture—would be subject to the income tax.

Perversely, from a tax perspective the downward pressure social mission exerts on a venture's profitability should constitute a blessing. Setting aside the limits considered below, an enterprise that sufficiently prioritizes a social mission should have little to fear from a tax on profits. Employing an unskilled labor force in order to provide those employees with valuable job skills imposes clear costs on an enterprise. So, too, does utilizing costlier, more environmentally sensitive production processes. The more urgently a firm pursues the social goal of training its employees or preserving the environment, the less likely it is to earn a profit that might be subject to tax.

Herein lies the rub. Unlike the typical costs of doing business, mission-driven expenditures may not be tax deductible—and could therefore be ignored for tax purposes.[70] Conceptually, extra training for nontraditional employees or using a costly and unconventional (yet greener) production process fall afoul of the requirement that deductible expenses be "ordinary and necessary."[71] In *Welch v. Helvering*, a taxpayer paid debts of his former employer despite the fact that, first, they were not his obligations and, second, they had been discharged in bankruptcy.[72] His motivation—"to reestablish his relations with customers whom he had known" as an employee of the bankrupt company "and to solidify his credit and standing"—prevented him from deducting those payments.[73]

While commendable, his actions were extraordinary. The Supreme Court explained, "Unless we can say from facts within our knowledge that these are ordinary and necessary expenses according to the ways of conduct and the forms of speech prevailing in the business world," no deduction is permitted.[74] The money that social enterprises devote to mission at the expense of profit may be—like the thousands of dollars that Welch paid although not legally required to do so—"well and wisely spent."[75] Some may be successfully cast as marketing, public relations, or research and development efforts, and deducted on that basis. But money expended purely because of a firm's dedication to a social mission will be nondeductible. As a result, when mission-driven expenditures extend beyond those a typical business would incur, through an income tax lens a social enterprise may be profitable, even if it loses money.

The SE(c)(3) regime attempts to reconcile this existing tax law skepticism with respect to mission-driven expenditures with social enterprises' confidence in their potential. It embraces the notion of a double bottom line by providing an exclusion for up to $250,000 of income attributable to a social enterprise's mission. Even if those mission-driven expenses might be deemed extraordinary—and therefore nondeductible—they could be used to shield income from taxation. For a firm that elects to participate, each dollar of mission-driven expenditures that it incurs results not in a deduction but in the exclusion of a dollar of otherwise taxable income. The exclusion helps to ensure that if a social enterprise merely breaks even financially, it will be taxed accordingly. An additional one-for-one feature doubles the amount of the exclusion to provide an additional cushion: a dollar of tax-free income for each dollar of excluded SE(c)(3) income. As a result, even a moderately profitable social enterprise would owe no tax so long as its revenues do not more than double its mission-driven expenditures.

Take a corporate social enterprise that spends $25,000 on conventional business expenses and another $25,000 a year on activities that arguably cross the boundary that divides profit from generosity, putting associated expenses in jeopardy of disallowance, while earning $100,000 in revenues. Were no deduction allowed for those extraordinary, mission-driven expenses, the enterprise would be subject to tax on up to $75,000 of income despite enjoying an economic profit of only $50,000.

The SE(c)(3) exclusion would protect such a social enterprise from the risk of that unwelcome tax result. By choosing the SE(c)(3) regime, the hypothetical social enterprise described above could shield a portion of its income with that mission-driven expense. The SE(c)(3) need only demonstrate that the mission-driven expenditures further a charitable purpose that would be broadly consistent with the tax-exempt activities of a section 501(c)(3) entity. Excluding $25,000 of the enterprise's income would help to ensure that this hypothetical social enterprise is taxed on net, rather than gross, income. This basic exclusion amount ensures that mission-driven expenses will not be treated less favorably than conventional expenses. The result simply brings tax results into line with cash flows.

The additional one-for-one exclusion goes further. Conceptually, the one-for-one exclusion allows for the possibility of mission-driven profits, perhaps as the product of an altruism premium. In other words, if mission-driven expenditures more than pay for themselves, a social enterprise could shield the resulting income from tax. The enhanced exclusion also acts as a multiplier to address the kinds of benefits social enterprises create that might not so easily show up in expenditures. For example, extra training for hard-to-employ workers not only increases their own earning power, but also affects the fortunes of their families and the education of their children. Finally, the one-for-one element provides a safety margin. Only when a social enterprise's taxable income more than doubles its mission-driven expenditures would it face a possible tax burden.

A different sort of social enterprise—for example, one that serves its mission not by incurring mission-driven expenditures, but by offering mission-focused discounts—might not be systematically taxed on more than its financial profits, but could still embrace the SE(c)(3) regime. If the one-for-one exclusion were linked either to extraordinary expenses or mission-driven discounts, it could shield an amount of income equal to the discounts it provides. Embracing this relatively modest tax benefit would allow the social enterprise to demonstrate its devotion to its mission.

In essence, a social enterprise that manages to be profitable despite the economic burden associated with its social mission could treat a portion of its income equal to that burden as excludable SE(c)(3) income. The additional resources a social enterprise devotes—as compared to a for-profit business—to training its employees, providing discounted services to customers, or deploying environmentally friendly production technology would serve as a benchmark for that burden. Moreover, managers would be offered a clear financial incentive to promote the enterprise's mission.

The Stick

Without more, providing an annual exclusion for up to $500,000 of income while requiring only that the enterprise in question incur what might be considered "extraordinary" mission-driven expenditures would invite abuse. Even defining mission-driven expenditures in terms used by the section 501(c)(3) tax exemption casts a wide net. Requiring an SE(c)(3) to articulate the charitable, educational, or other exempt goal an expenditure advances would only go so far in screening out strategic claimants. As Victor Fleischer notes, such a tax benefit would unleash "a flood of companies that currently pay taxes—for example, biotech and cleantech start-ups engaged in 'scientific' activities or web companies engaged in 'literary' activities—attempting to qualify as charities."[76] Such businesses could exploit the SE(c)(3) exclusion despite a ruthless focus on their financial bottom line.

The SE(c)(3) exclusion on its own would be vulnerable to such strategic claims, but our proposal taken as a whole is not. Stock in companies that opt into the SE(c)(3) regime will be excluded from the tax law's definition of "capital asset" and thereby become ineligible for the lower rates available for capital gains.[77] Dividends paid by SE(c)(3)s will be denied the similarly favorable treatment most dividends receive.[78] Currently, the gains from such assets are taxed at only 20 percent, rather than a top rate of 39.6 percent on ordinary income. This design exacts a price for the SE(c)(3) exclusion that, while palatable for a venture pursuing a double bottom line, would be steep for a strategic claimant. Simply put, for a purely profit-seeking firm, the relatively high rates imposed on distributions of SE(c)(3) profits and sales of SE(c)(3) shares would more than outweigh the advantages of the limited exclusion. Even a business with no shortage of plausibly mission-driven expenditures would be reluctant to assert a questionable claim to the limited $500,000 entity-level exclusion if the certain result would be an uncapped, permanent increase in shareholder-level taxes.

There are also other, less obvious, costs to SE(c)(3) status. To claim the SE(c)(3) exclusion, a social enterprise must operate in corporate form. In its start-up phase—precisely when the enhanced funding access provided by SE(c)(3) status would be most important—consenting to corporate tax treatment would represent a lost opportunity for a strategic claimant. Initial losses, such as those generated by an enterprise's product development expenses, would be trapped at the corporate level and unavailable to offset income from investors' other ventures.

Since the SE(c)(3) penalty targets only distributions of profits and gains from sales of shares, routine tax-planning techniques could also substitute economically equivalent transactions designed to skirt the edges of the regime. For example, the owner of an SE(c)(3) might contribute its shares to a holding company in order to sell shares of that new parent free of the SE(c)(3) taint, or strip away the entity's corporate shell entirely, replacing it with an ordinary corporation. Fortunately, the corporate tax has long experience defeating such efforts and can address them simply and easily with cures like extending the SE(c)(3) election to closely related corporations and applying the existing provisions on tax-free reorganizations. As elsewhere, those responses could impose broad limitations on the structure and operations of SE(c)(3)-electing entities or narrowly target specific abuses.

We also recognize that the SE(c)(3) regime complicates the principal-agent story of a traditional, purely for-profit firm. Investors always face risks when they place their capital in the hands of managers with the opportunity to shirk, squander, or steal. This problem imposes agency costs on investors who try to limit agents' misdeeds through monitoring, attempt to realign the incentives of principals and agents to coincide, or must make an untimely or unprofitable exit. The SE(c)(3) is designed to decrease the cost of monitoring—particularly monitoring compliance with a social mission far more difficult to track than profit alone—and to align the incentives of agents and principals by allowing them to preselect for commitment to a double bottom line. Yet its reduction of the after-tax value of profits investors take out of the firm could increase managers' existing temptation to retain earnings and magnify the cost of investor exit. One cannot be certain how this trade-off will turn out. In our view, though, SE(c)(3)s' focused protection for social mission is worth the risk—particularly in the typically small, illiquid social enterprise, whose investors' ability to sell is already limited. After all, SE(c)(3) represents a commitment device, and in turn a signal, designed to catalyze a primary market for small-scale social enterprise investments. Without a successful primary market, questions about a secondary market simply become irrelevant.

Finally, unless an adopting firm distributes profits to shareholders or those shareholders sell their shares, the SE(c)(3) regime leaves tax authorities unable to penalize an enterprise that abandons its social mission to pursue profits. If a motivation other than greed drives a social enterprise to abandon its mission, the Internal Revenue Service as judge would be powerless to preserve that mission. But greed is what insiders and outsiders alike fear most.

In the retail investment space, in which promises would be easy for insiders to make and impossible for small, dispersed investors to verify, a robust collective signal of commitment to a double bottom line is invaluable. The SE(c)(3) regime provides a commitment device capable of delivering such a signal. Even for sophisticated investors, SE(c)(3) would serve a useful role by limiting the impact of the complex assurance game confronted by every social enterprise. For retail investors, though, that signal would make SE(c)(3) status an indispensable trusted brand.

SE(c)(3) as Mass-Level Commitment Device

When a small number of deep-pocketed investors join forces with an entrepreneur, it is possible to manufacture the missing trust, effectively ridding the would-be stag hunters' forest of hares. They can, in other words, reach an "enforceable agreement" that would produce "the only possible focal point for the necessary subsequent tacit collaboration" so that "no one has a unilateral preference . . . to do anything but what he is expected to do."[79] Such an approach allows sophisticated entrepreneurs and investors to achieve the contractual equivalent of tearing a treasure map in half to ensure reciprocal loyalty.

Private agreement, like the treasure map gambit, has practical limits. At the risk of understatement, we suggest that retail investment illustrates those limitations. Drawing a substantial number of insubstantial investments to nurture the growth of an enterprise would inevitably involve groups too large to squeeze into the offices of a law firm where such an enforceable agreement might be crafted. No less important, the size of retail investors' stakes would almost certainly be too small to justify the costs of reaching such an agreement.

Fortunately, commitment devices need not be individually tailored. Moreover, if adoption of such a device is hard to fake, using one can also serve as a powerful signal. The SE(c)(3) tax regime does both at once. By allowing investors and entrepreneurs to embrace a tax regime that imposes costs on those that stray from the pursuit of a double bottom line, the SE(c)(3) regime offers a commitment mechanism within the reach of even the smallest investors. Pairing favorable treatment for mission-driven income with higher tax rates on share-holder profits also provides a ready-made signal of commitment to a double bot-tom line. Both individuals and investment platforms can use SE(c)(3) status as a sorting mechanism to help investors seeking blended value find true fellow travelers and reliably dual-mission firms.

Commitment devices have a pedigree every bit as distinguished as the notion of the assurance game. Ulysses, of course, bound himself to the mast to allow him to listen to the sirens without endangering him or his crew. Today, com-mitment devices employing the same core principles operate in a variety of con-texts. Smokers hoping to quit, dieters, and even policymakers aiming to reach a consensus have relied on commitment devices with varying levels of success.

Claiming the SE(c)(3) exclusion constitutes a commitment by a corporate social enterprise to pursuing a double bottom line. Like agreeing to send a big check to an unappealing charity for each cigarette smoked or pound gained, claiming the exclusion represents a "self-limiting act carried out . . . for the pur-pose of achieving a better outcome, as assessed by his preferences at the time of action, than what would occur had he retained his full freedom of action."[80] Agreeing to pay a higher tax on shareholder profits today constrains the SE(c)(3)'s freedom to prioritize profits in the future.

The exclusion element of the SE(c)(3) regime distinguishes it from a typical commitment device. In addition to the benefits of commitment—here increased access to capital rather than smoking cessation or weight loss—the SE(c)(3) regime compensates participating social enterprises by providing an exclusion for mission-driven income. The exclusion's immediate benefit takes some of the edge off the potential penalty of higher tax rates looming indeterminately in the uncertain future, making it more likely social enterprises will opt in. The resulting dynamic becomes closer to a "fair bet rather than a one way ratchet,"[81] contemplating both costs and benefits for parties seeking to constrain their own future behavior.

With or without this compensating benefit, two characteristics largely deter-mine the degree to which a commitment device will bind a group or individual to a chosen course of action.[82] For a commitment device to be effective, one must first be able to determine whether the promise has been kept. The European Union financial crisis might not have occurred had Greece not been able to disguise its borrowing, maintaining the appearance of a sober debt-to-GDP ratio without the burden of actually limiting its debt. Because it relied on an inadequate definition of a loan, the European Union Growth and Stability Pact proved to be a paper tiger despite its sophisticated monitoring and enforcement mechanisms.[83]

Once compliance can be reliably distinguished from cheating, the emphasis shifts to enforcement. Here the critical issue is the existence of an individual or entity with the authority to enforce a commitment. A would-be drunk driver who has given his keys to a sober companion will be better protected than one who merely enlists a friend to counsel him. Entrusting keys to a reliable third party will be more effective because it relies on the actions of the sober friend rather than on the willingness of an inebriated potential driver to accept advice after he has become intoxicated.

Along both dimensions, the SE(c)(3) regime's appealing combination of simplicity and strength relies on the government. For income to be shielded by the SE(c)(3) exclusion, the taxpayer must prove its eligible, mission-related expenses to tax authorities. The regime's key enforcement element—the relatively high rates imposed on shareholder profits—is also policed by the IRS. Neither asks tax authorities to step outside their traditional roles of measuring and taxing income. Further, even if it was easy for a venture to pass itself off as a dual-mission SE(c)(3), it would be unattractive to do so. Highly profitable social enterprises would certainly bear the substantial burden the SE(c)(3) regime promises. Investors and entrepreneurs intent on maximizing such profits would find little to love in the SE(c)(3) regime.

Finally, and crucially, SE(c)(3) status provides a strong but simple signal. If they can be made to understand the commitment SE(c)(3) status embodies, individual retail investors can interpret this signal on their own. Social enterprises will have incentives to brand themselves this way, as will others eager to increase their access to capital. Perhaps more importantly, however, the intermediaries that bring private placements, mini-IPOs, and crowdfunded and intrastate offerings to the investors' attention could use the SE(c)(3) brand to ease investor concerns about the dedication of social enterprise issuers. This signal may be especially useful for funding portals under the new crowdfunding exemption. The significant regulatory requirements imposed on these nascent platforms give them enough to worry about. Vetting the mission commitments of putative social enterprise issuers would be simple if SE(c)(3) were available as a proxy. By relying on the SE(c)(3) brand, these platforms could leverage the work of the tax system to match reliable social enterprises with mission-committed retail investors.

Why Turn to Government Now?

The SE(c)(3) regime's success as a commitment device, and in turn as a brand, hinges on the intervention of the federal government. The first generation of social enterprise law embraced a view of the public sector as a threat to, rather than an ally of, social enterprise. Tax and corporate laws that cater to the extremes, while creating obstacles for entrepreneurs and investors working at the intersection of profit and social mission, have made it difficult to resist that mindset. Of course, as the MPH demonstrates, policymakers could play a far more productive role. State organizational law could be amended to address the needs of dual-mission ventures. Instead, by failing to strike a balance between securing a venture's mission and preserving shareholder autonomy, chapter 3 showed the first-generation hybrid entities that have proliferated in the United States over the past few years have fallen short. A turn to private ordering, like FLY paper, represents one possible response to these failures and a skepticism that they will be remedied.

However frustrating, those failures should not be taken as proof that policymakers have no place in the second generation of social enterprise law. The SE(c)(3) regime calls on Congress to enact legislation authorizing the executive branch, specifically the Internal Revenue Service, to encourage honesty and penalize deception. Fortunately, though, this does not require regulators to stray beyond their comfort zone. In fact, as detailed earlier in this chapter, the SEC already plays precisely that role to promote trust between investors and entrepreneurs. Relying on mission-driven expenditures and shareholder profits as proxies for fidelity to mission and for faithlessness capitalizes on the tax law's strengths. In the absence of robust metrics capable of capturing a social enterprise's commitment to mission, the SE(c)(3) regime measures cash flows.

It will never warm the hearts of tax purists or tax phobics, but the use of the tax law to catalyze retail investment in social enterprise has much to recommend it. Governments frequently use tax laws to encourage or discourage particular behaviors. By offering individuals or businesses a credit or deduction for a particular expense or an exclusion for a specific type of income, a legislature can put a thumb on the scale in favor of owning a home or saving for retirement. These provisions, known as tax expenditures, provide a subsidy for favored activities. Tax penalties do just the opposite, discouraging disfavored behavior such as bribery and increasing the fisc.

Although they may escape the scrutiny imposed on other forms of spending, tax expenditures do reduce government revenues. This is another reason to support the SE(c)(3) regime's blend of carrot and stick. The combination of the tax penalty on shareholder profits with the tax benefit for mission-driven expenses could be calibrated to achieve a rough revenue neutrality. For individual ventures, the impact of the SE(c)(3) regime is a function of how they balance mission and profit. Social enterprises emphasizing mission would benefit from lower tax bills, while ventures that ultimately prioritize shareholder profits would suffer greater tax costs. Those increased taxes on SE(c)(3)s that de-emphasize mission in favor of the financial gains of their owners cross-subsidize the lighter burden enjoyed by more mission-focused enterprises. Rather than drawing resources away from or directing them to the social enterprise sector, the SE(c)(3) regime simply siphons from one set of social enterprises to another. The heavier burden imposed on SE(c)(3)s emphasizing shareholder profit would indirectly ease the load on mission-focused enterprises, and leave a light footprint on the federal budget.

Crafting a more generous exclusion or a more narrowly targeted penalty would make SE(c)(3) status more attractive for ventures, but more expensive for taxpayers. Either approach would allow government to support the growth of social enterprise without attempting to seize control of it. Rather than elevating a particular constituency or a specific approach, the SE(c)(3) regime invites social enterprises to choose for themselves. In fact, by offering a readily recognizable brand that small investors can use to identify enterprises committed to balancing social mission and profit, the SE(c)(3) regime cedes decision-making authority to the wisdom of the crowd.

A cynic might also note that tax breaks tend to fare better in the political process than economically equivalent government spending. That result may be neither logical nor desirable, but for whatever combination of reasons, "[t]ax expenditures have grown in importance to the point where they are now the dominant instruments for implementing new discretionary spending policies."[84] While the tax law need not be the only mechanism through which government promotes the pursuit of double bottom lines, its use as a mechanism for promoting social and economic objectives would hardly be extraordinary.

Of course, government is not the only entity capable of catalyzing social enterprise investment by offering signaling and enforcement tools. Private entities, too, could play such a role, in a variety of ways. Experiments in this vein are ongoing, from the certification efforts of B Lab to the creation of social stock exchanges with listing standards focused on issuers' contributions to social good. After exploring the contribution of metrics to driving capital to social enterprises, the next chapter will review these private efforts to develop organized signaling and enforcement capacity, and evaluate how they might reassure investors and entrepreneurs of each other's commitments.

Conclusion

Like other business owners, social entrepreneurs searching for capital will find the retail investment market's considerable resources extremely appealing. Until recently, however, for small and start-up social enterprises, reaching retail investors was little more than a pipe dream. Legal and practical impediments to accessing retail investors have long prevented all but the most spectacularly successful and well connected from reaching individual investors' shallow but numerous pockets. In the years since the enactment the 2012 JOBS Act, the SEC's actions allowing general solicitation for some private placements, increasing the raise caps for mini-IPOs, creating a framework for crowdfunded securities, and eliminating obstacles to the use of intrastate offerings have removed some of these limitations. We defer to the ample literature on securities law to debate the advantages and disadvantages of these various changes, but are cheered by the wealth of new capital-raising possibilities social enterprises can explore.

Even if these developments do result in greater retail investment in small and start-up businesses, however, they will not guarantee capital access for social enterprises. Without a robust legal infrastructure in place to promote trust and shore up investors' and entrepreneurs' confidence in one another, they will never get together. Individualized arrangements like FLY paper provide a workable solution for investors with the resources, sophistication, and sway to deploy them. These features, though, make them ill-suited to the retail investment context. Legislators could create specialized organizational forms to attract retail investment to social enterprises by compelling adopting entities to prioritize social good and deploying vigorous enforcement mechanisms. First-generation hybrid forms do not meet these criteria, and serious resource and political obstacles stand in the way of achieving them.

The SE(c)(3) regime offers a fittingly radical architecture to house double-bottom-line ventures, permitting them to embrace and advertise their dual pursuit of profits and social good. A measured tax benefit linked to the costs of pursuing social goals, paired with higher taxes when shareholders cash in, offers the appropriate balance of rewards and sanctions to ensure fidelity. The SE(c)(3) regime's use of tax rules to further goals far afield from measuring or redistributing income would certainly raise eyebrows in jurisdictions accustomed to relying on direct regulation to achieve social objectives. Much the same, those who favor private ordering over government intervention would no doubt prefer the market-based possibilities for signaling and enforcing social enterprises' commitments the next chapter canvasses. We decline to choose a favorite. Rather, we argue the SE(c)(3)'s simple, revenue-neutral, and uniquely American approach to the matter commends its adoption to increase social enterprises' access to capital.

6

The Promise of Metrics

Data has come to play a central role in almost every aspect of our lives. Algorithms help us do everything from avoiding traffic jams to finding love. We track steps to gauge our health and count likes to validate our choices. Whatever its limits, using metrics to quantify mission seems no less plausible than asking data to serve as the cornerstone of a relationship.

Pulling back the curtain on a venture's social returns would cement the leap to the second generation of social enterprise law. Investors, entrepreneurs, and regulators could not only track each venture's commitment to mission but could use legal tools to reward or punish them predictably and transparently. A reliable metric could allow a court to penalize a fallen social enterprise that chose to prioritize profit at the expense of mission. Calibrated just right—perhaps by quantifying the excess profit the venture earned—such a punishment would instantly render itself obsolete. Wavering ventures would recognize the futility of a midstream shift and maintain their focus on mission.

A range of public and private actors could harness such a metric with the aid of well-designed legal instruments and institutions. The lawsuit described above could, for example, have been brought as a derivative shareholder action or by an attorney general authorized to police the commitments made by social enterprises. Independent observers could employ the same metric to monitor and report on the success of double-bottom-line ventures in maintaining the promised balance between mission and profit, triggering contractual or statutory penalties for failures. Investors could capitalize on legally mandatory disclosures by making well-informed choices to buy or sell shares of a publicly traded social enterprise or simply embed metrics directly into the legal terms of their investments in start-ups.

If not a silver bullet, a robust metric for a venture's commitment to its social mission would undoubtedly serve as a linchpin. As described below, reinforced with legal rights and obligations, it could simultaneously serve as evidence of a social enterprise's aspirations and protection against disappointment. Completely reliable social performance metrics may never be developed, but half measures here can still do tremendous good. After surveying the emerging landscape of social performance metrics and those creating them, we return to the proposals detailed in the preceding chapters and show how they would dovetail with the evolution of social enterprise metrics. Then we discuss the role of metrics in enabling certification—private brands intended to signal quality and reliability. Certification has become a reality in the social enterprise sector. We show how metrics can be paired with legal tools to help entrepreneurs and investors find and trust each other.

Why Metrics Matter

The social enterprise concept covers a broad waterfront. Our definition draws in any for-profit business that pursues both profit for owners and one or more social goals. In practice, this big tent will cover companies with social missions as different as combating climate change, improving economic opportunity for people at the base of the economic pyramid, and increasing educational achievement in urban centers, along with a host of other goals too numerous and diverse to list comprehensively. It will also include firms that pursue these social objectives in varying degrees relative to their profit-making goals. Some social enterprises will be resolutely dedicated to social mission, with entrepreneurs and investors willing to cut marginal profit to the bone in order to achieve greater social good. Others will see their dual missions as more in balance, and have founders and funders who view a healthy financial profit as an important part of their vision of success.

For social enterprises to successfully access capital, entrepreneurs and investors must find counterparts who share their values. In essence, this is a matching problem. If an investor seeking a healthy profit invests with a social entrepreneur interested in maximizing social mission so long as he stays in the black, both will quickly find themselves dissatisfied. If a founder interested in increasing profitability as long as social good continues to be generated receives funding from an investor seeking to maximize social mission so long as his initial investment is protected, they may soon become disillusioned. Entrepreneurs and investors fearful of such misalignments may be unwilling to work together in the first place. Legal technologies like the MPH, FLY paper, and SE(c)(3) are designed to send reliable signals to entrepreneurs and investors, to help them avoid these blunders by making good matches.

Part of what makes these signals useful, of course, is their reliability. Funders will not invest and entrepreneurs will not accept investments without assurances that the claims each of them make about their appetites for a particular mix of profit and social good will be durable—at least for a reasonable period of time. Each of our proposals includes both measurement tools and mechanisms to provide these assurances. Improved metrics will serve as modular building materials that

private parties and public actors can use to construct better deals and more powerful regulatory regimes. Just as bankers and their clients incorporate published
interest rates into the terms of individual loans rather reinventing that particular
wheel for each transaction, robust metrics could greatly enhance the signaling and
enforcement potential of these innovative technologies. Each focuses on the law's
strength in clearly articulating legal rights and obligations—a strength that reliable metrics enhance—in order to access capital for social enterprise.

But crafting metrics for social performance is daunting. It is challenging
enough to select and track metrics for purely financial performance. Should one
focus on revenues or earnings? Return on invested capital or profits per employee?
Quarterly earnings or longer-term financial return? Dueling maxims tell managers, "You can't manage what you can't measure"[1] and to be wary that defining
metrics will create pressure to manage toward improving the metrics, if not necessarily the underlying objectives sought.[2] When a company pursues social mission
as well as profit, the task becomes harder still. How will an entrepreneur or investor track whether her social enterprise is combating climate change, alleviating
poverty, or improving education? And how much is enough? Fortunately for us,
we are not the first to identify the need for metrics in the social enterprise space,
and a number of entities are hard at work developing formulations.

Metrics for Social Performance

The first step in designing useful metrics involves developing a set of uniform
indicators to be tracked. These foundational metrics act as a kind of common unit
of measurement. Applying a consistent set of descriptors makes it possible to
compare assessments, both of a single entity or portfolio and across firms, funds,
or industries. Foundational metrics thus form the building blocks of evaluative
metrics. Evaluative metrics measure how much social good is achieved and compare social good generation over time and across entities. They are scores, ratings,
starred reviews—metrics that do not simply count, but render a judgment.[3]

The range of possible evaluative metrics for social enterprise exists on a
spectrum. On one end of this spectrum are highly specific measures of impacts
achieved by a particular type of entity, in a particular industry, perhaps in a particular geography. At the opposite extreme would be truly universal metrics: the
kind that provide an overall assessment of the good an organization creates and
that apply no matter what region, population, or problem a social enterprise
addresses. To develop that universal metric—a Rosetta Stone for mission—one
must make implicit or explicit trade-offs between various social goods, developing an "exchange rate" between the social value of children taught to read
versus species saved from extinction versus jobs created in low-income communities. The obvious incommensurability problem with such trade-offs likely

makes creating a perfect universal evaluative metric for social enterprise impossible.[4] Even approaching the universal side of the spectrum gets difficult. More narrowly targeted evaluative metrics pose fewer design challenges.

The First Step: Developing Foundational Metrics

Several major players in the social enterprise space came together to begin developing the most ambitious foundational metrics for social enterprises. The Rockefeller Foundation, Acumen, a nonprofit that uses charitable contributions to invest in social enterprises worldwide, and B Lab, the nonprofit behind the benefit corporation concept, initiated a project to create the Impact Reporting and Investment Standards (IRIS) in 2009.[5] IRIS is a set of "common metrics for reporting the performance of impact capital,"[6] and was soon made an initiative of the Global Impact Investing Network (the GIIN). The GIIN is a kind of industry association for social finance, made up of impact investor members and focused on improving "the scale and effectiveness of impact investing."[7]

IRIS offers a comprehensive set of descriptive metrics for social impact, creating a vocabulary for social enterprises and impact investors to communicate effectively about social mission achievements.[8] For example, its metric "Client Households: Provided New Access" identifies the "number of unique households that were clients of the organization and gained access, during the reporting period, to products/services they lacked prior to the reporting period."[9] Related metrics define how to count unique households and clients, and when one can be said to have obtained "new access" to water, energy, education, finance, and healthcare. The most recent version of the IRIS catalog includes over 550 individual items with specific definitions.[10] Social enterprises and investors are encouraged to select from this enormous menu the metrics that matter to them, and to adopt them to track and report on impact consistently.

IRIS itself developed many of the metrics in its catalog, but chose not to work on a blank slate. Instead, IRIS drew on existing metrics developed for a number of impact sectors and by a variety of groups. For example, IRIS aligned its metrics with those independently developed to assess social impact in the microfinance industry by the Microfinance Information Exchange and the Social Performance Task Force.[11] In other areas, IRIS spurred the development of new industry standards. Collaborating with the Center for Health Market Innovations, IRIS convened a special working group of industry experts to develop performance metrics in the healthcare arena.[12] The Center adopted the metrics the working group developed as part of its data collection activities, and IRIS made these aligned metrics part of its catalog. By folding these ideas into its system of metrics, IRIS has created a more comprehensive taxonomy. IRIS also welcomes feedback on metrics and suggestions for new ones, updating its catalog over time to the most recent 4.0 version in 2016.

Funds and others who collect impact performance data in IRIS-compliant form can opt to share this information with the GIIN for use in research and analysis. For example, in 2015, the GIIN issued "Data Brief: Focus on Beneficiaries"[13] using data culled from nearly 5,000 organizations reporting their performance using IRIS metrics at that time. This document reported exhaustively on beneficiary metrics in this sample, including such issues as the location and type of services offered, number of clients and female clients served, and growth in number of clients served over time. The GIIN is transparent about the limits of its current database, including data from only a few thousand organizations and compiled from just a handful of data partners that supply the information, and who are clustered heavily in the financial services industry.[14] If IRIS metrics become more widely adopted, however, it will extend the GIIN's ability to analyze and report on aggregated data.

Of course, IRIS is not the only foundational metric that has been developed for tracking, reporting, and benchmarking social impact. Big Society Capital, a UK social investment financial institution, developed an "Outcomes Matrix" with indicators in nine areas and across 15 potential beneficiary groups. For example, indicators in mental health include "understands their [mental health] condition" and "[h]as self-managed and sustained their mental well-being successfully for (x) months."[15] Like IRIS, the Outcomes Matrix is available free of charge. Social enterprises of all sizes are encouraged to select metrics that are relevant to them, and commit to tracking and reporting on them over time.

The Global Reporting Initiative (GRI) and the Sustainable Accounting Standards Board (SASB) standards are also foundational metrics, geared toward larger organizations. The GRI has been developing metrics to assess the environmental, social, and economic impacts of companies and organizations since the 1990s and reports that there are "thousands of [GRI] reporters in over 90 countries," making its products "the world's most widely used standards on sustainability reporting and disclosure, enabling businesses, governments, civil society and citizens to make better decisions based on information that matters."[16] The SASB was created by a group of Harvard University researchers "to develop and disseminate sustainability accounting standards that help public corporations disclose material, decision-useful information to investors."[17] These laudable efforts to provide a consistent vocabulary for impact measurement and reporting will continue to be refined and more closely integrated over time.

Evaluative Metrics along the Spectrum

Foundational metrics lay crucial groundwork for effective evaluative metrics. As noted earlier, evaluative metrics not only describe, but judge. By taking that next step, they provide comparative information, conveying to social enterprises and impact investors the relative gains in social impact generated by organizations over time and across entities. The scores and ratings these metrics produce can bolster other signals of a social enterprise's achievements or transmit such a signal standing alone. How potent an evaluative metric will be as a signal depends on a variety of factors, including its scope, reliability, and clarity.[18]

If foundational metrics permit observers to describe temperature and precipitation, evaluative metrics can tell you whether to expect a nice day. The more universally applicable an evaluative metric is, the wider the scope for its application. Evaluative metrics judging sustainability or educational impact can only assess social enterprises operating in those fields. Specific evaluative metrics can become widely used and powerful signals within a single issue area or geography, but, like a ski forecast in the Caribbean, will be of little use outside those fields. In contrast, an evaluative metric that ranks all social enterprises with a single score, regardless of geography, industry, size, and so on, could apply to everyone. But, as noted above, that Rosetta Stone for comparing social enterprises' commitment to mission remains elusive. Like the technical challenge posed by the deceptively difficult task of translating data into a reliable weather forecast, the need for expertise in ever more diverse realms, combined with the difficulty of assigning values to compare incommensurables, saps the accuracy and credibility of evaluative metrics as their scope of application expands.

These challenges have not chilled efforts to create evaluative metrics all along the spectrum. B Lab again figures prominently here. As discussed in chapter 3, B Lab created the B Impact Assessment tool as part of the initial launch of its B Corp certification program. The B Impact Assessment is a self-administered online survey available to dual-mission businesses free of charge. The following questions offer a sample of the types of information the assessment collects.

- Which is the broadest community with whom your environmental reviews/ audits are formally shared? Answer choices: Owners, Executives, Board; Employees; Broader community outside the company; N/A
- What % of energy used is from renewable on-site energy production for corporate facilities? Answer choices: 0%; 1–4%; 5–10%; 10–15%; 15%+
- Based on referenced compensation studies, how does your company's compensation structure (excluding executive management) compare with the market? Answer choices: Below market; At market; Above market; N/A (Have not referenced a compensation survey)
- Which of the following underserved populations does your business impact or target (check all that apply)? If you are a business-to-business focused company, think of who the ultimate user of your product or service is. Answer choices: Low-income, poor or very poor (including low-income minorities and other underserved populations); Minority, disabled, and other underserved (but not low-income); Nonprofits that serve the poor; Nonprofits (other than those that serve the poor); None of the above[19]

Responses can generate a total possible score of up to 200 points.

The B Impact Assessment grapples with the universality problem through dynamic design. Depending on a company's size, location, and industry, the precise questions the assessment will ask, as well as the weight that answers are given, will shift.[20] This means that the point scores are only roughly comparable, as a large company in the manufacturing sector in the developing world receiving a score of 90 will have compiled its score in response to different questions than a small consulting firm in the United States with the same score.

Applicants will typically spend one to three hours completing the survey and will be prompted to submit supporting documentation for some questions.[21] In a follow-up phone call with an applicant representative, a B Lab staff member will answer questions about the survey and obtain applicant-specific information to clarify answers. If the applicant's score is 80 or higher, B Lab will randomly select several questions for additional desk review. Applicants will be required to upload documentation supporting their answers, which B Lab staff will evaluate, and B Lab will perform background checks on the company. If everything checks out, and the applicant makes the governance changes to require its fiduciaries to consider nonshareholder constituencies in decision-making, the applicant will be certified a B Corp. Certification lasts for two years, during which 10 percent of certified companies will be randomly selected to participate in a more fulsome audit with B Lab staff, either in-person or virtually.[22]

The B Impact Assessment score provides an evaluative metric that social enterprises can use to quantify their impact, gauge progress over time, and compare their performance with peers. B Lab provides applicants long-form reports to aid in interpreting the primarily self-generated scores, including a composite score in each category for all other companies that have completed the survey to use in benchmarking. B Lab also offers "Customized Improvement Reports" to help companies track their performance and map out where they would like to do better in the future.[23]

B Lab has also leveraged the B Impact Assessment as part of a more extensive evaluative metric designed for impact investors. The Global Impact Investing Rating System (GIIRS) rates the social and environmental achievements of impact investors, in part by evaluation of the mission-driven companies in which they invest.[24] B Lab evaluates investee companies using the B Impact Assessment, extracting data to assess investee companies on two fronts. It considers the social content of a portfolio company's business model, rating it bronze through platinum, as well as the impact of its actual operations, rated on a scale from one to five stars. For fund ratings, these investee evaluations are rolled up into a weighted average, providing a portfolio-level report. GIIRS Fund ratings also evaluate fund management, and report into which of five percentile bands a rated fund falls. As the data for these ratings begins with the B Impact Assessment, it is initially self-reported information. For GIIRS reports, a combination of staff and contractors work to verify this self-reporting. Currently, B

Lab lists Deloitte & Touche as the preferred provider for document review, which appears more thorough than that required by the B Impact Assessment process alone, or even its on-site audit program.[25] Ten percent of all impact investing entities are subject to audit each year. This thorough review produces a robust and lengthy report on each applicant, valid for one year.

Perhaps unsurprisingly, given B Lab's involvement in IRIS's origins, GIIRS endeavors to use IRIS-compliant indicators whenever possible.[26] It is also one of the data-reporting partners that provides IRIS-compliant impact information to the GIIN. GIIRS and others have described the relationship between IRIS and GIIRS as analogous to that between the Financial Accounting Standards Board (FASB) and ratings agencies like Moody's, Standard and Poor's, or Morningstar.[27] IRIS provides objective measurement methodology, free for anyone to adopt and applied by funds and companies to themselves. GIIRS creates a meal out of those carefully weighed ingredients, offering objective and verified assessments based on the IRIS foundational metrics, which may be tracked over time and compared across entities.

Social Return UK (formerly the SROI Network) has also developed an evaluative metric designed to measure social, economic, and environmental outcomes. Its social return on investment (SROI) framework uses a ratio format, which looks at first glance like an easily digestible indicator of a given social enterprise's bang for the buck. In fact, SROI produces a result that tends to be even more idiosyncratic than the B Impact Assessment and GIIRS. Each entity applying the framework is instructed to engage in a comprehensive, multistakeholder analysis of the organization, to determine the appropriate impacts to measure and track. An organization may choose well-known and consistently applied indicators, like those developed by IRIS, but need not do so.[28] Thus, each SROI evaluation will be tailored to the organization undertaking it. Inevitable divergence in approaches means that while SROI will help each unique organization engage in self-reflection and self-improvement, either at a particular moment or across time, it will be of less use as a comparison across organizations. The fact that SROI ratios are expressed in currency, such as one pound of investment returns three pounds of social impact, suggests a universality and precision that belies that variance in method. Perhaps inevitably, because the measure intends to capture social impact rather than cost savings or financial return, the SROI does not facilitate a true apples-to-apples comparison among firms.

The Current State of Metrics

There are many more metrics available than the ones described here.[29] Indeed, the sheer number of organizations, their overlapping relationships, and corresponding abbreviations can be overwhelming. This discussion is not intended to provide an exhaustive list, but rather to introduce the reader to the types and range of metrics under development. These measures are intended to allow social enterprises, impact investors, and others to track and improve their own impact over time and aim to allow for comparison with peers. Foundational metrics like IRIS, the Outcomes Matrix, the GRI, and SASB standards focus on providing a consistent vocabulary for impact measurement and reporting. Foundational metrics like these can be incorporated into evaluative metrics like the B Impact Assessment, GIIRS ratings, and SROI. Social enterprises and impact investors can use evaluative metrics to bolster self-assessment efforts and legitimize and verify their claims of absolute and relative impact.

Currently available evaluative metrics are powerful, but far from perfect. Each represents a trade-off between offering a sufficiently accurate assessment of a venture's commitment to mission to compare very different organizations on the one hand and precise enough to track the evolution of a single social enterprise's mission on the other. Individually tailored metrics like SROI are hard to compare across entities; the plasticity of more universal metrics like the B Impact Assessment and GIIRS limits their capacity to convey results with a high level of precision. Their reliance on self-reporting and the limited consequences of misstatements makes verification and enforcement a serious challenge for all of them.

Folding Metrics into Second-Generation Social Enterprise Law

In time, high-quality impact metrics will enhance social entrepreneurs' and investors' ability to signal and enforce their commitments to each other. Each of the proposals described in the preceding chapters demonstrate how. Our FLY paper contemplates unique deal terms and thus can incorporate foundational and specific evaluative metrics idiosyncratically. Universal evaluative metrics would need to be significantly more robust to anchor proposals like the MPH and SE(c)(3) but could one day permit regulators to readily pierce the disguises of crooks and charlatans. Along with available foundational metrics, extant evaluative metrics already present an array of promising tools, and we look forward to their continued improvement.

FLY Paper

The FLY paper concept explored in chapter 4 showed how social enterprises can entice investors and reassure them of their bona fides with long-term, low-yield convertible bonds. Bonds are debt financing; investors lend money to an enterprise in return for the right to be repaid their principal at a stated time and to receive interim interest payments along the way. Bondholders are entitled to these interest payments, but not a role in governance, so entrepreneurs need not fear their interference in managing the enterprise as long as the bonds stay bonds.

Social enterprise investors would be wary of straight debt products, though, especially at low yields. Their lack of influence would risk entrepreneurs using investors' cheap money, but abandoning their social commitments to drive up the value of the enterprise. In the most extreme case, the entrepreneur would then sell the enterprise to the highest bidder without any upside participation for creditors. FLY paper's convertibility feature targets this risk in order to reassure investors. If the entrepreneur sells control, the bonds convert to equity and any upside must be shared with the (former) bondholders. In this way, FLY paper would improve access to patient, affordable capital for social enterprises.

The limitation of the FLY paper model, however, lies in its simplicity. Its single conversion trigger—sale of the entrepreneur's equity—protects investors from the ultimate loss of upside. By lowering the stakes for entrepreneurs, it also encourages them to live up to their social commitments. But this is only an indirect nudge. If investors and entrepreneurs cannot trust each other to continue to pursue social good in the firm's everyday operations, convertibility triggered by sale of entrepreneurs' equity may not suffice. If conversion could be triggered on midstream determinations that a social enterprise had veered off course toward a more fully profit-making orientation, FLY paper and vehicles like it could be made smarter.

Convertible bonds often have multiple triggers. Conversion may trigger at a particular stock price, missing an earnings goal, dipping below a specified capital ratio, or even upon regulatory action. Similarly, one could imagine bond documents that trigger conversion on failings determined by evaluative metrics. A FLY paper issue could trigger conversion rights on receipt of a B Impact Assessment score below a certain minimum or a SROI ratio lower than the prior year's. To correct for the possibility of outlier results, convertibility could be triggered only if these events occurred in multiple consecutive reporting periods.

Individual FLY paper deals can also adopt triggers tied to narrow metrics relevant to the specific entities they finance. Foundational metrics like IRIS offer a huge range of indicators from which to choose, and entrepreneurs and investors could agree on which ones to track and report. An impact investor interested in educational technology would be wise to develop expertise with indicators in the educational arena. Once she has, she can use them to design benchmarks that suit her preferences across a number of deals in that industry. By negotiating benchmarks to use as triggers, the parties can set their own terms for when the balance between mission and profit tips.

Links to metrics could also enhance other elements of FLY paper. As chapter 4 noted, rather than providing issuers a blanket payment holiday, the right to defer interest payments could be structured to fall in only on meeting particular benchmarks for social performance. Depending on the venture, evaluative metrics might offer a useful snapshot of deferral's wisdom. Alternatively, foundational metrics like those IRIS provides could provide more specific and incremental goals to motivate entrepreneurs and reassure investors.

If impact metrics can accurately track a venture's fidelity to social mission over time or compared to its peers, they would reassure investors fearful of being duped by entrepreneurs with altruistic rhetoric but avarice in their hearts. Likewise, committed social entrepreneurs would have little to fear from such additional conversion triggers. They could avoid triggering them by staying true to mission.

The underlying metrics must be reliable and clear for entrepreneurs and investors to build them into deals. One significant hurdle here is self-reporting, upon which current metrics rely heavily. Self-reported measures may not provide adequate comfort for investors, as they are prone to both inadvertent bias and deliberate fraud. For metrics to be embraced as reliable benchmarks, they will need to be applied rigorously by objective and independent experts able to engage in comprehensive review and auditing.[30] Even if this hurdle can be cleared, not all impact investors will be comfortable setting and tracking benchmarks keyed to metrics relevant in a particular industry or geography. Novice or general-interest investors may still prefer a trigger—like sale—with the advantage of consistency across deals. FLY paper is already a bespoke financial product. Adding negotiation over interim benchmarks, and the metrics to track them, would make it even more complex.

Some entrepreneurs and investors negotiating these deals will find including metric-based triggers in their deals attractive. For serial social entrepreneurs and impact investors, they may develop expertise regarding metrics relevant to their specific social goals and be able to use and improve them across an impact investment portfolio. Others, either preferring the simplicity of a single trigger or just skeptical of the current state of the impact metric art, will not. As metrics improve over time, however, more entrepreneurs and investors will experiment with using them to craft alternative or supplemental convertibility triggers. The availability of these additional triggers will make FLY paper a more appealing tool for enhancing capital access for social enterprises.

MPH

The mission-protected hybrid (MPH) articulated in chapter 2 tells a different story. This idealized model for a legal form for social enterprises imposes a prioritization mandate—that adopting entities prioritize social good over profit— and enforces it through a variety of mechanisms. The first is disclosure. All adopting entities must report to a regulator their expenditures on producing social good and those on producing profit. An imbalance in favor of social good expenditures suggests compliance with the prioritization mandate. The opposite triggers further scrutiny. Organizations breaching the prioritization mandate would be subject to significant, though not confiscatory, fines.

An expenditure test offers neither the only reasonable metric by which to assess a social enterprise's prioritization of its social mission nor the best. Its appeal instead lies in its bluntness. Because it speaks simply in the language of dollars and cents, state legislatures can adopt it, state agencies can employ it, and social enterprises can comply without imposing an undue administrative burden. But as other, more refined metrics for evaluating social impact are developed, they may provide useful additions or alternatives to expenditure reporting. For example, using IRIS-compliant indicators could add nuance and depth to an expenditure report and would better lend itself to cross-entity comparisons.

Chapter 2 also noted that states might delegate disclosure review to outside parties. Metric developers present an obvious choice for such a delegation. They will have valuable expertise in determining how and what to measure and in how to report on these measures in a way that is intelligible and useful. That said, the MPH model does not suddenly become easily adopted when metric experts surface. Like any delegation, handing over responsibility for reviewing MPH disclosures to a third-party expert would not discharge the state's responsibility for enforcement. The delegate or delegates must still be monitored and funded, which would leave the state still very much on the hook to make a solution like MPH a success.

It is important to note (perhaps for the final time) that standard benefit corporation statutes do not delegate enforcement to a metric developer. These statutes merely require adopting entities to self-report their achievements annually using a third-party standard as a yardstick. Such standards, which must be independent, transparent, comprehensive, and credible, emerge from the efforts of metric developers. In this limited way, benefit corporation statutes build on the valuable work of metric developers, including the improvements these developers make over time. But these statutes only require that benefit corporations apply such metrics to themselves and report on their achievements in relation to these metrics to shareholders. No government agency reviews these reports to determine if they effectively apply the relevant metric; nor must the metric developer vouch for the results a reporting benefit corporation generates. Indeed, it appears at present that few benefit corporations prepare the reports at all. Our MPH proposal differs from benefit corporation and other first-generation legal forms for social enterprise by providing the resources necessary for serious review of required disclosures.

In addition to disclosure, the MPH model empowers investors to enforce the prioritization mandate by challenging fiduciary failures in court. Improved metrics would also shore up this path to enforcement. Litigation challenging directors' decisions as failing to prioritize social good will require courts to make their own assessments of how much social good an entity generates. Foundational and evaluative metrics could assist them with this difficult task, as well as in crafting effective remedies. Perhaps injunctive relief could be designed with reference to benchmarks defined by the GRI indicators or the Outcomes Matrix. Damage awards might even be reverse engineered with reference to SROI.

The MPH represents an ideal. Distilling social good generation into enforceable metrics presents but one of several serious challenges that stand between its formulation and its implementation. Refining social impact metrics will help to close that gap and make MPH a reality. That said, the nature of MPH and its mandate to prioritize social good demands fairly universal metrics, and universal metrics represent little more than an ideal today. Moreover, without convincing legislators and taxpayers that new regulatory bodies deserve funding and bolstering the coffers of state treasuries to do so, gains in metric development alone will not bring the MPH to life.

SE(c)(3)

The development of improved metrics could help to bring SE(c)(3) to fruition. Remember, SE(c)(3) pairs a carrot with a stick to create a reliable signal of social purpose commitment and to enforce these commitments over time. Social enterprises that opt into the regime would qualify for an annual tax exclusion of up to $250,000 of demonstrated expenditures to achieve social mission. This benefit would be doubled in our own version of "one for one." The stick—to ensure SE(c)(3) status would not be attractive to companies seeking a tax benefit without a corresponding commitment to creating social good—would tax all gains generated by investing in SE(c)(3)-electing entities at ordinary income rates. Doubling the effective tax rate on extracted profits could be an acceptable trade for the conditional benefit of the exclusion for a company truly prioritizing mission, but not for a greenwasher seeking tax advantages alone.

Like the MPH, the SE(c)(3) regime uses expenditures as a key metric. And again, expedience, in particular tracking by electing firms and review by relevant regulators, makes that choice easy. Firms already track expenditures to document ordinary and necessary business expenses, charitable contributions, and a variety of other deductible items. In turn, the IRS has expertise auditing taxpayer claims about them. But even the basic terms of our SE(c)(3) proposal acknowledge the limitations of the expenditure metric. The one-for-one additional exclusion is embedded into the regime specifically to account for social good generation not easily linked to individual expenditures. With these limitations quite squarely in mind, we applaud the development of new and more sensitive metrics to assess social impact.

A new metric could more accurately measure social impact creation—or its absence. Congress or the Department of the Treasury could use a minimum B Impact Assessment score to gate access to the SE(c)(3) regime. Rather than calibrating the tax exclusion to expenditures, regulators could set a dollar amount for the exclusion, calculate a dynamic benefit based on a GIIRS score or its change over time, or use an algorithm drawing on SROI. As currently constructed—primarily or entirely self-assessed, with only moderate review at most—tax regulators will not likely find these metrics sufficiently robust to anchor the SE(c)(3) regime. But evaluative metrics will improve.

SE(c)(3) sends a reliable signal because it includes both carrot and stick. It bestows on electing entities an incentive tied to mission creation, which might be measured in various ways. But it also penalizes prioritizing profit generation by applying higher tax rates to those that opt in. Improving evaluative metrics like the B Impact Assessment and SROI enough to convince regulators to use them to unlock access to the SE(c)(3) regime and to calibrate incentives for entities that elect to participate will not eliminate the risk of abuse. The stick of an increased tax rate on distributed profits will remain pivotal. Without it, there is nothing to stop the many businesses that generate benefits for society from flooding into the SE(c)(3) exclusion and weakening its power as a brand.

What Metrics Can Do on Their Own

At the most basic level, foundational metrics simply provide social entrepreneurs and investors with the language they need to discuss their intentions precisely. Evaluative metrics go further, measuring and assessing the results foundational metrics yield, providing social enterprises and investors the ability to track social performance over time and, sometimes, across entities. Metrics can also be valuable tools for intermediaries and others in the social enterprise space. Those who wish to help social entrepreneurs and investors find each other, or to offer desirable products to either or both, will also benefit from metric development.

Metrics as Brands: Certification

One of the most obvious applications for impact metrics is certification. Certification creates a brand that can be deployed only by those who perform above some level on a specific set of metrics, and sells access to it. It is already a popular strategy in many industries that attract social enterprises and impact investors. Fair trade certifications are legion, running the gamut of products from coffee to handicrafts to wine, and ranging considerably in the depth of their standards and strength of their enforcement. To respond to critiques that microfinance firms were not sufficiently protective of customers, that industry developed the "Client Protection Certification."[31] Firms can be certified through a combination of self-reporting and on-site review of a number of measures designed to test treatment of borrowers and other consumers. If designed and policed effectively, certification sends a strong signal that the company or product displaying the brand can be trusted to possess particular qualities. For a certification to help social enterprises increase access to capital, the signal it transmits must help social entrepreneurs and investors reassure each other of their social commitments.

Certification can be described as a club good, meaning it is excludable but nonrivalrous. Excludability permits, for example, a supplier, to limit access to a service, providing it only on certain conditions. A good is nonrivalrous when, once created, its use by one does not leave less of it for others to consume. Access to a club good, like membership in the clubs for which they are named, signals something to others. To be an effective signal, though, club goods must take excludability seriously, and engage in reliable enforcement. Only if being "in the club" is meaningful will it create a brand. A person's membership in the Friars Club, applicants to which must be sponsored by two members and who are typically connected to the entertainment industry,[32] reveals far more about her than a membership in Sam's Club, whose big-box discount offerings anyone can access by paying the annual fee.[33] Certifications can engage in exclusion using all kinds of criteria, but using standardized and consistent metrics will make the brand they create more comprehensible and credible to those observing it.

A certification's power as a signal also depends on how trustworthy and relevant it will be to its intended audience. To develop a strong brand, certifications must elicit meaningful information from prospective recipients and rigorously enforce their standards of quality. They also must achieve a network effect, whereby enough applicants earn the certification that the brand achieves awareness among its target audiences.[34] Often, these two necessary elements will be in tension. On the one hand, if a certification's requirements are too easy to meet, they will fail to communicate valuable information. On the other hand, if the requirements to become certified are overly stringent, too few certifications will be sought and granted for the brand to become known in the marketplace. To be successful, certifiers must artfully balance these competing concerns, developing standards that are meaningful while still achievable.

B Corp Certification

B Lab has been working to strike this balance since its inception. The B Corp certification was B Lab's first product and remains its flagship. It licenses the "B Corp" mark to companies that score 80 points or more on the B Impact Assessment, along with making governance changes, submitting to the possibility of audits, and paying a licensing fee. Firms that qualify as B Corps and license the mark can post it on their websites, and many do. King Arthur Flour puts the B Corp logo on its bags of flour, and Dansko prints it on its shoeboxes. Certified B Corps also can participate in a range of partnerships and group discounts negotiated by B Lab, list open positions on the B Corp job board, and obtain a free GIIRS rating to share with investors or potential investors.

While it has not yet become a household name, B Lab continues to pour resources into developing awareness around its certified B Corp brand. It placed "print ads reaching 5MM conscious consumers" in a coordinated ad campaign, has developed relationships with major retailers to place special edition products and promotions from B Corps in their stores, and has a significant social media presence.[35] It works to promote certified B Corps to be included in various "best of business" lists, and trumpets their successes.[36] And B Lab's work on related issues like benefit corporation legislation and GIIRS ratings all draw upon and reinforce the B Corp certification process. At the B Corp launch in 2007, B Lab certified just 19 companies. As of this writing, over 2,000 companies are certified B Corps, representing 50 countries and 130 industries.[37] B Lab even has sister organizations certifying businesses in other markets around the globe.

B Lab has also devoted significant resources to its enforcement processes, which it recognizes are "critical in maintaining the authenticity of the Certified B Corp Seal."[38] Again, B Corp certification depends primarily on required governance changes—which are easy to verify but impose no prescriptions or proscriptions on organizational action, only making some paths more difficult to pursue—and a survey score. The B Impact Assessment survey is initially self-administered by the social enterprise applicant, but it is subject to documentation requirements and partial desk review, and one-tenth of certifications are audited each year.

The relative strength of the enforcement process for B Corp certification should reassure investors that B Corp certification can be trusted, but this reliability only matters if the information the certification communicates is meaningful to them. B Lab asserts that its B Corp certification denotes a company that has met "rigorous standards of social and environmental performance, accountability, and transparency."[39] All certified companies will have adopted governing documents requiring their fiduciaries to consider concerns beyond profit-making and constituencies beyond shareholders as they make decisions. This requirement alone, though, will not reassure entrepreneurs that investors in a B Corp will stay faithful to social mission. It requires only consideration, not prioritization of social good. Moreover, if it, or any of the B Corp requirements are breached, all that can be lost is certification. This penalty will be too little too late to reassure investors making long-term decisions to place their capital at risk.

Although a glass-half-full view might characterize the B Corp certification process as resilient, it would not be hard to see the signal it sends as ambiguous.

Relying on its broadly applicable metric, companies can achieve a score of 80 or higher in a wide variety of ways. Companies must earn at least some points in each of the B Impact Assessment's four issue areas—governance, workers, community, and the environment—to earn the necessary 80 points, but some may score more highly on environmental performance, making up for somewhat lower scores on worker protection.[40] Consumers may be satisfied with the general sense of "a good company" this package of information communicates, especially as they make little lasting commitment by purchasing a bag of flour or a pair of shoes. But investors facing the trust gap between themselves and social entrepreneurs will need more clarity than B Corp certification alone to part with their capital. Indeed, the fact that B Lab developed the much more fine-grained GIIRS rating process targeted at investors suggests the B Corp certification alone is insufficient to meet such needs.

Metrics as Facilitators

Metrics not only demonstrate their value to social entrepreneurs and private investors directly through programs like certification, but also serve as an engine driving public and private efforts to bolster the social enterprise sector. Foundational and evaluative metrics have already begun empowering government actors and other intermediaries who want to build the social enterprise and impact investment industries to better target subsidies and services to the right entities. For example, the US Small Business Administration (SBA) offers billions of dollars of funding each year through its Small Business Investment Corporation program. In this program, private investment funds can be licensed by the SBA to receive matching funding for their own investments in small businesses.[41] It has been supporting private funds investing in traditional small businesses for nearly 60 years. Beginning in 2011, the program began a special focus on impact investment funds, and has dedicated $200 million to this category since 2014.[42] To be licensed as an Impact Small Business Investment Corporation (ISBIC), the fund must deploy at least half of its investment capital in investments that pursue social, environmental, or economic goals along with financial ones.

Once licensed, an ISBIC has two years to submit a report on the impact of its investment strategy using one of the metrics described above.[43] A licensee may choose fund-level reporting, in which case it must obtain an overall rating of the fund's impact conducted by an independent third party using IRIS-compliant metrics. (The SBA suggests GIIRS ratings.) Alternatively, a licensee may report on the impact achieved by its underlying investee small businesses. Again, reports must be obtained from an independent provider; this time, permissible metrics include IRIS, the GRI standards, and SASB. Government infusions of investment capital can be a significant driver for industry development, and can unlock capital social enterprises need. Like other investors, however, the SBA needed assurances about the bona fides of proclaimed "impact" orientation by investors and enterprises alike. Metrics have already become a crucial link in this chain, delivering significant government benefits for mission-driven businesses.

Investment platforms targeting impact investors can likewise rely on metrics to facilitate their business models. For example, the Social Venture Connection (SVX) is a Canadian nonprofit that curates a list of impact-first investment opportunities for impact-oriented accredited investors. As part of its screening process to select appropriate for-profit companies for its platform, SVX requires applicants to submit impact documentation using (at least in part) IRIS-compliant metrics, and to be either B Corp certified or achieve a minimum GIIRS rating.[44] SVX advertises its screening process as assurance for investors that its site will contain reliably mission-driven investment opportunities.

> SVX . . . allows investors to identify screened impact investment opportunities, and share due diligence and collaborate on deals, reducing the burden of due diligence.[45]

The site's success rests on its ability to play this matchmaking role, and SVX relies in turn on evaluative metric providers and certifications to help.[46]

High-quality metrics will only enhance the ability of institutions dedicated to bolstering the social enterprise and impact investment industries. Metrics will provide an armature to support these efforts, as they do for the proposals outlined above. Metrics alone can be useful, but when paired with legal instruments and institutions, they not only say, they do.

Conclusion

The advent of reliable foundational and evaluative metrics holds great promise for propelling the legal concepts we describe beyond their current potential. Creating legal tools and institutions capable of nurturing social enterprises becomes much easier when investors and entrepreneurs can declare their intentions succinctly and all can judge how their results compare to their ambitions. The MPH, FLY paper, and SE(c)(3) all show that the absence of perfect metrics need not keep investors and entrepreneurs apart. Each simultaneously highlights the latent impact of well-calibrated metrics.

Developing accurate and usable metrics to track and assess social impact presents a daunting task. Social good is difficult to quantify, and creating comparable measures engenders serious incommensurability problems. Like many hard things, though, metric development proves to be worth the trouble, and even partial success will generate benefits. High-quality metrics will enhance the ability of many legal tools to persuade investors and entrepreneurs to trust each other. Among the three approaches described above, the potential upside appears greatest for FLY paper. Parties to such heavily negotiated deals can use foundational or evaluative metrics they find meaningful as additional triggers for convertibility, refining and defining the particular balance of profit and purpose that suits them. Presently available evaluative metrics do not possess the strength to satisfy regulators of a venture's sincerity standing alone, but even today's foundational and evaluative metrics can enhance MPH and SE(c)(3) transparency. As they are improved and refined, some of these metrics might directly capture the commitments these proposals measure only through the rough proxy of expenditures.

Today, metrics already offer an inkling of that possibility, helping to tame the assurance game between social entrepreneurs and investors by paving the way for a variety of institutions to target their support toward worthy ventures. Of these, certification shows the greatest near-term potential. A powerful certification can send a signal reassuring would-be investors that they will not be duped, and that the enterprise in which they invest can be trusted to maintain its dedication to social mission over time. By creating a brand that communicates reliable devotion to mission, a certification can likewise reassure entrepreneurs that investors in a certified entity or fund can be trusted to remain committed to generating social good.

Developing a potent brand through certification requires clarity and robust enforcement, each a worthwhile investment. Metrics also empower institutions facilitating investment in social enterprises, like the nascent social stock exchanges only now beginning to emerge,[47] by actively identifying mission-driven investors and businesses. Institutions with the capacity to build metrics may well be those best positioned to deploy them to match like-minded partners.

There can be no argument that metrics have great potential to fuel the growth of social enterprise, and there can be no argument that developing high-quality metrics poses profound challenges. A variety of institutions are engaged in this admirable work. Particularly when coupled with legal mechanisms such as MPH, FLY paper, and SE(c)(3), foundational and evaluative metrics could enhance access to capital for social enterprise. They can help social entrepreneurs and impact investors find and trust each other enough to make an initial investment, and help them to deepen—or prod them to end—their relationship by revealing and interpreting critical information.

7

Social Enterprise Exits

Beginnings, of course, tell only part of the story of social enterprise. To fully understand the pressures that shape ventures as they strive to balance mission and profit, it helps to consider those no longer in pristine condition. Just as an autopsy can reveal a great deal about how a person lived and why he died, examining social enterprises' endings offers fresh insights into the challenges they face. This shift in perspective demonstrates that rather than a fair-weather friend, the law can be a powerful ally of social enterprise.

Until now, this book has addressed the obstacles a social entrepreneur faces as she accesses capital to save or scale up her organization while remaining at the helm. This is the sunny success story in which every social entrepreneur wishes to star. But it is all too clear—from the failure rates of small businesses generally, from the special challenges of staying in the black while pursuing profit and social mission simultaneously, and from the simple law of averages—that many social entrepreneurs will have quite different experiences.

Some will never find fully committed impact investors willing to retain the founder, but may find or be approached by a buyer interested in purchasing their business or its assets. Many such social entrepreneurs will accept these offers, exiting one venture to pursue another with social or nonsocial aims. Other ventures will simply fail. On this end of the spectrum, social entrepreneurs and their investors may consider utilizing bankruptcy protection. Even in such turbulent moments, the law can offer shelter for missions and succor for entrepreneurs and investors.

Sale and dissolution could scarcely represent more divergent outcomes. Nevertheless, both take their shape from deal structure and governance. Planning a sale raises two key questions. What will be transferred? What will be received in exchange? The choice of what to jettison and what to take in return will profoundly affect social mission's trajectory. Mission commitments can also be integrated directly into a deal's terms. For example, parties could expressly agree to contract terms requiring a buyer to meet foundational metric targets (retain employees, continue charitable activities or contributions), to satisfy evaluative metric benchmarks, or to maintain certifications. Negotiating these

items will reveal to sellers valuable information about buyers' level of commitment to social good. The interplay of metrics and legal rights present throughout
Social Enterprise Law can be seen clearly in these moments of disruption. Robust
metrics and potent legal protections can preserve a balance between mission
and profit even in the face of radical change.

Governance plays a related role. Governance actions, like a resolution of the
board of directors, shareholder approval, or an LLC member vote, will often
be necessary to accomplish a sale. Depending on the place entrepreneurs and
investors inhabit in a selling social enterprise's hierarchy, they can deploy those
approvals to influence the terms of a deal. In some cases, sellers may even negotiate retention of governance roles after a purchase. Since courts can and do
enforce governance rights, this approach can be particularly useful for enforcing
contract terms in the postsale environment.

Although dissolution differs from sale in myriad ways, transaction structure
and governance remain key levers available to entrepreneurs and investors concerned with maintaining social mission. The financial state of the social enterprise at the time of dissolution will determine how much influence they will
provide. If assets remain, they may be used to secure future mission commitments. Those with claims to these assets can bargain for their preferred mix of
financial and social return. Avoiding insolvency puts control over these negotiations in the hands of the social enterprise's managers and investors, and their
roles in governance can bolster their power. But if the insolvency line is crossed,
by formal petition for bankruptcy or practical reality, control will shift to noninvestor creditors. If trade and other noninvestor creditors take on negotiating
and governance roles, financial concerns will likely come to dominate.

Conceptually, of course, sales and dissolutions just represent different species of exit. For ordinary entrepreneurs and investors, designing an exit strategy
is a key part of building a business. But in the social enterprise world, this likely
eventuality remains hidden—lurking in the shadows as the potential bogeyman
threatening mission. In fact, exit is a natural part of the life of a business and
its founders, and social enterprises are businesses—not charities. Charities are
outliers, endowed with perpetual life and responsible for serving their mission
until it becomes well-nigh impossible. Businesses must be nimble, and while
their lifetimes need not be finite, there is nothing sinister about them coming
to an end. Exits can happen in all kinds of ways for social enterprises, and bring
along with them a variety of potential risks and benefits. Legal tools can help
social entrepreneurs and investors plan for and configure exits, to make them
smoother, more predictable, and satisfying for all.

The legal regimes and instruments discussed in previous chapters harness the
power of exit. An MPH can draw down; FLY paper has a term; certifying entities
and exchanges can decertify and delist. Even SE(c)(3) status typically terminates
at a claimant's dissolution. By incorporating endings into their architecture,

these tools help bring entrepreneurs and investors together in the first place. But social enterprises that have not been so careful or prescient also confront exit opportunities in one form or another, some forced upon them. Fortunately, just as the preceding chapters showed that social entrepreneurs and investors can adapt standard legal tools to give their dreams flight, conventional legal mechanisms can help them pursue their dual-mission goals through this final phase.

Selling . . . and Selling Out

For many entrepreneurs, the prospect of selling their business to a buyer who will run it independently or as part of a larger firm offers one vision of success. The business will go on in some form and the founder and other early investors will receive the purchase price. For the struggling small business with as-yet negative cash flow, an offer to purchase can provide a founder with the liquidity to start a new venture or simply pay her home mortgage. Even very successful small and growing businesses may distribute no profits to owners. They may not yet be earning net profits—just showing great potential and paper value. Or the profits they do earn are needed for reinvesting, in order to continue the business' growth trajectory. Selling a business can allow an entrepreneur to realize the gains he has built, providing a moderately ambitious goal to cultivate. If entrepreneurs' wildest dreams involve an IPO, their next best outcome is often an acquisition.

Of course, not every firm's sale constitutes a victory for lap for its founder. Lots of businesses fail to thrive. Attracting a buyer to pick up the pieces of an entrepreneur's broken dreams may be a Pyrrhic victory even for ordinary firms. Still, even here, sales can provide substantial value for founders and even investors. An exit through sale, albeit at a lower price than one aspired to, can allow a founder to cut her losses and move on to her next project. Selling a venture can be an important element in failing fast—a mantra for success according to many serial entrepreneurs. Investors too will be cheered by a variety of paths for potential exits. They have reason to be wary when asked to risk their capital on an unproven business. Identifying ways out can make it easier to draw investors into a project in the first place.

The Exit Experts

The mantra of exit pervades the venture capital (VC) environment. VC firms consider exit opportunities early and often, and they consciously design deal structures and governance provisions to maximize their control over them. The most successful VC investments often culminate in the initial public offerings described in chapter 5. These sensational triumphs represent but a highly

publicized minority. Many VC investments never become profitable and are liquidated, sometimes with no return to the VC fund. Among VC investees that do
well, more exits occur through sales than IPOs. Some of these are trade sales,
in which a larger, more established industry player purchases the investee firm.
Other buyers, including other VC firms, act with purely financial motives. VC
funds carefully design their investments to maximize their influence over how
and when these exits will happen.

Venture capital firms become exit experts because their business models
demand it.[1] A VC firm forms each of its funds as a limited partnership. Investors
contribute their capital as limited partners and have a passive role. The general
partner VC firm must invest in a portfolio of companies for a set period of time
and handles all of the day-to-day management. The VC firm itself commits little
capital to the fund—frequently only 1 percent of the total. Yet it receives a large
portion of the profits it generates; the going rate is 20 percent. The gap between
the VC firm's capital contribution and its return rights can be justified only if the
firm offers access and expertise the limited partners cannot match on their own.
VC firms make their reputations by identifying pools of companies with attractive risk/return profiles and structuring and managing investments in them to
generate and protect returns.

For this business model to work more than once, successful exits are crucial.
VC fund investors accept that they cannot reclaim their capital until the investment period—often 10 years—elapses.[2] At this point, though, the VC fund dis-
solves and must be able to cash out the limited partners. The greater the gains
it yields, the more successful the firm will be in attracting investors to future
funds. The mandatorily limited time horizon means VC firms must always keep
one eye on the door. Doing so allows them to capitalize on moderate and smash
successes, and identify losing ventures early enough to limit loses. Several legal
tools help VC firms ensure their influence, and at times control, over exit timing
and terms.

Anticipating exit starts with the deal structures VC funds use to invest.
Rather than making their investment in a portfolio company in one fell swoop,
VC funds stage their investments over time. A promising company will receive
a cash infusion only large enough for it to reach "the next milestone in its business plan."[3] Staging financing allows the VC to obtain more information about
an investee's uncertain product—about which the entrepreneur will always have
more information—before it invests more capital. The results of that effort will
determine whether and how much the fund will invest at the next stage. VC
funds also often negotiate rights to have their shares repurchased by the portfolio company.[4] Along with downside protection, these redemption rights further
enhance their control over exit alternatives.

VC deal structures also exert influence over exit by deploying a particular type
of investment vehicle: convertible preferred stock.[5] Preferred stock is equity; it

entitles holders to a share of the residual earnings of the firm. But it enjoys a privilege over common stock in terms of payout. Preferred stock holders collect payment first in dividend distributions. More importantly here, on liquidation they receive the return of their entire initial investment before common stockholders receive anything. Sometimes they receive even more. VC funds often negotiate liquidation preferences, which entitle preferred shareholders to receive a multiple of their initial investments, again before any returns are paid to common shareholders. The convertibility component mirrors the conversion right described in chapter 4's discussion of FLY paper. Holders of convertible preferred shares can convert their shares to common stock, and generally must do so in the event of an IPO. Convertibility, along with other rights attendant to their preferred shares, give VC funds flexibility to maximize their returns in a variety of exit scenarios.

Either at the outset, or over time through incremental share purchases, VC funds also obtain substantial board representation in their portfolio companies. Input, if not control, at the board level ensures the VC a key role in determining the timing and type of exit because exits are initiated at the board level. The board must propose any merger, consolidation, or sale, and it must decide on any initial public offering of securities. If the fund ultimately holds sufficient voting power, it can backstop its board role with a shareholder veto.

Finally, VC funds demand an active role in management. Participation in management provides the fund with information necessary to evaluate whether performance justifies an additional round of funding and to make exit decisions. VC contracts can also include rights to approve important business decisions, even when they do not rise to the level of requiring a board or shareholder vote. These negative covenants supplement or substitute for VC influence in governance, providing additional power over business decisions that will make exits more or less feasible down the line.

These rights combine to allow VC funds to reduce the uncertainty, information asymmetries, and agency costs inherent in investing, and dovetail with VC firms' business models.[6] Limited partner investors are willing to put up virtually all of the capital and give away a large proportion of the profits from a VC fund because they value the contacts, expertise, and business savvy that a VC firm can provide—not only in selecting but also in stewarding investee companies. VC firms use deal structure and governance to secure significant control over the time and terms of any exit, and to ensure they can pay out investors and live to raise another fund.

Lessons from the VC Experience

Although there is no mature social venture capital market per se as yet, impact investors in a social enterprise can learn a great deal from the VC experience.

Like VCs, impact investors contribute capital rather than creating enterprises. They too can negotiate for power over exit through deal structures and governance rights agreed to ex ante. But if impact investors do not build in these protections on the front end, many of them will be impossible to retrofit when a sale opportunity arises. Moreover, the analogy is far from perfect.

Social enterprise investors care about mission achievement, not only the ability to extract their capital and (hopefully) a return.[7] Not all of the tools VCs utilize can be repurposed for the social enterprise context, and using some of them could be counterproductive. Venture capital firms and the tech start-ups associated with them operate in a very different milieu than social enterprises, and they do not face the unique assurance game created by a double bottom line. But in both settings, success means aligning incentives and creating trust, and many of the insights developed by these exit experts will apply measure for measure to social enterprises.

We have already taken the VC experience to heart in other parts of this book. Our FLY paper proposal demonstrates that creative deal structures like those VCs have mastered can constrain future exits and operate as powerful signals. Instead of contingent convertible bonds, impact investors could seek convertible preferred shares to limit entrepreneurs' potential upside gains from jettisoning a social enterprise's mission. But convertible stock creates a very different power dynamic than convertible debt. As equity, preferred shares will endow investors with just the type of control rights that make skeptical social entrepreneurs nervous. Adding liquidation preferences to the mix would further raise entrepreneurs' concerns about investors' true motives. We fear a simple copy-paste from the VC environment would tilt the balance of power too far away from entrepreneurs in favor of investors.

If impact investors demand the additional governance power VCs gain through a portfolio company's board, the imbalance would only increase. Controlling the board means wielding authority to initiate decisions, not only to stop them. There may be deals in which the entrepreneurs prove trusting and impact investors sufficiently skittish that such lopsided arrangements satisfy both. In the typical case, however, such asymmetric relationships between entrepreneurs and investors will not improve the flow of capital to social enterprises. The relentless timeline of venture investing and the unique combination of rights VC funds hold can also place their exit preferences at odds with those of portfolio company's founders and other investors. But even when used aggressively, venture capital firms' preferred tools serve them well because reputational concerns in the tightly knit VC and start-up communities constrain VCs' willingness to mistreat entrepreneurs.[8] In the relatively chaotic impact investment space, such dominance will send negative signals to social entrepreneurs and make them suspicious of investors who advocate for them.[9]

Other VC practices offer more promising models for social enterprise. Social entrepreneurs and impact investors unsure of each other's commitments to mission might use staged investment to test them. Investors concerned about the possibility that exits they disfavor will jeopardize mission can extend their courtship period by parceling out capital over time, perhaps using foundational or evaluative metrics as benchmarks. Setting social goals that will trigger additional investments limits what impact investors will have to lose from a sale they disfavor. Staging investment can also increase the seriousness with which entrepreneurs take impact investors' claims of social commitment, and their resolve to achieve them.

Active management can also build trust. Philanthropic donors practicing "venture" or "high impact" philanthropy echo VC techniques. These practices

> distill[] . . . down to five key elements: 1) Investments in a long-term (3–6 year) plan for social change; 2) A managing partner relationship; 3) An accountability-for-results process; 4) Provision of cash and expertise; and 5) An exit strategy.[10]

Venture capital strategies can be an awkward fit for donors and charities, but impact investors and social entrepreneurs should be comfortable adapting all of these elements in their deals. What is more, when social entrepreneurs and impact investors engage with each other on business decisions small and large, each can see what the other values—even if they do not share formal governance rights.

Big Corporate M&A and the Real Scoop on Ben & Jerry's

For both impact investors and social entrepreneurs, the prospect of selling a mission-driven business takes on a decidedly different cast than planning an exit for a VC-funded tech start-up. Social enterprise founders worry purchasers will not share their mission or continue it, and stories like the apocryphal tale of Ben & Jerry's don't help. Ben & Jerry's—an early adopter of a double-bottom-line approach—found itself drawn into what has become something of a ghost story that social entrepreneurs tell one another. The complex narrative described below often fails to account for the simple fact that Ben & Jerry's ultimately answers to its owners, just like every other for-profit corporation. When Unilever swallowed Ben & Jerry's, it did so with the approval of those shareholders. To those who view the transaction as a whodunit, suspicion usually—and unfairly—falls on the corporate law.

Virtually every social entrepreneur can relate how Ben Cohen and Jerry Greenfield started selling ice cream with a commitment to supporting the social causes they favored, grew into a laudable publicly held corporation, but then sold out to a major international food conglomerate. Many believe that corporate law made them do it. In fact, the true story of Ben & Jerry's is one of trust, and the role of corporate law is one of object lesson—not arch villain.

After growing their premium ice cream business as a private company for a handful of years, Ben & Jerry's went public in 1984. They first sold shares in a limited, intrastate offering for Vermont residents only. They went national a year later, with a full IPO and listing on the Nasdaq. Early investors were rewarded; the share price rose from $10.50 in the intrastate offering to $13 in the Nasdaq issue and further from there.[11] The scale of Ben & Jerry's ice cream operations grew as well, along with the company's outspokenness on social issues. It introduced environmentally friendly packaging, continued sourcing arrangements to support local farms and sustainably harvested ingredients, and donated 7.5 percent of profits to charitable causes (considerably more than other firms at the time).[12] It seemed that Ben and Jerry had created a new market category— premium ice cream for conscious consumers. Plus, they did it all while proclaiming an unofficial motto of "If it's not fun, why do it?"[13]

Over time, however, growth stalled. The share price stagnated, generating critiques of current management and attempts to replace them.[14] Dreyer's Grand Ice Cream Company submitted its first bid to acquire Ben & Jerry's in 1998. Over the next two years, more bids materialized, including interest from Unilever. Cohen worked with a group of investors to attempt to take the company private, but failed. Dreyer's made another formal offer in 2000, and Unilever soon joined the bidding.

Here, in the standard account, comes the unmasking of corporate law as the nemesis of the double bottom line, when the Ben & Jerry's board was forced to sell by their fiduciary obligations to maximize value for shareholders. As chapter 2 explained, Delaware corporate law's *Revlon* doctrine imposes that strict mandate to maximize shareholder value in an endgame scenario—when the corporation is put up for sale or the board has decided to undertake a transaction that will irreversibly alter the shareholders' investment.[15] Somewhat more leeway is granted to directors defending against a hostile takeover under the *Unocal* line of cases. Outside the endgame situation, they may adopt reasonable defenses and consider the impact of a change of control on nonshareholder constituencies like "creditors, customers, employees, and perhaps even the community generally."[16] Ben & Jerry's had not been officially put up for sale, but if it rejected Unilever's offer and wanted to make that rejection stick, it would have had to employ takeover defenses. Precedents like these Delaware cases confront boards with the difficult choice between negotiating an acceptance with—to some, a surrender to—an acquirer that avoids litigation risk and rejecting the offer and gearing up to defend their decision and future tactics in court. When arbitrageurs purchase stock in anticipation of an acquisition, the likelihood of litigation increases.

While compelling, that narrative here encounters its first key flaw: Ben & Jerry's was not subject to Delaware law. As a Vermont corporation, Vermont law would apply, including its constituency statute, which gave directors discretion to

> consider the interests of the corporation's employees, suppliers, credi-
> tors and customers, the economy of the state, region and nation, com-
> munity and societal considerations, including those of any community
> in which any offices or facilities of the corporation are located, and any
> other factors the director in his or her discretion reasonably considers
> appropriate in determining what he or she reasonably believes to be
> in the best interests of the corporation, and the long-term and short-
> term interests of the corporation and its stockholders, and including
> the possibility that these interests may be best served by the continued
> independence of the corporation.[17]

We will never know how the Vermont courts would have decided the question of whether Ben & Jerry's directors could lawfully refuse the Unilever offer under the protection of this statute. We cannot say what defensive steps it would have allowed the board to take without violating their fiduciary duties. Had they taken that route, however, running the company in the face of caustic litigation would certainly have become less fun. With much public denouncement of the role of corporate law, the board negotiated with Unilever to accept their offer. [18]

In the public company M&A space, much is made of preemptive measures potential target companies can use to avoid selling under duress. In the hot take-over markets of the 1980s, corporate lawyers unleashed remarkable creativity in developing (and naming) an arsenal of defensive techniques including lockups, shark repellents, and poison pills.[19] Although the law offered an array of tools that could have prevented the sale, Ben & Jerry's did not rely on them to manage the succession of the business. Like the myriad social entrepreneurs and investors who will not have deployed FLY paper, the MPH form, or an SE(c)(3) election, Ben & Jerry's acted in the moment to respond to a perceived threat to its undefended double bottom line. Just as a VC might, Ben & Jerry's used deal structure and governance creatively, here to embed mission protections directly into the transfer of ownership.

The sale contracts included several specific terms to institutionalize Ben & Jerry's social commitments postsale.[20] Unilever agreed to contribute over a million dollars per year to the Ben & Jerry's Foundation, and to continue increasing the size of this contribution as sales grew. It promised to pay all full-time Ben & Jerry's employees a living wage set based on realistic estimates of living costs in Vermont, and this commitment was backed by enforcement authority lodged in two individuals with long-standing ties to Ben & Jerry's. They were empowered to sue Unilever if it failed to comply, and Unilever would pay for that litigation. Unilever also made a one-time payment of $5 million to fund bonuses for workers at the Vermont plants, agreed to keep substantial Vermont operations for a minimum of five years, promised not to lay off workers or cut benefits for two, and made a host of other concessions to entice Ben & Jerry's to sell. The time limits on the provisions that had them have run, with mixed results. On the one hand, Ben & Jerry's maintains substantial operations in Vermont more than 15 years later. On the other, layoffs occurred just after the two-year anniversary of the sale.

This series of express contract terms was bolstered by a unique governance arrangement established for the company going forward. Ben & Jerry's became a wholly owned subsidiary of Unilever, which means Unilever owns all of the shares of Ben & Jerry's—not an unusual structure. The rules of the road for the Ben & Jerry's board of directors, however, are extraordinary. The board has 11 seats, and Unilever selects the people who fill only two of them.[21] The remaining seats were initially filled by Cohen, Greenfield, and others with history and commitment to Ben & Jerry's and its social mission. When vacancies arise, the board itself—not Unilever—selects and appoints new members to fill them. This power to staff the overwhelming majority of Ben & Jerry's board without Unilever's approval is not a concession for a transitional period; it lasts forever.

This would all be window dressing unless the board was granted significant control over the business. The sale agreements do this too. The board has

> primary responsibility for "preserving and enhancing the objectives of the historical social mission of the company as they may evolve," and for "safeguarding the integrity of the essential elements of the brand." Unilever has primary responsibility for the financial and operational aspects of the business, and it also retains all powers not expressly given to the board.[22]

The Ben & Jerry's board is explicitly empowered to prevent changes to product standards and the use of its trademark, and is entitled to be consulted on hiring and firing the CEO.

It took several years for this vision of shared authority to settle into practice.[23] Early on, Unilever directed changes in product standards without board notice and consent. While the board may have been frustrated with the lack of progress on the company's social mission, it did little to counter it. Since 2007, though, the board has taken a more active role—even considering litigation to enforce the sale agreement's provisions. After personnel changes at both Ben & Jerry's and Unilever, the board has become a forceful steward of the company's social mission, and the two parties have begun working in concert. In fact, Unilever touted its socially responsible brands as its strongest, and it and its CEO, Paul Polman, have become a recognizable leaders in this area.[24] Recent events suggest Unilever may have pushed its social agenda too far—making itself a target for acquisition. In February 2017, Kraft made an unsolicited offer to acquire all of Unilever's shares at an 18% premium over market, which the board promptly rejected.[25] In the wake of the offer, however, Unilever undertook a "comprehensive review of options available to accelerate delivery of value for the benefit of our shareholders,"[26] and announced changes designed to "unlock sustainable value faster."[27]

Whatever the results of this latest challenge, the Ben & Jerry's acquisition starkly illustrates the gap between the perception and the reality of the relationship between social enterprise and the law. Although convicted in the court of public opinion for compelling the sale, the applicable Vermont corporate law offered assurances to directors that they need not blindly maximize shareholder value. In truth, the terms of an apparently voluntary sale underscore the law's capacity to shelter mission even in the midst of radical change.

Lessons from M&A Practice

This more nuanced version of the Ben & Jerry's story demonstrates that even in the context of large company mergers and acquisitions, the basic insight of *Social Enterprise Law* remains relevant. The law can empower those concerned about mission longevity after a sale. By negotiating about mission expressly, carefully crafted and agreed-upon terms can be made clear and enforceable. Buyers may be willing to accept a transaction including express commitments to social mission post-transition. Sellers can negotiate not only the content of these commitments, but also whether they will be time-limited or enduring. The Ben & Jerry's sale agreement included a complex web of these commitments, many of which have had lasting impact not only on Ben & Jerry's but on Unilever as well.

In the case of Ben & Jerry's, mission-enhancing contract commitments came along with a windfall purchase price for exiting shareholders. In a social enterprise with less bargaining power, selling entrepreneurs and investors will likely need to trade mission commitments for a more painful decrease in the purchase price they receive. Some social entrepreneurs and impact investors will accept such a trade-off happily. But it will not always be simple. Taking less profit out of the sale of a social enterprise means founders and initial investors take less with them to their next venture (mission-driven or otherwise). This is no small matter; nor is it black and white. The attraction of social enterprise for founders and investors lies not only in its ability to achieve social mission, but also in its capacity to provide a financial return. Social entrepreneurs and investors who want to maximize financial returns at the time of sale betray no commitment to serve social mission forever, because social enterprises make no such commitments. Sales can be structured to include mission-enhancing contract terms, but only if selling parties desire them. And sellers may disagree. Conflicts over the balance of profit and social good among the various parties on the selling side will need to be resolved at the time of exit. Doing so will frequently complicate negotiations toward mission-enhancing contract terms.

If a social enterprise's sellers do bargain for buyers' promises to continue mission, mechanisms to enforce them are crucial. If buyers renege on their commitments, former entrepreneurs or investors will find standard breach-of-contract damage remedies quite unsatisfying. What are the damages for failing to continue local or sustainable sourcing commitments? To whom would they be paid? Even if they were calculated and appropriately distributed, a damage remedy would not reassemble the prior supply chain. Moreover, litigation is expensive, and by default each party bears its own costs.

The Ben & Jerry's deal included significant planning for enforcement, from Unilever's agreement to fund litigation to enforce its living wage obligation to the power-sharing arrangement with the non-Unilever-controlled board. Undoubtedly, the power and value in the Ben & Jerry's brand gave the sellers its exceptional bargaining power. Entrepreneurs and investors selling more modest social enterprises are unlikely to be able to negotiate so many potent enforcement mechanisms. Still, these terms are a powerful reminder of the importance of bargaining with enforcement in mind—the loftiest promises to continue mission should be traded for little if enforcement options are weak.

As potent as enforceable contractual terms may be on their own, the Ben & Jerry's sale demonstrates that they can also work in tandem with governance rights. Establishing an independent board with control over the Ben & Jerry's brand and its commitment to social mission was the crux of the Ben & Jerry's sale agreement. A founder or impact investor in a selling social enterprise could emulate this tactic precisely, and attempt to bargain for a continuing governance role postsale. But it is the rare buyer who would be willing to agree. The more general point about the power of governance is more practically useful. The governance roles held by Cohen, Greenfield, and those who sympathized with them put them in the negotiating seats. The roles they do or do not play in governance will often too determine how much control entrepreneurs and investors will have in shaping a contemplated sale.

Finally, there is the road not taken by Ben & Jerry's. Managers and investors often clash over takeover defenses because of fears that they maintain the offices of the former at the cost of losses for the latter. Entrepreneurs and investors in a social enterprise, however, might agree to costly defenses in order to protect mission commitments from being undermined by a hostile sale. Prior chapters bristle with attempts to broker such deals. The benefit corporation, public benefit corporation, and social benefit corporation forms all ease boards' paths to reject offers to buy, often citing the Ben & Jerry's sale as an example of a transaction that these forms will avoid.[28] Chapter 4's FLY paper also functions as a type of defense. It deters changes of control by making sale of the entrepreneurs' shares less valuable and, therefore, less attractive. Social enterprise boards could also use traditional takeover defenses to reject acquirers whose dedication to social mission they doubt—at least in states with constituency statutes, and as long as they are willing to face down potential litigation.

Ben & Jerry's is far from the only readily recognizable business with social commitments to have traveled the acquisition road. As consumers' interest in organically produced and sustainably sourced products has grown, major players in the food and personal care products industries have responded by purchasing companies recognized as leaders in these areas. Examples like these abound. Clorox bought Burt's Bees in 2007; Campbell's Soup Company bought Plum Organics in 2013; General Mills bought Annie's Homegrown in 2014. Unilever itself acquired green cleaning and paper products company Seventh Generation in 2016. The deal created an independent Social Mission Board for Seventh Generation including its founder, and which is "tasked with preserving the commitments" the company has made to the environment.[29]

Other than the Seventh Generation acquisition, however, none of these deals included the kind of contractual and governance protections for social mission seen in the Unilever–Ben & Jerry's deal. Annie's and Burt's became mere labels within the stable of their acquirers; only the strength of the acquirers' public pronouncements of their commitments to the acquired firms' social practices and their value to consumers prevent them from walking them back.[30] As a separate subsidiary of Campbell's, Plum Organics has been able to maintain its B Corp certification and its status as a Delaware public benefit corporation.[31] That said, Campbell's owns all of Plum's shares and can drop the B certification or convert to a standard corporation at will.

Burt's and Annie's received private equity investments before being acquired, and private equity investors continue to be interested in mission-driven businesses—at least those with the highest profiles. Blake Mycoskie, founder of one-for-one espadrille titan TOMS Shoes, negotiated with mission preservation in mind when he sold 50 percent of the company's equity to Bain Capital in 2014. Mycoskie retained his position as "chief shoe giver" and, more importantly, the other 50 percent of the company's shares.[32] This substantial stake will give him leverage in governance to protect against Bain's early commitment to TOMS's social mission waning over time.

Selling does not have to be selling out. Social enterprise exits are not all bad, and a lawyer's tools can be used to help buyers and sellers continue to generate social good postsale if they wish. The increasing prominence of social enterprise will make attention to mission in dealmaking ever more important. Rather than a nadir, the Ben & Jerry's acquisition appears to represent a remarkable success story in terms of the law's ability to nurture a balance between mission and profit. Not every sale of a social enterprise will satisfy the dual-mission goals of its founders and investors. Certainly few will satisfy the demanding rhetoric of much social enterprise literature. Deal structure and governance are powerful—if underused—tools for sellers and buyers to negotiate the longevity of a social enterprise's mission commitments.

The Little Deals on the Block

Insights from the M&A and VC experiences can help avoid the pitfalls often associated with selling a social enterprise. But few social enterprises operate in the rarified air occupied by public companies or even VC-funded start-ups, or benefit from the advice they enjoy. Small social enterprises may find it difficult to adapt the tools these very different entities deploy as a way to channel exits toward retention of social mission. Fortunately, small businesses are bought and sold every day. Each of these little deals on the block also harnesses deal structure and governance rights, and many techniques common to them can also be used to negotiate postsale mission commitments.

What to Sell and What to Buy

Small businesses can sell their assets or their equity, and the preferred route depends on a combination of tax consequences, liability concerns, and the practical and legal requirements of each option. In broad terms, sellers of incorporated small businesses achieve clear tax advantages by selling equity, while buyers achieve them by buying assets.[33] Good nontax reasons bolster these tax-driven preferences.[34] An asset sale allows a buyer to take on the liabilities of the selling entity selectively. A buyer can purchase the firm's intellectual property, but not its inventory, or its real property, but not its large piece of equipment subject to a lien. By structuring a transaction as an asset sale, any assets (and accompanying liabilities) the buyer does not wish to accept can be left with the seller. This means, of course, a seller wishing to divest herself of liabilities from the business she is exiting will prefer to sell equity. Equity buyers take all of the assets and liabilities of the business together. They cannot pick and choose. The legal steps required to complete asset versus equity sales also differ, often making asset sales costlier to complete.

The acquisition structure chosen will determine some of the mechanisms entrepreneurs and investors can use to cement a social enterprise's mission. Imagine a social enterprise in the food business, which hires from groups facing barriers to employment and trains them for work in the culinary field. Perhaps it also sources the majority of its ingredients from local suppliers. Transferring the equity in this firm will result in a purchaser taking on the obligations of the entity it acquires; existing obligations to employees and suppliers will transfer to new ownership. The social enterprise can protect these commitments after a sale of equity by making them legally durable for the firm presale. It can eschew at-will employment or ink long-term supplier agreements, which obligations will then persist after the equity transfers. In an asset sale, the seller will need to bargain expressly for the buyer to accept constraints like these, even if they are already in place. Of course, such commitments may reduce the purchase price a seller can obtain, and they may be just the type of obligations purchasers will try to avoid with an asset sale structure. Negotiations over these points may reduce the number of interested buyers and the attractiveness of other purchase terms offered, but they will also reveal valuable information about potential buyers' level of interest in continuing social mission.

Coming to Terms

Small business sales have many terms beyond their basic structures as asset or equity sales. Among them, financing is paramount. The luckiest small-business sellers find a buyer who can pay the purchase price in cash. In most sales, though, sellers make a down payment and agree to pay the remainder of the purchase price over time.[35] These payments can be fixed as general debt obligations by the seller or made contingent upon the transferred business' future profits, called an "earnout."[36] In fixed seller-financing, the purchaser agrees to pay the portion of the purchase price beyond the down payment in installments, with interest. If the buyer defaults, such as by missing payments, the seller-lender will have the right to retake control of the business. To improve recourse, sellers sometimes also take a security interest in assets of the transferred business or demand other collateral or personal guarantees.

Seller-financing not only is good for buyers wishing to delay payment, but also helps sellers attract buyers in the first place. By agreeing to forestall receipt of the full purchase price, often for a few years or more, seller-financing demonstrates a seller's faith that her business will remain profitable after she exits. It is powerful proof that the seller is not unloading a lemon, and an earnout structure puts additional seller skin in the game. In an earnout, if the business surpasses agreed-upon profit goals, the buyer will increase his payments to the seller according to a negotiated schedule. It is challenging to set goals for an earnout structure, and to specify seller and purchaser obligations sufficiently clearly in the contract of sale. If the deal can be written, though, an earnout mechanism can create an even more powerful bonding effect than seller-financing alone. The seller will receive a higher price only if profits warrant it, creating downside protection particularly comforting to skeptical buyers.

Like the VC staged-funding technique, these familiar legal tools for bringing buyers and sellers together in small business sales are ripe for adaptation to the social enterprise context. As is true for other small business owners, social enterprise sellers are unlikely to find an all-cash deal. Seller-financing will help them expand the universe of potential buyers for their business. Sellers also can use the flexibility seller-financing offers to enforce postsale social mission commitments to which buyers assent. Imagine a social enterprise formed to design, manufacture, and sell inexpensive water filtration systems in developing countries, to improve water quality and health. The owners build their business for a while and then need to sell, but want their mission to continue. They might offer seller-financing with mission-related as well as financial terms. The sellers would agree to take a down payment and installments for the remainder of the purchase price. Sellers would resume control not only if the buyer fails to make payments, but also if it raises prices above agreed-upon levels, leaves particularly needy markets, or abandons product lines designed for the poorest communities.

A traditional earnout, whereby profit or revenue benchmarks increase the overall purchase price, might be used to assuage a buyer's concerns that pursuing social good would undermine profitability. Mission-related benchmarks could also be used to design a kind of reverse earnout feature to motivate buyers to continue mission. Sellers could negotiate a price for the deal, but agree to lower future installment payments if the buyer demonstrates achievement of mission-related goals. Earnouts can be challenging to document, and eschewing specifics in favor of vague requirements for parties to use their "best efforts" can lead to dissatisfaction and litigation down the line. Moreover, as chapter 6 elaborates, metrics for social performance have some distance to go before they can offer the bright lines and sharp edges dealmaking often demands. Still, seller-financing and earnout structures are proven methods for getting small business buyers and sellers to yes, and enforcing their commitments to each other. Mechanisms like these offer too much upside in the social enterprise context to overlook their potential.

Additional opportunities for sellers to contract with buyers to maintain social mission arise when some of the consideration for the sale is transferred outside the exchange of cash and notes for a business' assets or equity.[37] Small business sellers frequently agree to covenants not to compete with the transferred business and are paid for consulting services they promise to provide after the transfer. In some sales, certain assets are transferred to the purchaser by license or lease rather than outright—often with an option to purchase later.

Social entrepreneur and early local-food enthusiast Judy Wicks used just such a license to safeguard the mission of her social enterprise postsale. Ms. Wicks founded the White Dog Café in West Philadelphia in 1984 with a commitment to local sourcing.[38] Over two and half decades, she made the restaurant into a local institution and became a leader in the sustainable food movement. When she sold the cafe to a local restauranteur in 2009, she wanted to ensure it would keep up its social commitments under new ownership. To do so, she licensed the "White Dog Café" name to the new owner separately for 15 years. To retain the license, the licensee was required to use renewable energy, purchase fair-trade ingredients, and meet a range of other sustainable sourcing, green production, and local ownership commitments.[39] Contractual arrangements like these allow sellers and buyers to bargain over the extent to which a social enterprise's mission will be maintained over time—and to reveal their true preferences to each other.

Governance Rights as Leverage

Governance will be operating in the background of these negotiations, influencing what deal structure is possible. Asset and equity sales trigger different governance requirements, which matter the most when minority interests enter the picture. The organizational structure of the selling company determines these governance rights, but regardless of the company's form, governing statutes demand a high level of formal consensus for an asset sale.[40] In a social enterprise with minority owners committed to mission, governance rights can be used as a bargaining chip—among sellers and with buyers that strongly prefer an asset sale structure. Investors committed to mission maintenance, and who hold a sufficient ownership stake, can use this leverage to secure mission going forward.

Equity sales do not trigger statutory consent requirements, but will not always provide a route to sidestep minority opposition. In unincorporated businesses, statutory limits prevent equity holders from transferring management rights along with ownership.[41] To provide new owners of transferred partnerships or memberships with management rights, fellow partners or members must agree. Unless a buyer is willing to acquire an equity stake in a small business without rights to influence its activities, other equity holders can powerfully impede a sale they oppose. Owners of unincorporated small businesses usually bolster these statutory limits with agreements that further restrict transfer of ownership. For example, LLCs' operating agreements often grant the LLC the right to purchase the interests of members who wish to transfer, and detail a process for setting the purchase price.[42]

At first glance, equity sales appear to provide a more effective workaround in incorporated small businesses, as corporate statutes place no limits on a shareholder's sale of her shares. Even a controlling shareholder may transfer her stake to whomever she pleases, so long as doing so will not breach her fiduciary duties to the corporation and its shareholders.[43] The content of this fiduciary obligation is somewhat uncertain. Selling a controlling stake to buyers the seller knows or should know will loot the corporate coffers is a breach.[44] And courts often speak of heightened fiduciary obligations in the context of closely held corporations: those with a small number of shareholders, active owner participation in management, and little or no market for the corporation's shares.[45]

The law leaves no doubt, however, that if a seller can find a purchaser willing to buy a controlling—but not complete—equity stake, minority shareholders have no formal vote on the matter.

This lack of formal power over transfer creates such obvious concerns in small incorporated businesses that those with two or more owners typically limit their transfer rights in buy-sell agreements.[46] These agreements, like those limiting transfer in unincorporated businesses, will address the process by which owner-ship stakes may be transferred. Commonly, such arrangements will grant share-holders the option to purchase the shares of their colleagues who wish to sell, and describe the process for valuation. Buy-sell agreements can also be used to ingrain a company's social mission by limiting even majority shareholders' abil-ity to sell shares unilaterally.

Making Mission Part of the Deal

If sellers want to trade value in exchange for mission commitments from new owners, the legal tools discussed here provide a means to encourage fidelity to mission and some greater enforcement than empty words. As metrics evolve and dealmakers gain experience, acquisitions of all sizes can be structured to make mission more secure, not more vulnerable. The process of bargaining over these commitments will also reveal far more about a buyer's intentions than words alone. It is a buyer's values and preferences for the social enterprise he is purchasing that will ultimately determine the fate of its social mission. No legal machinations can promise 100 percent certainty that the dual-mission nature of a social enterprise will endure after its sale to new owners. Once sellers leave the picture, even the strongest contractual terms and governance provisions will leave new owners with flexibility. Devotion to social mission will wane unless new owners and managers want to preserve it.

This fear about buyers' commitments mirrors that faced by entrepreneurs seeking investors, and it creates a similar trust gap the next generation of social enterprise law can help to close. Here, though, the trust deficit need not run in both directions. Buyers seeking to purchase a mission-driven business may be quite concerned, as committed impact investors are, about the firm's bona fides in terms of social goals. If a buyer for a social enterprise values its social mission, given the current state of metrics, it will have a challenging diligence process ahead of it. But sellers worry that buyers might be attracted to their social enterprise not because of its social mission, but despite it. Buyers might see the firm's upside if stripped of its social commitments, or may find them incidental. This is not always bad. Sometimes the value sellers can take out of a social enterprise from a purely profit-seeking buyer will fuel their next social venture, or is the safety net that allows entrepreneurs and investors to form a mission-driven business in the first place. For sellers that do want their ventures to continue their social missions, however, carefully negotiating deal structure and governance rights can help them identify the best buyers, and trust them enough to make the sale.

Dissolution

Social entrepreneurs and investors will find the prospect of failure just as upsetting as that of sale, perhaps more so. But many, if not most, businesses fail. Social enterprises, along with their founders and investors, need to be prepared for the possibility of failure and to know when to close their doors. One trenchant criticism of the charitable form is that it provides insufficient incentives to quit.[47] Social enterprise adopts business forms and practices in part to create these incentives to fail, and failing fast has advantages. The process can cull poor ideas and teach social enterprise participants valuable lessons. The network of connections and the wisdom gained through an ultimately unsuccessful venture are legacies that investors and entrepreneurs take with them. Realizing and accepting that a social enterprise will fail while some assets remain will allow entrepreneurs and investors to preserve their resources, energy, and reputation for future endeavors.

Closing a social enterprise, though, is not simply a matter of accepting reality and walking away. Governance actions must be taken to legally dissolve it. For example, in a corporation, the board of directors recommends dissolution to shareholders, and a majority of shareholders must vote to approve it. Notice of corporate dissolution must also be provided to state officials.[48] Even this process of legal dissolution does not terminate a business' existence immediately. It must wind up its affairs by paying creditors and distributing to its owners any property that remains. The firm may liquidate its assets to satisfy these debts, and distribute the proceeds that remain in cash. Alternatively, so long as the interests of creditors are protected, owners may agree to distribute some or all of a firm's remaining assets in kind. These decisions can be shaped by an agreement concluded in advance, or in negotiations at the time of dissolution.

The transactions used to wind up a business can be designed to shield mission or to forsake it. But assets are crucial; they are the currency in which these deals will be struck. If a dissolving social enterprise has assets beyond those needed to satisfy creditors, investors can bargain over what remains. If some or all of them desire to make mission part of that deal, they can do so. Imagine a health-oriented social enterprise formed as a corporation to sell low-cost insecticide-treated bed-nets in base-of-the-pyramid markets. Its fiduciaries resolve to dissolve, and shareholders approve. So long as the corporation can pay its debts without liquidating its remaining inventory, shareholders could agree to donate those nets to charities that will distribute them to needy individuals free of charge. Terms agreeing to such a process could be included in a share-holder agreement concluded in advance or adopted at the time of dissolution.

Provided there are assets to work with, a dissolving social enterprise can also use the process of distributing them among residual owners to further mission. Once creditors' interests are satisfied, owners have significant flexibility in negotiating how their own claims to the business' assets will be met. Particular patterns of distribution or distribution in kind rather than liquidation might improve the ability of former owners to continue pursuing mission postdissolution. For example, members of a green-technology LLC might negotiate a plan for dissolution that would liquidate its real property and use the proceeds to satisfy creditors and most investors, but distribute intellectual property rights and machinery to its engineer founder in kind, for use in a successor social venture. If no such advance plan should exist, the founder might try to negotiate for it in the course of dissolution. She might offer to discount the value of her distribution relative to other members in exchange for it taking such a form. She might even withhold a vote for dissolution to encourage her fellow members to agree, so long as doing so would not run afoul of any fiduciary obligations or contractual duties, such as the duty of good faith and fair dealing.[49]

Negotiating to protect mission in the shadow of dissolution will not be easy. Participants in many social enterprises will fail to reach such accords in advance, and crafting them with proverbial vultures circling will, at the risk of understatement, be difficult. By that point, minds may have turned from devoting assets to achieving social good to preserving them for oneself. The particular assets held by a social enterprise also may not lend themselves to mission-conserving maneuvers such as those hypothesized above. And plenty of dissolving social enterprises will not have assets beyond what is needed to satisfy creditors. Many may not even have enough to do that.

When a venture's obligations swamp its reserves of cash and valuable rights and property, once clear lines of ownership and control become blurred. Insolvency increases the power of creditors and can create fiduciary obligations to them. Once insolvency gives way to the formal process of bankruptcy, power further shifts in favor of creditors and away from a venture's owners. This shift will sharply reduce the options to steward mission through exit. Social entrepreneurs and investors should take this additional risk insolvency poses to heart. Using their governance rights to trigger dissolution while assets remain will enhance their ability to structure wind-down transactions that account for mission-related concerns.

Bankruptcy: A Special Case

Bankruptcy law's complexity cannot be summarized comprehensively here. The federal bankruptcy code provides a variety of bankruptcy options, the choice among which is itself a complex legal question. For our purposes, this array of choices can be reduced to two major categories of outcomes from bankruptcy filings. Bankruptcy can be used either to liquidate a filing company's debts or to restructure them. The ultimate takeaway from each is the same. Neither will give much consideration to a social enterprise's social mission, which makes bankruptcy a perilous option for social enterprises, even for ventures that adopt first- or second-generation hybrid forms.

Bankruptcy liquidation follows a more stringent process than liquidation outside of bankruptcy. Filing a bankruptcy petition starts a formal procedure in which an automatic stay on claims against the debtor is issued, a bankruptcy trustee is appointed and empowered to liquidate and distribute the debtor's assets, state and federal law exemptions are the only way to prevent assets from being liquidated, and the bankruptcy court is able to force a decision even if some creditors object.[50] Bankruptcy also follows very strict rules of seniority in distributing a debtor's assets.[51] Secured creditors—whose debts are secured by specific property identified as collateral—must be paid first, in order of priority. These secured creditors must receive the full amount they are owed before any payments will be made to other claimants. Next in line stand priority unsecured creditors, which include specific types of claims like taxes and recent wages. Ordinary unsecured creditors like suppliers will be paid only after—and if—priority unsecured debts are satisfied. Finally, if anything is left, it will be available to equity holders.

The values and structure of the bankruptcy system for liquidation do not map well onto the goals of social enterprise. Bankruptcy trustees manage the process of liquidation—not debtor companies themselves. Trustees are charged with obtaining the most value for creditors and, when possible, with giving debtors a fresh start.[52] Concerns about preserving social mission have no place in bankruptcy proceedings, and when mission-enhancing approaches will diminish the value available to creditors, bankruptcy law will disfavor them.[53] Although insolvency itself will impose significant restraints, social entrepreneurs and investors concerned with furthering mission through turbulent times will be better served by the flexibility of liquidation outside this system than the rigidity within it. Moreover, business entities (unlike individuals and sole proprietorships) may not discharge their indebtedness through the bankruptcy system. Without this benefit, social enterprises have even less reason to pursue bankruptcy liquidation.

Reorganization in bankruptcy has somewhat more to recommend it to social enterprises, but not much. As in bankruptcies seeking liquidation, filing a petition for reorganization will trigger an automatic stay of claims, offering debtor companies a moment of relief to consider the way forward. In a reorganization, the debtor will remain in control of its assets during the pendency of the proceedings as "debtor-in-possession," and courts rarely appoint trustees.[54]

Debtors-in-possession have a number of powerful tools to manage the business, including the ability to undo certain types of prepetition transfers, to reject the obligations of unexpired leases and executory contracts, and to sell assets (provided the creditors will retain their interests in the proceeds of sale). This control and flexibility compares favorably with the lack of control and rigidity in trustee-managed liquidations. But debtors-in-possession and their managers must also exercise their powers in compliance with fiduciary obligations to the creditors.[55] Rather than pursuing mission, or even balancing it with a concern for financial return for owners, debtors-in-possession must preserve the enterprise's assets to satisfy creditors' claims.

The debtor-in-possession puts forward an initial plan of reorganization—essentially a business plan for how the debtor will return to solvency. The plan proposes payments to creditors, often reducing the total amount to be repaid or extending the time for repayment. Again creditors are treated by class, with secured creditors holding the first-priority position. Negotiations begin. If, through them, all parties can agree to a plan of reorganization, the court will be asked to confirm it.[56] If parties cannot agree, the bankruptcy court may force acceptance of the plan by creditors through the "cramdown" procedure. This procedure allows the court to approve a plan without full creditor consent, but only if it finds that each class of creditors either has accepted the plan or is treated no worse than if the company had undergone liquidation by a bankruptcy trustee.[57] The "absolute priority rule" poses a final important obstacle. For a plan to be crammed down on unconsenting unsecured creditors, equity interests of former shareholders must be extinguished.[58]

As in bankruptcy liquidation, the formal processes and core values of the bankruptcy reorganization process will do little to help founders and investors of financially distressed social enterprises attend to their entity's social mission. For example, a debtor-in-possession would breach its fiduciary obligations to creditors by refusing to undo a prepetition transfer that served social goals at the expense of value creation or cost savings. The negotiation and cramdown processes too give creditors the ultimate power, and protecting mission will depend on whether creditors—and which creditors—share a commitment to this goal. Imagine an insolvent social enterprise with a dedicated impact investor as its sole secured creditor. Perhaps this creditor could be persuaded to allow some of the property securing its loan to be sold or encumbered in order to generate cash to satisfy more unsecured trade debt than would otherwise be possible. In exchange, all creditors would agree to retain mission-enhancing practices. Reorganization in bankruptcy might be used to formalize such an arrangement, though if the parties could agree informally to such a plan, it would be far less costly. Bankruptcy reorganizations are expensive, even for those entities that qualify for the fast-track designated for small businesses.[59] Formal reorganization under bankruptcy law would only be preferable to informal negotiation with creditors if the facilitative role of the bankruptcy court or the possibility of cramdown was needed to make such an arrangement work. Moreover, cramdown's absolute priority rule may simply shift the risks to social mission into the future, requiring mission-committed owners to give up control going forward.

As assets decline, so do opportunities to structure transactions to enhance mission, and insolvency's introduction of a governance role for creditors further limits entrepreneurs' and investors' ability to make mission-enhancing trade-offs. Bankruptcy is an especially fraught type of exit for social enterprises, and will rarely make strategic sense as a voluntary move for those concerned with mission preservation. Although creditors seldom use their ability to initiate involuntary bankruptcy proceedings,[60] the prospect of such actions too should prod financially distressed social enterprises to take corrective actions or dissolve outside of bankruptcy. Notably, charities need not fear involuntary bankruptcy. Such proceedings may be initiated "against a person, *except . . . a corporation that is not a moneyed, business, or commercial corporation*."[61] A social enterprise could argue its dual mission distinguishes it from the typical type of "moneyed, business, or commercial corporation" and merits exceptional protection from involuntary bankruptcy as well.

We do not recommend such an extension. The possibility of involuntary bankruptcy enhances social enterprises' credibility as borrowers—and they need all the help they can get. Suppliers, trading partners, and landlords will already worry that a social enterprise's double bottom line will make it a poor credit risk. There is no need to pile on immunity from involuntary bankruptcy. In fact, even the exception for charities is subject to powerful critiques. The exception adds to the difficulty charities have in accessing debt, and it can discourage voluntary use of the bankruptcy system early in situations of financial difficulty, when it can be the most useful.[62] This book is not the place to debate the merits of the exception for charities, but we strongly oppose expanding it to cover social enterprises.

Social Enterprise Is *Not* Charity—Nor Should It Be

After all, social enterprises are not charities. The point of a social enterprise is the value—both financial and social—to be gained from operation in a business form rather than a charitable one. Part of this benefit comes from the content of social enterprise production. Many nonprofit charities run job-training programs. But a social enterprise can offer employment opportunity and training in an entity more like the companies at which trainees will seek future employment. It can become a true part of the marketplace, and prove the dual-mission concept for its other for-profit players. Nonprofit charitable universities and research institutions engage in unparalleled pure science. In contrast, the social enterprise thesis argues that a dual-mission business is poised to extend this basic research to develop practical applications that address climate change or persistent poverty.

But perhaps the greater part of the value of social enterprise is its ability to attract capital seeking financial returns, and which would never be contributed for perpetual altruistic use. This ability to access investment capital creates capacity for a greater scale of production and distribution of social goods. Social enterprise entrepreneurs and investors are devoted to these goals, and will often be willing to await returns patiently. But they make investments, not donations. For these parties to embark on a social enterprise, exit cannot be entirely off limits. The possibility of an eventual financial return—in addition to the social one—is a key part of the equation. It is also what differentiates social enterprises from charities.

Assets contributed to charity are, quite simply, locked in. The clear and abiding nondistribution constraint serves as the defining economic characteristic of a charitable entity. A variety of doctrines accomplish this legal result. For example, charitable trusts are governed by the ancient doctrine of cy pres.[63] Any assets impressed with a charitable trust must remain devoted to the trust's charitable purposes forever. Only a court order will release this obligation, and courts will grant such relief only in dire situations when continuation of the original mission has become unlawful, impossible, or highly impracticable. Even when they do, the assets cannot be distributed to the trustees or owners. They must remain dedicated to some other charitable use, and courts try to hew closely to the original purpose, often attempting to find a new purpose as near as possible to it. For charities formed as nonprofit corporations, there is somewhat greater discretion to depart from the original charitable mission—in some states even without court approval. But assets still cannot be diverted from the charitable stream. On dissolution, a nonprofit corporation must transfer its remaining assets to another charity.[64] Once contributed to a charitable vehicle, assets cannot exit to private owners.

There are good arguments for this complete asset lock for charities. The nondistribution constraint offers protection against lapses by fiduciaries and other agents. When, as is common, the purchasers of charitable goods do not consume them, they cannot judge the adequacy or quality of their provision. These contract failures limit the capacity of donors and other patrons to discipline charity managers.[65] Although the law provides for government oversight, resource constraints will keep attorney general intervention well below the level needed to fully deter fiduciary breaches. Barring the transfer of a charity's assets to its members or managers discourages those seeking profit distributions from forming or operating charities in the first place. Further, perpetual dedication to charitable purposes goes a long way to justifying various special benefits charities can receive. Charitable tax advantages are well known, but charities also benefit from a series of other legal perks ranging from reduced postal rates to limited tort liability.[66] Donors are also empowered to impose perpetual restrictions on assets contributed to charities—dead-hand control otherwise shunned by property law.[67] Of course, the nondistribution constraint far from fully protects against mismanagement, and it significantly constrains charities' access to capital. These are precisely the challenges of nonprofit production that social enterprise is designed to overcome. Social enterprise has to be different from charity to do that, and exit is where the distinction lies.

Conclusion

Legal creativity can prevent the specter of exit from undermining the trust required to capitalize social enterprises. In fact, structuring exit has formed the core of each of this book's proposals. The unilateral and immediate dissolution and payout available in the L3C and hybrid corporate forms gave way to the MPH's insistence that investors and entrepreneurs negotiate exit together and that investors only gain access to a social enterprise's assets over time. FLY paper's convertible debt structure likewise ties entrepreneurs and investors to the mast for a considerable stretch, but provides opportunities for exit and liquidity after a sustained and patient period. SE(c)(3) imposes no set time restrictions, but incentivizes dedication to mission by aggressively taxing—though not forbidding—liquidity events. Much of the value of certifications and exchange listing standards lies in the fact that companies can fall out of them; in this context metrics essentially succeed by triggering and communicating exit from such systems. All our proposals contemplate an end to a social enterprise's social commitment. But they reassure entrepreneurs and investors that this end will not be blithely forced upon them.

Exit is a fact of life for businesses, and it produces valuable liquidity and learning for founders and investors alike. Social entrepreneurs and impact investors have different fears about exit than their traditional counterparts—and rightly so. They worry a buyer will abandon the dual-mission ethic that built their business. They worry dissolution will focus all parties on financial return, crowding out concerns for social good. They worry about empowering creditors in this process, when those creditors may not have bought into the double bottom line. They are right to worry; these things can happen. Sometimes legal tools can be used to ease these fears.

Of course, the ultimate way to protect social mission is for it to be intrinsically intertwined with firm value in a way that cannot be undone. When the value in a business is tied up with achieving its social mission, exit no longer represents an existential threat. New owners seeking value will produce social good because it is the surest way for them to realize value for themselves. Creditors will remain committed to the firm's social mission because doing so will be the best route to generate revenues to pay their unpaid claims. This is the ideal social entrepreneurs strive to reach and on which the concept of social enterprise is based.[68]

But great good can be done in the world by firms, entrepreneurs, and investors that fall short of this ideal. When the moment of exit arrives for them, deal structure and governance can be used to give mission a place in the process—if that is what entrepreneurs and investors want. Taking a page from the VC book, social enterprise investors may be able to ensure influence over these decisions in advance. But even without advance planning, entrepreneurs and investors can still consider mission as they choose what to sell and how to sell it, what to liquidate and to whom. They can use governance rights to negotiate for the bargain they want and for terms that continue a firm's dedication to social mission. Any such terms should be designed with an eye to enforcement. Sellers with substantial bargaining power may be able to maintain a governance role to ensure compliance, but more pedestrian tools like seller-financing terms can also provide meaningful discipline. Even for those social enterprises that have not planned for exit in advance, in this moment of crisis law can be harnessed to preserve mission.

These approaches will go some distance toward easing the minds of entrepreneurs and investors who want to retain their enterprises' social missions, especially if planning for exit begins before insolvency has set in. Contract provisions and governance structures can provide some confidence that new owners of a social enterprise or its assets will continue its mission commitments, when sufficient value exists to justify their retention. In dissolution, options become more limited, but the transactions used to the wind up a business and the governance actions required to approve it remain powerful levers for preserving mission. Entrepreneurs and investors who seek continuation of their mission should deploy these tools when they can be most powerful—before insolvency. Insolvency, within or outside the bankruptcy context, will elevate creditors' positions and make preservation of social mission beyond dissolution considerably more difficult.

All this said, there is no shame in sale or in dissolution—even without retaining mission commitments. Entrepreneurs and investors should be proud of what they have been able to accomplish in a social venture that comes to an end. Exit will help them emerge with the liquidity and experience to try again. The social enterprise game need not be one played only once. Social enterprises will end, but their entrepreneurs and investors can take the lessons learned from that venture and apply it to improve the next.

Conclusion

The law can be a powerful ally. To raise the capital necessary to flourish, the social enterprise sector needs the stability the law excels at generating. Like the gyroscopes that guide ships and aircraft, the legal mechanisms considered above can prevent double-bottom-line ventures from losing their way. Collectively, the MPH, FLY paper, and SE(c)(3) testify to the law's power and versatility, empowering the crowd just as deftly as they offer bespoke mission security to those that can afford it. More importantly, they offer a starkly altered vision of the relationship between the law and the burgeoning community of dual-mission ventures and impact investors. Rather than a threat to be contained, *Social Enterprise Law* reveals the law to be a wellspring of trust.

As radical as the notion of an entirely new generation of social enterprise law might seem, its aims represent something of a throwback. The L3C ultimately served the same symbolic ends—allowing entrepreneurs to trumpet the dual nature of their ambition—as the other first-generation hybrids that came after it. At its inception, though, this earliest hybrid form aspired to connect a particular type of investor with social enterprises in need of capital.[1] Targeted not at the trust deficit, but at a narrow technical requirement, the L3C could not bring investors and entrepreneurs together like the MPH, FLY paper, or SE(c)(3). Nevertheless, the parallels between the L3C's original purpose and the goals of the second generation suggest that the unorthodox proposals described above could be seen as a homecoming just as easily as a departure.

The law has the power to formalize a shared set of expectations into enforceable rights and obligations. When it succeeds in doing so, the results can provide prosperity for those directly affected and positive spillover benefits for the broader community. Real property law, for example, creates mutual gains for buyers and sellers at the same time that its requirements work to keep industrial and residential uses safely separate. The corporate law has long done much the same, creating great wealth on the one hand and promoting charity on the other. Social enterprise law could go further, integrating mission and profit to ensure that investors and entrepreneurs can keep their eyes on their twin bottom lines and not on one another.

The trust deficit that inhibits the flow of capital to social enterprises presents a serious problem, but not an intractable one. Recognizing that the law poses no threat to social enterprise, but instead offers private and public actors an array of tools to nurture its growth represents the first step toward creating a more robust social enterprise sector. Lawyers have long experience supplying investors and entrepreneurs with frameworks in which they can build mutually beneficial relationships.

Whatever forms the second generation of social enterprise law may take, the trust it nurtures will offer a solution to the assurance game that keeps investors and entrepreneurs on the sidelines. FLY paper may never play the prominent role that high-yield debt long has, and dual-mission SE(c)(3)s will certainly never supplant 501(c)(3) charities, but the second generation of social enterprise law nevertheless has the potential to revolutionize all corners of the field. Mom-and-pop ventures and public corporations that may share noting beyond a commitment to simultaneously doing well and doing good can find strength in its insights.

NOTES

Introduction

1. The venture formerly known as Google X (now simply X) describes its aims in these terms. Its ambitions are technological, rather than legal, but the effort to "to invent and launch 'moonshot' technologies that we hope could someday make the world a radically better place" mirror our attempts to fundamentally rethink how the law can serve social enterprise. *See* X, *About* https://x.company/about (last visited Dec. 5, 2016).

2. Although this book will focus primarily on the US context and experience, social enterprise is a global phenomenon. *See generally* SOCIAL ENTERPRISE: A GLOBAL COMPARISON (Janelle A. Kerlin, ed. 2009); Marieke Huysentruyt et al., "Market-Oriented and Mission-Focused: Social Enterprises Around the Globe" [Stanford Social Innovation Review Online, Oct. 19, 2016] *at* https://ssir.org/articles/entry/market_oriented_and_mission_focused_social_enterprises_around_the_globe (last visited Dec. 1, 2016); *see also* e.g., UK Advisory Panel to Government Mission-Led Business Review, *On a Mission in the UK Economy*, 9, *at* https://www.gov.uk/government/uploads/system/uploads/attachment_data/file/574694/Advisory_Panel_Report_-_Mission-led_Business.pdf (last visited Dec. 7, 2016) (discussing the increasing prevalence of "mission-led businesses" in the United Kingdom).

3. Goldman Sachs, *Selected Highlights from the Environmental, Social and Governance Report*, at 2, *at* http://www.goldmansachs.com/citizenship/esg-reporting/esg-content/esg-report-2015-highlights.pdf (last visited July 14, 2016).

4. *Etsy, Mission & Values, at* https://www.etsy.com/mission?ref=hp (last visited July 14, 2016).

5. *Id.*

6. TOMS, *Improving Lives, at* http://www.toms.com/improving-lives (last visited July 14, 2016).

7. Warby Parker, *History, at* https://www.warbyparker.com/history (last visited July 14, 2016).

8. Harvest Power, *Who We Are, at* http://www.harvestpower.com/company/ (last visited Dec. 7, 2016).

9. Nisolo, *Our Vision, at* https://nisolo.com/pages/about-page (last visited Dec. 7, 2016); *see also* Nisolo, *Ethically Made, at* https://nisolo.com/pages/ethically-made (last visited Dec. 7, 2016) (describing these and other benefits provided to employees).

10. Seeds Green Printing, *Facts, at* http://www.seedsgreenprinting.com/index.php?option=com_content&view=article&id=109&Itemid=126 (last visited Dec. 7, 2016).

11. This aspect of our work is in line with a substantial literature describing and documenting the value of lawyers as "transactional engineers." *See* Nestor M. Davidson, *Values and Value Creation in Public-Private Transactions*, 95 IOWA L. REV. 937, 940 and n. 1 (2009).

Chapter 1

1. For a discussion of embedding social mission across the value chain, see J. Gregory Dees and Beth Battle Anderson, *For-Profit Social Ventures*, at 3–5 *in* SOCIAL ENTREPRENEURSHIP (Marilyn L. Kourislsky & William B. Walstad, eds. 2003).

2. Chan Zuckerberg Initiative, *FAQs*, *at* http://chanzuckerberg.com/faq/ (last visited June 21, 2016).

3. *See* Deepa Seetharaman, *Zuckerberg Funds Startup*, WALL ST. J., June 16, 2016, at B3.

4. Andela, *Helping IBM Recruit Future Data Scientists*, *at* https://andela.com/client/ibm/ (last visited June 22, 2016).

5. Andela, *Series B Press Release*, June 16, 2016, *at* http://press.andela.com/d/zcY9f3OJeDAG/ andela-press-kit (last visited June 21, 2016).

6. *See* Katie Smith Milway, *How Social Entrepreneurs Can Have the Most Impact*, HARV. BUS. REV. ONLINE, May 2, 2014, *at* https://hbr.org/2014/05/how-social-entrepreneurs-can-have-the-most-impact/ (last visited June 23, 2016) (reporting that according to a "recent release of data from The Great Social Enterprise Census [a survey of over 500 social enterprises], only a fifth are larger than $2 million in budget, just 8% employ more than a 100 people, and 60% were founded in the past 8 years").

7. *See* Archi's Acres, *About*, *at* http://archisacres.com/page/about (last visited June 21, 2016).

8. *See* Katie Smith Milway and Christine Driscoll Goulay, *The Rise of Social Entrepreneurship in B-Schools in Three Charts*, HARV. BUS. REV. ONLINE, Feb. 23, 2013, *at* https://hbr.org/2013/ 02/the-rise-of-social-entrepreneu (last visited June 21, 2016).

9. *See, e.g.*, Advisory Panel to Government Mission-Led Business Review, *On a Mission in the UK Economy*, 11, *at* https://www.gov.uk/government/uploads/system/uploads/attachment_ data/file/574694/Advisory_Panel_Report_-_Mission-led_Business.pdf (last visited Dec. 7, 2016) (reporting research demonstrating millennials' particular devotion to mission-led business and impact investment). Tom Petruno, *Social Net Worth*, L.A. TIMES, Dec. 7, 2014, at B1 (reporting that millennials are "embracing 'socially responsible' investing").

10. Many commentators describe raising capital as a key challenge for social enterprises. *See, e.g.*, Julie Battilana, Matthew Lee, John Walker, & Cheryl Dorsey, *In Search of the Hybrid Ideal*, STAN. SOC. INNOV. REV. (Summer 2012) at 51, 53; John Tyler, Even Absher, Kathleen Garman, & Anthony Luppino, *Producing Better Mileage: Advancing the Design and Usefulness of Hybrid Vehicles for Social Business Ventures*, 33 QUINNIPIAC L. REV. 235, 285–86 (2015). Social entrepreneurs themselves agree. *See* CATHERINE H. CLARK ET AL., ACCELERATING IMPACT ENTERPRISES: HOW TO LOCK, STOCK AND ANCHOR IMPACT ENTERPRISES FOR MAXIMUM IMPACT 6 (2013) (finding based on a survey of entrepreneurs that "IEs [impact enterprises] need capital that matches their growth trajectory"); ALLIANZ, DUPONT, SKOLL FOUNDATION, & SUSTAINABILITY, GROWING OPPORTUNITY: ENTREPRENEURIAL SOLUTIONS TO INSOLUBLE PROBLEMS 15 (2007) ("Overwhelmingly, social entrepreneurs cited access to capital as one of their two primary challenges (72%)"); Kate Goodall & Ryan Ross, *Building "Silicon Valleys of Impact"*, STAN. SOC. INNOVATION REVIEW, June 29, 2016, *at* http://ssir. org/articles/entry/building_silicon_valleys_of_impact (last visited July 13, 2016) (reporting that funding was the first of "four pillars" of support social entrepreneurs stated they need to succeed).

11. *See* DOUGLAS G. BAIRD ET AL., GAME THEORY AND THE LAW 35–36 (1998); Richard H. McAdams, *Beyond the Prisoners' Dilemma: Coordination, Game Theory, and Law* 82 S. CAL. L. REV. 209, 220–22 (2009).

12. *See* McAdams, *supra* note 11, at 221.

13. Consultative Group to Assist the Poor and Center for Financial Inclusion, THE ART OF THE RESPONSIBLE EXIT IN MICROFINANCE EQUITY SALES 4 (2014) [hereinafter RESPONSIBLE EXIT] ("No other aspect of an equity sale looms quite as large as the selection of the buyer").

14. This is precisely the reason why many technology company founders have recently pursued dual-class stock structures, which maintain founder control even while selling a large proportion of a company's common stock to the public. *See* Steven Davidoff, *Thorny Side Effects in Silicon Valley Tactic to Keep Control*, N.Y. TIMES, Sept. 4, 2013, at B8.

15. *See* Responsible Exit, *supra* note 13, at 4.

16. *See* Arthur Fleischer, Jr., Alexander R. Sussman, & Gail Weinstein, Takeover Defense: Mergers and Acquisitions § 5.01 (2016).

17. *See* Cox & Hazen, Business Organizations Law §§ 23.6–7 (3rd ed. 2011) (discussing defensive tactic jurisprudence in general, and the treatment of poison pills in particular, with an emphasis on positions of the influential Delaware courts).

18. *See* Air Products & Chemicals, Inc. v. Airgas, Inc., 16 A.3d 48, 121–29 (2011) (noting a staggered board combined with a poison pill was permissible takeover defense as the acquirer could run proxy contest to seek control of the board).

19. Ford Foundation, *From Dollars to Change, at* http://www.fordfoundation.org/about-us/ (last visited April 4, 2017).

20. *See* Dana Brakman Reiser, *Nonprofit Takeovers: Regulating the Market for Mission Control*, 2006 BYU L. Rev. 1181 (2006).

21. *See* Marion Fremont-Smith, Governing Nonprofit Organizations 54, 448 (2004).

22. *See* Thomas Lee Hazen & Lisa Love Hazen, *Duties of Nonprofit Corporate Directors-Emphasizing Oversight Responsibilities*, 90 N.C. L. Rev. 1845, 1879 n. 163 (2012) (cataloging the many scholarly articles referencing this troubling lack of resources).

23. *See* Fremont-Smith, *supra* note 21, at 445–48 (describing trends in AG charity enforcement); Linda Sugin, *Strengthening Charity Law: Replacing Media Oversight with Advance Rulings for Nonprofit Fiduciaries*, 89 Tul. L. Rev. 869, 876–80 (2015) (describing the emphasis on financial accountability in charity enforcement); Dana Brakman Reiser, *Enron. org: Why Sarbanes-Oxley Will Not Ensure Comprehensive Nonprofit Accountability*, 38 U.C. Davis L. Rev. 205, 219–43 (2004) (describing the incentives for AG charity enforcement).

24. *See* Henry B. Hansmann, *The Role of Nonprofit Enterprise*, 89 Yale L.J. 835, 838 (1980) (describing this limitation and designating it the "nondistribution constraint").

25. 382 P.2d 109 (Okla. 1962).

26. *See* Baird et al., *supra* note 11, at 50–57.

Chapter 2

1. American Marketing Association, Dictionary, *at* https://www.ama.org/resources/pages/dictionary.aspx?dLetter=B (last visited July 19, 2016).

2. Jean-Noel Kapferer, The New Strategic Brand Management 9 (5th ed. 2012).

3. K.L. Keller, Strategic Brand Management 51–53 (1998).

4. *See* Matthew 6:24 ("No one can serve two masters, for either he will hate the one and love the other, or he will be devoted to the one and despise the other. You cannot serve God and money.").

5. Other scholars have reached similar conclusions in favor of a social good prioritization standard. *See, e.g.*, John Tyler, Even Absher, Kathleen Garman, & Anthony Luppino, *Producing Better Mileage: Advancing the Design and Usefulness of Hybrid Vehicles for Social Business Ventures*, 33 Quinnipiac L. Rev. 235, 289–96 (2015) (arguing for "a crystalized concept of a hybrid form entity with a social purpose mandate as its dominant purpose" and designing a form to incorporate one); J. Haskell Murray, *Choose Your Own Master: Social Enterprise, Certifications, and Benefit* Corporations, 2 Am. U. Bus. L. Rev. 1, 27–33 (2012) (asserting that a prioritization requirement would facilitate fiduciary accountability); J. Haskell Murray & Edward I. Hwang, *Purpose with Profit: Governance, Enforcement, Capital-Raising and Capital-Locking in Low-Profit Limited Liability Companies*, 66 U. Miami L. Rev. 1, 39–40 (2011) (arguing that the primacy of charitable mission is necessary to develop a social enterprise enforcement scheme).

6. For an overview of these debates, see Kevin V. Tu, *Socially Conscious Corporations and Shareholder Profit*, 84 George Wash. L. Rev. 121, 127–41 (2016). The influential views of Delaware Chancellor Leo Strine Jr. are summarized in his article *Our Continuing Struggle with the Idea that For-Profit Corporations Seek Profit*, 47 Wake Forest L. Rev. 135 (2012).

7. 170 N.W. 668 (Mich. 1919).

8. *Id.* at 684.

9. *See, e.g.,* Lynn Stout, The Shareholder Value Myth 26 (2012); *see also* Andrew A. Schwartz, *The Perpetual Corporation*, 80 Geo. Wash. L. Rev. 764, 779–80 (2012) (arguing *Dodge* v. *Ford* supports the view that the purpose of the corporation is to promote long-term value).

10. *eBay Domestic Holdings, Inc.* v. Newmark, 16 A.3d 1 (2010).

11. *See* State of Delaware, Department of State, Division of Corporations, *About Agency, at* http://corp.delaware.gov/aboutagency.shtml (last visited June 23, 2016).

12. *See* Cox & Hazen, Business Organizations Law § 2.8 (3rd ed. 2011) ("With very limited exceptions, internal affairs are governed by the law of the state of incorporation").

13. *eBay*, 16 A.3d at 34.

14. *Id.*

15. *Id.*

16. 134 S. Ct. 2751 (2014).

17. *Id.* at 2771.

18. *See* Larry E. Ribstein, Robert R. Keatinge, Ribstein & Keatinge on Limited Liability Companies § 4.10 (2016 Update).

19. *See* Henry Hansmann, *Reforming Nonprofit Corporation* Law, 129 U. Pa. L. Rev. 497, 510 (1981).

20. *See* Marion Fremont-Smith, Governing Nonprofit Organizations 126–27 (2004); Hansmann, *supra* note 19 at 509–10.

21. *See* Dana Brakman Reiser, *Charity Law's Essentials*, 86 Notre Dame L. Rev. 1, 18–30 (2011).

22. *See* Henry B. Hansmann, *The Role of Nonprofit Enterprise*, 89 Yale L.J. 835, 838 (1980) ("A nonprofit organization is, in essence, an organization that is barred from distributing its net earnings, if any, to individuals who exercise control over it, such as members, officers, directors, or trustees."); *see also*, e.g., Rob Atkinson, *Unsettled Standing: Who (Else) Should Enforce the Duties of Charitable Fiduciaries?*, 23 J. Corp. L. 655, 665 (1998) (referring to the nondistribution constraint as the "defining feature" of nonprofits); Daniel Halperin, *Income Taxation of Mutual Nonprofits*, 59 Tax L. Rev. 133, 136 (2006) (noting the nondistribution constraint as the distinguishing feature of nonprofit, versus for-profit, entities); Geoffrey A. Manne, *Agency Costs and the Oversight of Charitable Organizations*, 1999 Wis. L. Rev. 227, 230 (describing the nondistribution constraint as the "[t]he defining characteristic of a charitable nonprofit").

23. *See* Cox & Hazen, Business Organizations Law § 10.1 (3rd ed. 2011) (explaining the rule and courts' general reticence to impose liability on corporate directors due to "imprudence or honest errors of judgment").

24. *See id.* §§ 10.9–15 (3rd ed. 2011) (canvassing the law on corporate director conflicts of interest and other duty of loyalty violations).

25. Occasional nonprofit law cases reference a duty of obedience for fiduciaries, which might be seen as a possible model for review of prioritization obligations. *See* Linda Sugin, *Resisting the Corporatization of Nonprofit Governance: Transforming Obedience into Fidelity*, 76 Fordham L. Rev. 893, 897–905 (2007) (describing this doctrine and its limitations). While the MPH prioritization mandate draws lightly on this experience with the duty of obedience, it is not a direct analog. The area itself is quite underdeveloped. Further, the idea of obedience is too easily conflated with slavish fidelity to the original mission of a charity, even when the utility of this function has been dramatically reduced.

26. Other commentators have also noted the importance of enforcement. *See, e.g.,* Tyler et al., *supra* note 5, at 291–320 (suggesting a range of enforcement tactics to hold their proposed "Social Primacy Company" accountable, including "noisy withdrawal" and dissenters' rights); Murray, *supra* note 5, at 33–44 (describing various means by which accountability for social mission prioritization might be secured); *see also* Colin Mayer, Firm Commitment 195–236 (arguing traditional corporations can be made more socially responsible through use of a supervening board of trustees to steward prosocial values, modeled on European industrial foundations).

27. *See, e.g.,* Revised Uniform Partnership Act § 101(6) (defining "partnership"); Uniform Partnership Act § 6(1) (same).

28. Interestingly, one motivating factor driving the creation of the existing hybrid corporate forms detailed in chapter 3 may have been to combat the perceived reluctance on the part of those officials to accept articles of incorporation that explicitly combine mission and profit. Although the significance of allaying such concerns should not be underestimated, defusing such bureaucratic booby traps represents only the start of a long process of creating a state law regime safe for dual-mission enterprises.

29. *See* State of Delaware, Department of State, Division of Corporations, *Expedited Services*, *at* https://corp.delaware.gov/expserv.shtml (last visited Dec. 12, 2016).

30. *See* Fremont-Smith, *supra* note 20, at 315–17 (describing state AGs' registration and reporting requirements).

31. I.R.C. § 6033(a).

32. For a brief introduction to periodic reporting requirements under the federal securities law, designed for the lay reader, see US Securities and Exchange Commission, *Fast Answers, Form 10-K*, *at* https://www.sec.gov/answers/form10k.htm (last visited Dec. 12, 2016).

33. *See* Jonathan Scott Goldman, *Just What the Doctor Ordered? The Doctrine of Deviation, the Case of Doctor Barnes's Trust and the Future Location of the Barnes Foundation*, 39 Real Prop. Prob. & Tr. J. 711 (2005).

34. The Sweet Briar story has a happy conclusion. A year after an AG-brokered settlement, it experienced a significant increase in applications and appears poised to remain in business for the near term. *See* Colin Diersing, *Sweet Briar College Gets Record Number of Applicants*, USA Today College, Feb. 1, 2016, http://college.usatoday.com/2016/02/01/sweet-briar-record-number-applicants/ (last visited July 19, 2016).

35. *See* IRC § 4958.

36. *See* One World Play Project, *at* http://www.oneworldplayproject.com/ (last visited July 19, 2016).

37. It is possible to imagine an increase in sales so large that the shift from 1-to-1 to 1-to-100 could be accomplished while still sending a constant number of free balls to distressed communities. There must be, however, some ratio at which the balance will shift and social good will diminish appreciably. For the sake of this example, we assume the 1-to-100 ratio does so.

38. Tyler et al. also suggest personal liability for social enterprise fiduciaries that fail to prioritize social mission, and would empower courts to order such awards paid to the organization, noncomplicit owners, a government agency or a charity. *See* Tyler et al., *supra* note 5, at 290 and Appendix A.

39. *Cf.* Manne, *supra* note 22, at 252–64 (proposing the creation of a similar set of contract plaintiffs, in this case for-profit monitoring companies empowered to challenge lapses by charitable fiduciaries); Dana Brakman Reiser, *Enron.org: Why Sarbanes-Oxley Will Not Ensure Comprehensive Nonprofit Accountability*, 38 U.C. Davis L. Rev. 205 269–72 (2004) (proposing a variation on Manne's concept empowering foundations and other nonprofit stakeholders to play a similar role).

Chapter 3

1. *See Social Enterprise Law Tracker*, *at* http://socentlawtracker.org/#/bcorps (last visited July 11, 2016). The model has also spread overseas. Italy adopted its own version of the benefit corporation in late 2015. *See* Law 28 December 2015 (Stability Law), n. 208, article 1, par. 376–84.

2. Benefit corporation statutes in many states closely track the structure and language of the Model Benefit Corporation Legislation. *See* Model Benefit Corporation Legislation, *at* http://benefitcorp.net/sites/default/files/documents/Model_Benefit_Corp_Legislation.pdf (last visited July 11, 2016). Rather than exhaustively reviewing the content of statutory provisions in dozens of states, we will use this model legislation as our authoritative source. For those seeking state-specific details, a continuously updated compendium of links to individual states' benefit corporation statutes can be found at Benefit Corporation, *State by State Status of Legislation*, *at* http://benefitcorp.net/policymakers/state-by-state-status (last visited Dec. 12, 2016).

3. Some statutes restrict formation to corporations with "the purpose of engaging in any lawful *business*." *See, e.g.*, Model Bus. Corp. L. § 3.01 (emphasis added). Others are even more expansive, permitting incorporation "to conduct or promote any lawful business *or purposes*." *See, e.g.*, Del. Gen. Corp. L. § 101(b) (allowing broad purposes in a statute governing both for-profit and nonprofit corporations) (emphasis added).

4. Model Benefit Corporation Legislation § 201(a).

5. *Id.* § 201(b).

6. *Id.* § 102 (emphasis added).

7. *See id.* § 102.

8. The model statute defines a standard as

   Comprehensive because it assesses the effects of the business and its operations upon the interests of . . . (ii) the employees and work force of the benefit corporation, its subsidiaries, and its suppliers; (iii) the interests of customers as beneficiaries of the general public benefit or specific public benefit purposes of the benefit corporation; (iv) community and societal factors, including those of each community in which offices or facilities of the benefit corporation, its subsidiaries, or its suppliers are located; (v) the local and global environment. *Id.* §§ 102, 301(a)(1)(ii)–(v).

9. *Id.* § 201(c).

10. *Id.* § 301(a)(1).

11. *Id.* § 301(a)(2).

12. *See id.* § 301(a)(3).

13. *See* Thomas A. Hemphill & Francine Cullari, *The Benefit Corporation and the For-Profit Social Entrepreneur*, 119 Bus. & Soc'y Rev. 519, 524–26 (2014) (pointing to 41); John Tyler, *Negating the Legal Problem of Having "Two Masters": A Framework for L3C Fiduciary Duties and Accountability*, 35 Vt. L. Rev. 117, 132–33 (2010) (citing 31); *see also* Lisa M. Fairfax, *Doing Well While Doing Good: Reassessing the Scope of Directors' Fiduciary Obligations in For-Profit Corporations with Non-Shareholder Beneficiaries*, 59 Wash. & Lee L. Rev. 409, 460 (2002) (counting 32).

14. Unocal v. Mesa Petroleum, 493 A.2d 946 (1985).

15. *See Unocal*, 493 A.2d at 955.

16. *Unocal*, 493 A.2d at 955.

17. Revlon Inc. v. MacAndrews & Forbes Holdings, Inc., 506 A.2d 173 (1986).

18. *See* Fairfax, *supra* note 13, at 459–60.

19. *See* Model Benefit Corporation Legislation § 301(c). For extended discussion of how courts might apply fiduciary duty law in the benefit corporation context, see Brett McDonnell, *Committing to Do Good and Doing Well: Fiduciary Duty in Benefit Corporations*, 20 Fordham J. Corp. & Fin. L. 19, 37–70 (2014).

20. Model Benefit Corporation Legislation § 305.

21. *See id.* §§ 301(c), 303(c), 305(b).

22. *See id.* § 102.

23. *Id.* § 401.

24. *See id.* § 402.

25. *See, e.g., id.* § 402(d).

26. Minnesota's statute contemplates revocation of benefit corporation status for failure to file required reports. *See* Minn. Stat. § 304A.301 (2015). A recent bill creating the benefit corporation form in Alaska included a similar provision. *See* H.B. 49, 29th Legis., First Sess. § 1(8) (Alaska 2015) (stating that the Commissioner of Commerce may dissolve a benefit corporation that "is delinquent six months or more in including its benefit report in its biennial report" or in paying the associated fee therefor).

27. Model Benefit Corporation Legislation § 401(a)(4).

28. *Id.* § 302.

29. *Id.* § 304.

30. Laureate's IPO is discussed further in chapter 5.

31. Model Benefit Corporation Legislation § 302(e).

32. B Lab, *About B Lab*, *at* http://www.bcorporation.net/what-are-b-corps/about-b-lab (last visited July 20, 2016); *see also* Brett McConnell, *Benefit Corporations and Strategic Action Fields (or the Existential Failing of Delaware)*, 39 SEATTLE U.L. REV. 263, 281–83 (2016) (describing the role of B Lab in creating and advocating for benefit corporation legislation).

33. *See* B Lab, *About B Lab*, *at* http://www.bcorporation.net/what-are-b-corps/about-b-lab (describing these three interrelated initiatives to "drive systemic change," as well as a recent fourth addition, "Inspiring millions to join the movement through story-telling by B the Change Media") (last visited June 24, 2016).

34. For a helpful comparison of the B Corp and benefit corporation concepts, see the chart provided by B Lab *at* https://www.bcorporation.net/what-are-b-corps/certified-b-corps-and-benefit-corporations.

35. *See* B Lab, *About B Lab*, *at* http://www.bcorporation.net/what-are-b-corps/about-b-lab (last visited June 24, 2016); B Lab, Benefit Corporations, http://benefitcorp.net/ (last visited June 24, 2016).

36. *See* B Lab, *Our History*, *at* http://www.bcorporation.net/what-are-b-corps/the-non-profit-behind-b-corps/our-history (last visited June 24, 2016).

37. *See* B Lab, *Benefit Corporations & Certified B Corps*, *at* http://benefitcorp.net/businesses/benefit-corporations-and-certified-b-corps (last visited June 24, 2016).

38. *See* B Lab, *Term Sheet for Certified B Corporations for Corporations in States That Do Not Have Constituency Statutes Where Benefit Corporation Is Available*, *at* http://www.bcorporation.net/sites/default/files/documents/term_sheets/2015/BCorpTermSheet-NonConstituencyBenefitStates-2015.pdf (last visited June 24, 2016); B Lab, *Term Sheet for Certified B Corporations For Corporations in States That Do Not Have Constituency Statutes Nor Benefit Corporation Legislation*, *at* http://www.bcorporation.net/sites/default/files/documents/term_sheets/2015/BCorpTermSheet-NonConstituencyNonBenefitStates-2015.pdf (last visited June 24, 2016).

39. *See* B Lab, *B Analytics*, *at* http://b-analytics.net/ (last visited July 20, 2016).

40. *See* B Lab, *Creating Benefit Reports Using the B Impact Assessment*, *at* http://benefitcorp.net/creating-benefit-reports-using-b-impact-assessment (last visited June 24, 2016).

41. 11 V.S.A. § 3001 (27)(A).

42. *See* Social Enterprise Law Tracker, *at* http://socentlawtracker.org/#/l3cs (last visited June 24, 2016).

43. *See* Sandra K. Miller, *The Best of Both Worlds: Default Fiduciary Duties and Contractual Freedom in Alternative Business Entities*, 39 J. CORP. L. 295 (2014).

44. *See, e.g.*, 11 V.S.A. § 3001 (27)(A). As most state L3C adoptions are similar to the inaugural Vermont effort and no model legislation exists, the Vermont statute provides a workable reference for L3C terms generally.

45. 11 V.S.A. § 3001 (27)(B).

46. *See, e.g.*, 11 V.S.A. § 3001 (27)(C).

47. *See, e.g.* 11 V.S.A. § 3001 (27)(D).

48. Americans for Community Development, *What Is the L3C?* (2013), *at* https://www.americansforcommunitydevelopment.org/downloads/What%20is%20the%20L3C%20(0312513-1).pdf (last visited June 24, 2016).

49. *See id.; see also* Robert Lang & Elizabeth Carrott Minnigh, *The L3C, History, Basic Construct, and Legal Framework*, 35 VT. L. REV. 15 (2010); Cassady V. Brewer & Michael J. Rhima, *Using the "L3C" for Program-Related Investment*, 21 TAX'N EXEMPTS 11 (2009).

50. I.R.C. § 4942.

51. *See* Tyler, *supra* note 13, at 119–23; Brewer & Rhima, *supra* note 49 at 12–13.

52. I.R.C. § 4944.

53. *See* J. Haskell Murray & Edward I. Hwang, *Purpose with Profit: Governance, Enforcement, Capital-Raising and Capital-Locking in Low-Profit Limited Liability Companies*, 66 U. MIAMI L. REV. 1, 25 (2011); Tyler, *supra* note 13, at 122. Some advisers caution against making a PRI without first obtaining a legal opinion or a private letter ruling from the Internal Revenue Service. Both processes can create cost and delay. *See, e.g.*, Carter G. Bishop, *The Low-Profit LLC (L3C): Program Related Investment by Proxy or Perversion?*, 63 ARK. L. REV. 243, 266 (2010).

54. *See* The Forum for Sustainable and Responsible Investment, *Report on US Sustainable, Responsible and Impact Investing Trends 2014*, Executive Summary, at 12, *available at* http://www.ussif.org/Files/Publications/SIF_Trends_14.F.ES.pdf (last visited June 24, 2016).

55. *See* Americans for Community Development, *Model L3C Operating Agreement*, *at* https://www.americansforcommunitydevelopment.org/downloads/ModelL3CArt.ofOrg.&Oper.Agree.-VermontCompliant.pdf (last visited June 24, 2016).

56. *See* Americans for Community Development, *Legal, Operating Agreements*, *at* http://americansforcommunitydevelopment.org/legal/ (last visited June 24, 2016).

57. *See* Americans for Community Development, Legislation, *at* http://americansforcommunity development.org/laws/ (last visited June 24, 2016) (providing links to legislation).

58. *See* Philanthropic Facilitation Act, H.R. 2832, 113th Cong. (2013); Philanthropic Facilitation Act, H.R. 3420, 112th Cong. (2011).

59. *See* Md. Code Ann., Corps. & Ass'ns §§ 11-4A-1201 to 11-4A-1208, 11-1-502, 5-6C-03 (2013); Ore. Rev. Stat. §§ 60.750 to .770 (2014).

60. *See* John Tyler, Even Absher, Kathleen Garman, & Anthony Luppino, *Producing Better Mileage: Advancing the Design and Usefulness of Hybrid Vehicles for Social Business Ventures*, 33 Quinnipiac L. Rev. 235, 289–96 (2015).

61. *See* S.B. 201, 2011–12 Legis. Sess. (Cal. 2011) (approved by Governor Jerry Brown on Oct. 9, 2011).

62. California's statute was drafted by a committee of attorneys. *See* Dana Brakman Reiser, *The Next Big Thing: Flexible Purpose Corporations*, 2 Am. U. Bus. L. Rev. 55, 62 (2012).

63. Cal. Corp. Code § 2602.

64. *Id.* § 2700; Wash. Rev. Code § 23B.25.040.

65. Cal. Corp. Code § 3500; Wash. Rev. Code § 23B.25.050.

66. Wash. Rev. Code § 23B.25.040.

67. *See* Cal. Corp. Code §§ 3500, 3501 (requiring extensive retrospective and forward-looking disclosure and timely reports of changes between annual reports); Wash. Rev. Code § 23B.25.150 (imposing slightly less onerous standards and authorizing courts to enforce noncompliant SPCs' responsibility to issue reports).

68. Cal. Corp. Code §§ 1152(d)(1), 3002, 3301; Wash. Rev. Code § 23B.25.140.

69. Cal. Corp. Code §§ 1300, 3305; Wash. Rev. Code § 23B.25.120; *see also* J. Haskell Murray, *The Social Enterprise Law Market*, 75 Md. L. Rev. 541, 558 (2016) (noting this distinction).

70. Florida adopted "social purpose corporation" legislation in 2014, but its version differs substantially from California's and Washington's and is more properly viewed as a mix of SPC and benefit corporation forms.

71. *See* Press Release, Governor Markell Signs Public Benefit Corporation Legislation, *at* http://news.delaware.gov/2013/07/17/governor-markell-signs-public-benefit-corporation-legislation/ (last visited June 24, 2016); see also Frederick H. Alexander, The Public Benefit Corporation Guidebook (2016) (providing extensive discussion and analysis of the PBC form); Alicia E. Plerhoples, *Delaware Public Benefit Corporations 90 Days Out: Who's Opting In?*, 14 U.C. Davis L. Rev. 247 (2014) (detailing the legislation's history and provisions, as well as tracking early adoptions of the form).

72. Del. Code Ann. tit. 8 § 362(a).

73. *Id.* § 365.

74. *See id.* § 363.

75. *See id.* § 366. Standard appraisal rights would apply in certain corporate transactions. *See* Frederick H. Alexander, Lawrence A. Hamermesh, Frank R. Martin, & Norman M. Monhait, *M&A Under Delaware's Public Benefit Corporation Statute: A Hypothetical Tour*, 4 Harv. Bus. L. Rev. 255, 257–66 (2014) (describing the challenge of applying existing appraisal law in the PBC context).

76. B Lab features the adoption of Delaware's statute, referring to it as a "benefit corporation" statute, as a milestone in its history. *See* B Lab, *Our History*, *at* http://www.bcorporation.net/what-are-b-corps/the-non-profit-behind-b-corps/our-history (last visited June 24, 2016). It also touted the enactment as a victory for the benefit corporation concept in an open letter to business leaders and a feature on its blog. *See* B Lab, *Open Letter to Business*

Leaders, (July 30, 2013), *at* https://www.bcorporation.net/open-letter-to-business-leaders (last visited July 11, 2016); B Lab, *Today Marks a Tipping Point in the Evolution of Capitalism* (July 17, 2013, blog entry), *at* http://www.bcorporation.net/blog/today-marks-a-tipping-point-in-the-evolution-of-capitalism (last visited June 24, 2016).

77. *See* Murray (Maryland), *supra* note 69, at Appendix A; *see also* Kate Cooney, Justin Koushyar, Matthew Lee, & Haskell Murray, *Benefit Corporation and L3C Adoption: A Survey*, Stanford Social Innovation Review Online, Dec. 5, 2014, *at* http://ssir.org/articles/entry/benefit_corporation_and_l3c_adoption_a_survey (last visited June 24, 2016) (finding about 2,000 such organizations); B Lab references "more than 3000 existing benefit corporations across the country" in answering one of the frequently asked questions on its benefit corporation website. *See* B Lab, Frequently Asked Questions, *Will it Be More Difficult for Benefit Corporations to Get D&O Insurance?*, *at* http://benefitcorp.net/faq (last visited June 24, 2016).

78. Del. Code Ann. tit. 8 § 362(a).

79. Wash. Rev. Code § 23B.25.020.

80. *Id.* § 23B.25.040.

81. *See* Model Benefit Corporation Act § 201(a); Cal. Corp. Code § 2602(b).

82. *See, e.g.*, Cal. Corp. Code § 14610(a); Md. Code Ann., Corps. & Ass'ns § 5-6C-06(a)(2); N.J. Stat. Ann. § 14A:18-5(a).

83. Model Benefit Corporation Act § 301(a)(3).

84. Cal. Corp. Code § 2700(c); Wash. Rev. Code § 23B.25.050.

85. Del. Code Ann. tit. 8. § 365(a).

86. N.Y. Bus. Corp. Law § 1706(a).

87. N.Y. Bus. Corp. Law § 1707(a)(3).

88. Minn. Stat. § 304A.201(2)(3); *see also* McDonnell (Fordham), *supra* note 19, at 42–43 (discussing Minnesota's provisions and their potential to create personal liability for director failures to pursue social mission).

89. Connecticut's benefit corporation statute allows adopting entities to adopt a "legacy preservation provision." *See* Conn. Gen. Stat. § 33-1355 (2014). Those entities taking this option may "distribute [their] remaining property only to one or more (1) charitable organizations, or (2) other benefit corporations that have enacted a legacy preservation provision." *See id.* Connecticut benefit corporations that choose legacy protection have even greater asset protection than our MPH proposal advocates, essentially mirroring the charitable nondistribution constraint. But, as an opt-in feature, it cannot help the legal form function as a clear brand.

90. *See* Tyler et al., *supra* note 60, at 266–69; Tyler, *supra* note 13, at 141; Murray & Hwang, *supra* note 53, at 27–28.

91. *See* Alan R. Palmiter, *Duty of Obedience: The Forgotten Duty*, 55 N.Y.L. Sch. L. Rev. 457, 466–69 (2010–11).

92. *See* Katie Cunningham & Marc Ricks, *Why Measure?*, Stan. Soc. Innovation Rev. (Summer 2004) 44, 51 (finding "at best, a lack of enthusiasm for performance measurement" in a qualitative study of large individual donors); Hope Consulting, *Money for Good II* (2011), *at* http://static1.squarespace.com/static/55723b6be4b05ed81f077108/t/55d24c66e4b05537993238fc/1439845478132/%24FG+II_2011_Full+Report.pdf (last visited June 24, 2016) (finding that only 33 percent of individual donors described themselves as doing research on charities prior to donating funds). Prior and subsequent studies by the same firm reported similar findings. *See* Hope Consulting, *Money for Good* (2010), *at* http://static1.squarespace.com/static/55723b6be4b05ed81f077108/t/566efb6cc647ad2b441e2c55/1450113900596/Money+for+Good+I.pdf (last visited June 24, 2016); *Money for Good III* (2015), *at* http://static1.squarespace.com/static/55723b6be4b05ed81f077108/t/56957ee6df40f330ae018b81/1452637938035/$FG+2015_Final+Report_01122016.pdf (last visited June 24, 2016).

93. *See* Brian Trelstad, *The Elusive Quest for Impact: The Evolving Practice of Social-Impact Measurement*, 583–603, *in* Frontiers of Philanthropy (Lester M. Salamon, ed. 2014), at 598 (raising just this concern, citing the same donor research as well as experience of interviewees).

94. *Compare* CAL. CORP. CODE § 3502(h) (2011) (including exemption) *with* CAL. CORP. CODE § 3502 (as amended in 2014 with the exemption removed).
95. *See* J. Haskell Murray, *An Early Report on Benefit Reports*, 118 W. VA. L. REV. 25, 35 (2015).
96. *See* CIC Regulator, *Community Interest Companies Annual Report 2014/15*, at 38, *available at* https://www.gov.uk/government/uploads/system/uploads/attachment_data/file/445334/cic-15-15-annual-report-14-15.pdf (last visited July 20, 2016).
97. Office of the Regulator of Community Interest Companies, *Information and Guidance Notes* [hereinafter CIC Regulator Guidance], Ch. 4 (May 2016) at 17, *available at* https://www.gov.uk/government/uploads/system/uploads/attachment_data/file/524152/13-781-community-interest-companies-chapter-4-creating-a-cic.pdf (last visited July 12, 2016).
98. *See id.* Ch. 1, at 3, *available at* https://www.gov.uk/government/uploads/system/uploads/attachment_data/file/524148/cic-12-1333-community-interest-companies-guidance-chapter-1-introduction.pdf (last visited July 12, 2016).
99. UK Companies Act 2006, § 174.
100. *See* CIC Regulator Guidance 2013, Ch. 9 (March 2013) at 4, *available at* https://www.gov.uk/government/uploads/system/uploads/attachment_data/file/211749/13-712-community-interest-companies-guidance-chapter-9-corporate-governance.pdf (last visited July 12, 2016).
101. *See* CIC Regulator Guidance, Ch. 8 (May 2016) at 3–4, *available at* https://www.gov.uk/government/uploads/system/uploads/attachment_data/file/524156/13-711-community-interest-companies-guidance-chapters-8-statutory-obligationstions.pdf (last visited July 12, 2016).
102. *See id.*, Ch. 11, at 4, *available at* https://www.gov.uk/government/uploads/system/uploads/attachment_data/file/524158/13-714-community-interest-companies-guidance-chapter-11-the-regulator.pdf (last visited July 12, 2016).
103. *See id.*, Ch. 6, *available at* https://www.gov.uk/government/uploads/system/uploads/attachment_data/file/524154/14-1089-community-interest-companies-chapter-6-the-asset-lock.pdf (last visited July 12, 2016) (describing the asset lock in detail).
104. UK Companies Act 2004 § 30.
105. *See* CIC Regulator Guidance 2014, Ch. 7 (May 2016) at 4–5, *available at* https://www.gov.uk/government/uploads/system/uploads/attachment_data/file/524155/14-1090-community-interest-companies-chapter-7-financing-cics.pdf (last visited July 12, 2016).
106. *See* CIC Regulator Annual Report, *supra* note 96, at 35.
107. *See id.* at 38.
108. For an exploration of the expressive and norm-shifting value of social enterprise legislation, see Joseph W. Yockey, *Does Social Enterprise Law Matter?*, 66 ALA. L. REV. 767 (2015).

Chapter 4

1. The investor-focused mechanism described here represents only one form a privately crafted mission-protection device could take. Others might empower employees or customers to protect a venture's mission. See Dana Brakman Reiser and Steven A. Dean, *The Social Enterprise Lifecycle, in* CAMBRIDGE HANDBOOK OF SOCIAL ENTERPRISE LAW (Joseph Yockey & Benjamin Means eds., forthcoming) (describing this class of private law mission protections as mission-protecting poison pills (MP3s)).
2. Warren E. Buffett, Letter to Shareholders, at 15, *available at* http://www.berkshirehathaway.com/letters/2002pdf.pdf (last visited July 12, 2016).
3. *See* David P. Hariton, *The Taxation of Complex Financial Instruments*, 43 TAX L. REV. 731, 732 (1988) (noting that "debt-equity hybrids" were "being issued with increasing frequency by Fortune 500 companies and quasi governmental entities" by the late 1980s).
4. Stephen Labaton, *The Men Behind the Biggest Stories on Wall Street and in Washington: Michael R. Milken, Drexel Burnham Lambert; "Junk Bond" King Waits Uneasily as Prosecutors Prepare Their Case*, N.Y. TIMES, JAN. 3, 1989, at D4.
5. *See, e.g.*, Douglas MacMillan, *Uber Raises $1.15 Billion From First Leveraged Loan*, WALL ST. J., July 8, 2016, at B2.

6. *See* Al Yoon & Katy Burne, *Investors Clamor for Risky Debt Offerings—Buyers Grab Securities with Weak Ratings, Tired of Lower Yields on Safer Deals*, WALL ST. J., Apr. 3, 2014, at C1.

7. *See, e.g.*, John F. Coyle & Joseph M. Green, *Contractual Innovation in Venture Capital*, 66 HASTINGS L.J. 133 (2014) (describing the increasing use of convertible debt in early-stage venture funding in the last decade); Douglas MacMillan et al., *Spotify Raises Cash—at a Price*, WALL ST. J., Mar. 30, 2016, at B1 (noting that "[t]ech startups are increasingly turning to convertible debt—bonds that can be exchanged for stock").

8. *See* I.R.C § 1273(c)(2) (describing the tax treatment of investment units).

9. Michael S. Farber, *Equity, Debt, Not—the Tax Treatment of Non-Debt Open Transactions*, 60 TAX LAW. 635, 649 (2007) (observing that the special status of convertible debt stands "on grounds that historically have never been entirely clear but that do clearly represent a view that convertible debt is not 'like' other debt").

10. *See* John D. McKinnon & Greg Hitt, *Double Play: How Treasury Lost in Battle to Quash a Dubious Security—Instrument Issued by Enron and Others Can Be Used as Both Debt and Equity—Win for Flotilla of Lobbyists*, WALL ST. J., Feb. 4, 2002, at A1. Enron was one of many companies that issued these instruments with the help of banks such as Goldman Sachs and Merrill Lynch.

11. Vipal Monga, *"Green" Bonds Raise Worries—Firms Find Growing Market for Them, but Lack of Standards Is Stirring Concern*, WALL ST. J., June 3, 2014, at B4 (noting that when issuers sell green bonds, but do not memorialize environmental commitments in the instrument's terms "investors have no recourse if firms spend the money on something else, because there are no covenants to enforce green promises").

12. *See* J.P. MORGAN, IMPACT INVESTMENTS: AN EMERGING ASSET CLASS 11 (2010), *at* https://www.jpmorganchase.com/corporate/socialfinance/document/impact_investments_nov2010.pdf (last visited July 12, 2016) (estimating the impact investment market would have "invested capital ranging from $400bn to nearly $1 trillion over the next ten years"); HOPE CONSULTING, MONEY FOR GOOD 10, 61 (2010), *at* http://www.hopeconsulting.us/pdf/Money%20for%20Good_ Final.pdf (last visited July 12, 2016) (estimating the impact investment market at $120 billion); *see also* GLOBAL IMPACT INVESTING NETWORK & J.P MORGAN, EYES ON THE HORIZON 5–8, 17–22 (2015), *at* https://thegiin.org/assets/documents/pub/2015.04%20Eyes%20on%20the%20Horizon.pdf (reporting the results of a study of impact investors "report[ing] having committed USD 10.6bn in 2014 and intend[ing] to invest 16% more—USD 12.2bn—in 2015" and that "progress was made in 2014 across several indicators of market growth") (last visited July 12, 2016); *see also generally* KEITH ALLMAN & XIMENA ESCOBAR DE NOGALES, IMPACT INVESTMENT 1 (2015); Drew Lindsay, *New Venture Connects Socially Minded Artists with Cash*, CHRON. OF PHILANTHROPY, Oct. 4, 2016, at 8; Paul Sullivan, *Investing to Make a Difference Is Gaining Ground*, N.Y. TIMES, Sept. 6, 2014, at B5.

13. *See* The Impact Terms Project *at* http://impactterms.org/, (last visited Apr. 4, 2017) (describing structures used in real-world impact-driven transactions).

14. *See* Jacob Gray, Nick Ashburn, Harry Douglas & Jessica Jeffers, GREAT EXPECTATIONS: MISSION PRESERVATION AND FINANCIAL PERFORMANCE IN IMPACT INVESTING 17 (2015), *at* http://socialimpact.wharton.upenn.edu/wp-content/uploads/2013/11/Great-Expectations_Mission-Preservation-and-Financial-Performance-in-Impact-Investing_10.7.pdf (last visited July 12, 2016) (reporting 60 percent of impact private equity funds surveyed sought market-rate returns); EYES ON THE HORIZON, *supra* note 12 at 5 (reporting a finding that 55 percent of impact investors surveyed principally targets "competitive, market rate Returns," 27 percent "below market rate returns: closer to market rate," and 18 percent "below market rate returns: closer to capital preservation"); *see also* Julie Petersen & Shauntel Poulson, *New Approaches to Ed-Tech Funding*, STAN. SOC. INNOVATION REV. (Spring 2016) at 41–42 (arguing that impact-first and finance-first investors can sometimes invest in the same company, and chronicling this development in the educational technology space).

15. Such debt, often referred to as PIK, or pay-in-kind, debt, has a long pedigree, tracing its roots as far back as the iconic leveraged buyout of RJR Nabisco. *See* Glenn Ruffenach &

Randall Smith, *RJR Nabisco Gets Major Jolt in Debt Ratings—Reports by S&P, Moody's Are Setback in Firm's Bid to Pare Its Borrowings*, WALL ST. J., Jan. 29, 1990, at A3 (noting that "PIK debt represents notes that accumulate interest in more notes and don't require cash payments for several years").

16. Tranched investments represent precisely such a strategy, with one investor subsidizing the returns of another investor. *See* Benjamin M. Leff, *Preventing Private Inurement in Tranched Social Enterprises*, 45 SETON HALL L. REV 1, 21 (2015) ("a tranched investment strategy means that a federally recognized tax-exempt charity will provide funds to a for-profit business enterprise with the expectation that it may not receive any of its money back").

17. *See generally* Edward D. Kleinbard et al., *Contingent Interest Convertible Bonds and the Economic Accrual Regime*, 95 TAX NOTES 1949 (2002) (tracing the development of the treatment of contingent convertible debt instruments).

18. Tom Fairless, *Banks Ordered to Boost Capital*, WALL ST. J., Feb. 20, 2016, at B1 (observing that contingent convertible debt, or CoCos, represented an "avenue of funding used by European banks in the past several years to boost capital buffers").

19. Features used in many bonds issued by publicly traded corporations that provide bondholders a right to acceleration or prepayment in the event of a change of control are frequently called "poison puts." *See* ARTHUR FLEISCHER JR., ALEXANDER R. SUSSMAN, & GAIL WEINSTEIN, TAKEOVER DEFENSE: MERGERS AND ACQUISITIONS § 6.11 (2016). Recent Delaware cases have expressed extreme skepticism about a particular kind of poison put—the "dead-hand proxy put"—which essentially triggers anytime a majority of the board becomes composed of directors elected in response to an actual or threatened proxy contest. *See id.* This especially powerful species of poison put, however, is quite different from the terms we propose for FLY paper. First of all, unlike in poison puts generally, the trigger in FLY paper would activate only conversion rights. It would not accelerate payment of the debt in which it is included and, through cross-acceleration provisions, potentially require immediate prepayment of all of a corporations' debt, to calamitous effect. Second, FLY paper includes no dead-hand feature, the aspect of these provisions the Delaware courts found particularly problematic.

20. *See* Unocal v. Mesa Petroleum, 493 A.2d 946 (1985).

21. *See, e.g.*, Kopin Tan, WALL ST. J., May 1, 2001, at C13 (noting that "complex option spreads" can have names like "iron butterfly, double box, condor—seemingly plucked from a childhood fantasy").

22. *See* Darian M. Ibrahim, *The (Not So) Puzzling Behavior of Angel Investors*, 61 VAND. L. REV. 1405, 1408, 1439–40 (2008) (describing the angel investment community and noting that many of them "invest for nonfinancial as well as financial reasons").

23. *See* Alex Daniels, *Ford Foundation to Put $1 Billion from Endowment into Social Investments*, CHRON. OF PHILANTHROPY, Apr. 5, 2017, *available at* https://www.philanthropy.com/article/Ford-Foundation-Makes-1/239692; Rockefeller Foundation, *Innovative Finance at* https://www.rockefellerfoundation.org/our-work/initiatives/innovative-finance/ (last visited Dec. 12, 2016); Kresge Foundation, *Social Investment Practice, at* http://kresge.org/how-we-fund/social-investing (last visited Dec. 12, 2016); *see also e.g.*, Schmidt Family Foundation, *Mission Investing, at* http://tsffoundation.org/impact-investing/ (last visited Apr. 7, 2017).

24. IRS, Notice 2015-62, Investments Made for Charitable Purposes, *at* https://www.irs.gov/pub/irs-drop///n-15-62.pdf (last visited July 20, 2016).

25. *See, e.g.*, Gray et al., *supra* note 14, at 3 (reporting results of a survey of "53 impact investing private equity funds from around the world").

26. *See* sources cited, *supra*, at note 12.

27. *See* Lester M. Salamon, *The Revolution on the Frontiers of Philanthropy*, 39–52 *in* FRONTIERS OF PHILANTHROPY (Lester M. Salamon, ed. 2014), at 3–87 (describing a plethora new tools emerging in the social investment space); Antony Bugg-Levine, Bruce Kagut, & Nalin Kulatilaka, *A New Approach to Funding Social Enterprises*, HARV. BUS. REV. (Jan.–Feb. 2012) (discussing various financial tools available for impact investment).

28. Chapter 5 will discuss the many impediments to a public offering of social enterprise stock. For the purposes of this example, assume these can be overcome.

29. Assuming the payments are deferred and "baby bonds" are issued instead, the amount of stock into which the FLY paper would be converted would grow as the amount of FLY paper does.

30. *See* Louis Kaplow, *Rules versus Standards: An Economic Analysis*, 42 DUKE L.J. 557, 560 (1992).

31. One need look no further than the contingent convertible debt that banks had issued to boost capital. Quite recently, those bonds fell out of favor, the risks associated with those bonds coming to life long after they were issued. *See* Richard Barley, *Heard on the Street*, WALL ST. J., Feb. 18, 2016, at C8 ("The big risk that investors have woken up to isn't that these bonds can be bailed in if a bank hits trouble—it is that interest payments on them can be skipped under certain circumstances.").

32. William T. Plumb Jr., *The Federal Income Tax Significance of Corporate Debt: A Critical Analysis and a Proposal*, 26 TAX L. REV. 369, 404–13 (1971) (describing evolution of judicial efforts to determine which instruments denominated debt should receive debt treatment—and the attendant benefits of debt treatment—from those that should be recharacterized as equity).

33. Treasury regulations provide that both conversion features and contingencies that are very unlikely to occur are to be ignored for purposes of the contingent payment debt rules. *See* Treas. Reg. § 1.1275-4(a)(4) (a "debt instrument does not provide for contingent payments merely because it provides for an option to convert the debt instrument into the stock of the issuer") and Treas. Reg. § 1.1275-4(a)(5) ("A payment is not a contingent payment merely because of a contingency that, as of the issue date, is either remote or incidental").

34. *See* Salamon, *supra* note 27, at 39–52; Antony Bugg-Levine et al., *supra* note 27 at 5–6.

35. *See* Coyle & Green, *supra* note 7, at 169 (describing the SAFE as "a contract for deferred equity investment"); *see also* Y Combinator, *Startup Documents*, *at* http://www.ycombinator.com/documents/ (outlining the terms of a SAFE and providing links to sample documents); *see also generally* Dana Brakman Reiser & Steven A. Dean, *Financing the Benefit Corporation*, 40 SEATTLE L. REV. 793, (2017) (canvassing a variety of financial tools that could be structured to engender trust between social entrepreneurs and impact investors).

36. Echoing Green, a nonprofit that provides fellowship seed funding to social entrepreneurs, recently announced it had developed the Seed Impact Investment Template Note ("SeedIIT") template with the assistance of elite law firm Sullivan & Cromwell. *See* Echoing Green, *The Seed Impact Investment Template Note Developed by and for Entrepreneurs*, *at* http://www.echoinggreen.org/blog/seed-impact-investment-template-note-developed-and-entrepreneurs (last visited July 12, 2016). SeedIIT is a convertible debt product intended for "investment into an early-stage social enterprise by investors who are primarily concerned with advancing the social or environmental mission of the company and not with earning a speculative financial return on their investment." *Id.*

Chapter 5

1. JESSE BRICKER ET AL., CHANGES IN U.S. FAMILY FINANCES FROM 2010 TO 2013: EVIDENCE FROM THE SURVEY OF CONSUMER FINANCES (Sept. 2014) 18, Box 6, *at* http://www.federalreserve.gov/pubs/bulletin/2014/pdf/scf14.pdf (last visited July 12, 2016). Although retail investors' portfolios have moved steadily toward pooled investment products and retirement-related managed accounts, direct investment in bonds and, particularly, stocks remains high. The same report found over 15 percent of US families invested directly in stocks and bonds outside of these professionally managed contexts. *See id.* at 16, Table 3.

2. *See id.* at 18, Box 6.

3. *See* Product (Red), *(Red) Products*, *at* https://red.org/red-products/ (last visited April 4, 2017).

4. *See* Amazon, *About AmazonSmile*, *at* http://smile.amazon.com/gp/chpf/about/ref=smi_aas_redirect?ie=UTF8&qid=1455115796&ref=spkl_3_1_2279808162 (last visited July 12, 2016).

5. *See, e.g.*, Sarah Dadush, *Profiting in (Red): The Need for Enhanced Transparency in Cause-Related Marketing*, 42 N.Y.U. J. Int'l L. & Pol. 1269 (2010); Angela Eikenberry, *The Hidden Costs of Cause Marketing*, 7 Stan. Soc. Innovation Rev. 51 (2009).

6. US/SIF Foundation, The Forum For Sustainable and Responsible Investment, Report on U.S. Sustainable, Responsible and Impact Investing Trends 2014, Executive Summary 12 (2014), *at* http://www.ussif.org/Files/Publications/SIF_Trends_14.F.ES.pdf (last visited July 12, 2016). This represents a tenfold increase since the US/SIF Foundation began tracking this data in 1995, *see id.* at 12–13, although it is worth noting that US/SIF uses an extremely expansive definition of assets managed using SRI strategies.

7. *Id.* at 13 (reporting 925 distinct ESG funds managing $4.31 trillion in net assets in 2014).

8. *See* Kathryn Judge, *The Future of Direct Finance: The Diverging Paths of Peer-to-Peer Lending and Kickstarter*, 50 Wake Forest L. Rev. 603, 637 (2015); Christine Hurt, *Pricing Disintermediation: Crowdfunding and Online Auction IOPs*, 2015 U. Ill. L. Rev. 217, 258–61; Chance Barnett, *Will Crowdfunding Ignite Investing for Profits and Purpose?*, Forbes.com (Aug. 9, 2012), *at* http://www.forbes.com/sites/chancebarnett/2012/08/09/will-crowdfunding-ignite-investing-for-profits-purpose/#28b432402f6a (last visited July 13, 2016).

9. *See* Usha Rodrigues, *Securities Law's Dirty Little Secret*, 81 Fordham L. Rev. 3389, 3430–32 (2013) (describing these limitations); Janet Kiholm Smith, Richard L. Smith, & Karyn Williams, *The SEC's "Fair Value" Standard for Mutual Fund Investment in Restricted Shares and Other Illiquid Securities*, 6 Fordham J. Corp. & Fin. L. 421, 446–47 (2001). *But see also* William A. Birdthistle, Empire of The Fund: The Way We Save Now 99-111 (2016) (describing how unscrupulous mutual funds may seek to use overvaluation of assets, particularly of illiquid assets, to increase their compensation); Jeff Schwartz, *Should Mutual Funds Invest in Startups? A Case Study of Fidelity Magellan Fund's Investments in Unicorns (and other Startups) and the Regulatory Implications*, 95 N.C. L. Rev. __(forthcoming 2017) (describing and critiquing some actively-managed mutual funds' recent investments in startups in search of high returns index funds cannot match, though still as a very small percentage of assets invested).

10. *See* Phillip Vidal, US Census Bureau, Annual Survey of Public Pensions: State- and Locally-Administered Defined Benefit Data Summary Report: 2014 2 (2015), *at* https://www.census.gov/content/dam/Census/library/publications/2015/econ/g14-aspp-sl.pdf (finding "[t]otal cash and investment holdings for state- and locally-administered pension systems increased 12.8 percent, from $3,280.7 billion in 2013 to $3,700.1 billion in 2014") (last visited July 13, 2016); *see also* Towers Watson, Global Pension Assets Study 2015 4, 6 (2015), *at* https://www.towerswatson.com/en-US/Insights/IC-Types/Survey-Research-Results/2015/02/Global-Pensions-Asset-Study-2015 (detailing the trillions of dollars in value in global pension funds) (last visited July 13, 2016).

11. *See* Interpretive Bulletin, 29 C.F.R. § 2509.2015-01 (Oct. 26, 2015), *at* https://www.federalregister.gov/articles/2015/10/26/2015-27146/interpretive-bulletin-relating-to-the-fiduciary-standard-under-erisa-in-considering-economically/ (last visited July 13, 2016).

12. *Compare* Rodrigues, *supra* note 9, at 3430–34 (proposing removal of these limitations to allow mutual funds specializing in private companies, in order to democratize access to these investments) *with* Schwartz, *supra* note 9, at 14-61 (identifying investor protection concerns with mutual fund investment in startups).

13. *See* New York Stock Exchange, Listed Company Manual, § 102.01C, *at* http://nysemanual.nyse.com/LCMTools/PlatformViewer.asp?selectednode=chp_1_2_2_1&manual=%2Flcm%2Fsections%2Flcm-sections%2F (last visited July 13, 2016).

14. *See* Nasdaq, Initial Listing Guide at 6, *at* https://listingcenter.nasdaq.com/assets/initialguide.pdf (last visited July 13, 2016).

15. Etsy, *Mission*, *at* https://www.etsy.com/mission (last visited July 13, 2016).

16. *See* Telis Demos, *Online Marketplace Etsy Files for IPO*, Wall St. J., Mar. 5, 2015, at B1.

17. *See* Suzanne Kapner, *Etsy Crafted Tax Strategy in Ireland*, Wall St. J., Aug. 17, 2015, at B1.

18. Laureate International Universities, Press Release, *Laureate Education Files Registration Statement for Proposed Initial Public Offering*, Feb. 10, 2015, *at* http://www.laureate.net/ NewsRoom/PressReleases/2015/10/Laureate-Education-Files-Registration-Statement-For-Proposed-Initial-Public-Offering (last visited July 13, 2016).

19. *See id.*

20. *See* Brookings Institution, *Brookings Papers on Economic Activity, Fall 2015 Conference, Media Summary: A Crisis in Student Loans? How Changes in the Characteristics of Borrowers and in the Institutions They Attended Contributed to Rising Loan Defaults*, *at* http://www.brookings.edu/ about/projects/bpea/papers/2015/looney-yannelis-student-loan-defaults (last visited July 13, 2016).

21. *See* Lauren Gensler, *The World's Biggest For-Profit College Company, Laureate Education, Raises $490 Million In Public Debut*, FORBES.COM, Feb. 1, 2017, *at* https://www.forbes.com/sites/ laurengensler/2017/02/01/laureate-education-initial-public-offering/2/#ee9c4ae454d4 (last visited Apr. 6, 2017); *see also* Gary Gately, *The For-Profit Education Company Targeting the Whole World*, CNBC.COM, Dec. 15, 2015, *at* http://www.cnbc.com/2015/12/15/a-controversial-education-model-us-is-exporting-to-the-world.html (last visited July 13, 2016).

22. Kickstarter, *About*, *at* https://www.kickstarter.com/about?ref=footer (last visited July 13, 2016).

23. Mike Isaac & David Gelles, *Kickstarter Focuses Its Mission on Altruism over Profit*, N.Y. TIMES, Sept. 20, 2015 at B1.

24. Alexandra Alper, *Obama Signs Bill to Boost Business Startups*, REUTERS, *at* http://www.reuters.com/article/us-usa-jobsact-idUSBRE83414F20120405 (last visited July 13, 2016).

25. Regulation D—Rules Governing the Limited Offer and Sale of Securities Without Registration Under the Securities Act of 1933, 17 CFR § 230.506 [hereinafter Rule 506]. Other private placement exemptions are also available, but we focus on Rule 506 as it has been the most popular exemption both prior to and after the JOBS Act, and was the one revised in response to it.

26. Securities issued under some private placement exemptions may also be sold to 35 or fewer nonaccredited investors. *See* 17 CFR §§ 230.505, 230.506(b). As 35 is hardly a crowd, we ignore this limited permission.

27. *See* 17 CFR § 230. 501(a)(5)–(6).

28. *See* US GOV'T ACCOUNTABILITY OFFICE REPORT TO CONGRESSIONAL COMMITTEES 18 (July 2013) *at* http://www.gao.gov/assets/660/655963.pdf (last visited July 13, 2016).

29. *See* Jason Parsont, *Crowdfunding: The Real and Illusory Exemption*, 4 HARV. BUS. L. REV. 281 (2014) (describing and critiquing these proposals).

30. *See* SEC Staff, *Report on the Review of the Definition of "Accredited Investor"*, Dec. 18, 2015, at 48 & tbl.4.2, *at* https://www.sec.gov/files/review-definition-of-accredited-investor-12-18-2015.pdf (last visited April 6, 2017).

31. *See* SCOTT BAUGUESS, RACHITA GULLAPALLI, & VLADIMIR IVANOV, CAPITAL RAISING IN THE U.S.: AN ANALYSIS OF THE MARKET FOR UNREGISTERED OFFERINGS, 2009–2014, at 6 (Oct. 2015), (report prepared for SEC, Division of Economic and Risk Analysis), *at* https://www.sec.gov/ dera/staff-papers/white-papers/unregistered-offering10-2015.pdf (last visited July 13, 2016).

32. *See* Elizabeth Pollman, *Information Issues on Wall Street 2.0*, 161 U. PA. L. REV. 179, 193–202 (2012); Rodrigues, *supra* note 9, at 3402–06.

33. *See* Rutherford B. Campbell Jr., *The New Regulation of Small Business Capital Formation: The Impact—If Any—of the JOBS Act*, 102 KY. L.J. 815, 827 (2013–14). *But see* BAUGUESS ET AL., *supra* note 31 at 12–14 (noting early data on the use of Rule 506(c) show slow initial uptake of this option).

34. *See* US GOV'T ACCOUNTABILITY OFFICE, GAO-12-839, SECURITIES REGULATION: FACTORS THAT MAY AFFECT TRENDS IN REGULATION A OFFERINGS 16–20 (2012), *at* http://www.gao. gov/assets/600/592113.pdf.

35. *See* JOBS Act, § 401(a)(2).

36. *See* SEC Press Release, *SEC Adopts Rules to Facilitate Smaller Companies' Access to Capital*, Mar. 25, 2015, *at* https://www.sec.gov/news/pressrelease/2015-49.html (last visited July 13, 2016).

37. *See* Securities Exchange Commission, *Regulation A Amendment Final Rules*, at 7, *at* https://
www.sec.gov/rules/final/2015/33-9741.pdf (last visited June 8, 2017).

38. *See, e.g.*, North American Securities Administrators Association, NASAA's Coordinated Review Program for Regulation A Offerings, *at* http://www.nasaa.org/
industry-resources/corporation-finance/coordinated-review/regulation-a-offerings/
(last visited July 13, 2016).

39. *See, e.g.*, Stacy Cowley, *New Rules Let Companies Sell Stakes to Investors of Modest Means*,
N.Y. Times, June 19, 2015, at B3. *But see* Neal Newman, *Let Sleeping Regs Lie: A Diatribe
on Regulation A's Futility Before and After the J.O.B.S. Act*, 18 U. Pa. J. Bus. L. 65 (2015);
Rutherford B. Campbell Jr., *The SEC's Regulation A+: Small Business Goes Under the Bus Again*,
104 Ky. L.J. 325 (2015–16).

40. Gofundme.com, *How it Works*, *at* https://www.gofundme.com/tour/ (last visited July 13,
2016).

41. *See* Suzanne Perry, *Legal Experts Weigh Regulations Best Suited to Crowdfunding Sites*, Chron.
of Philanthropy, Sept. 25, 2014, at 8, 10. A coalition of state charity officials agreed to
a loose set of principles for when Internet charitable appeals fall within their jurisdiction, called the Charleston Principles. *See* National Association of State Charity Officials
(NASCO), *The Charleston Principles: Guidelines on Charitable Solicitations Using the Internet*,
Mar. 14, 2001, *at* http://www.nasconet.org/wp-content/uploads/2011/05/Charleston-
Principles-Final.pdf (last visited July 13, 2016). These standards, however, were developed
prior to the explosion of crowdfunding and have not been updated to evaluate this phenomenon fully. NASCO did, however, recently post a "tips" document on its public website
advising funding platforms to "[m]ake sure you understand your legal status and any corresponding reporting or contractual responsibilities in each state that you operate." NASCO,
Internet and Social Media Solicitations: Wise Giving Tips, *at* http://www.nasconet.org/wp-
content/uploads/2013/12/Internet-and-Social-Media-Solicitations-Wise-Giving-Tips.pdf
(last visited Dec. 13, 2016).

42. SEC v. W. J. Howey Co., 328 U.S. 293, 301 (1946).

43. *See* Kickstarter, *Help the Candyman Make His Comeback*, *at* https://www.kickstarter.com/
projects/thecandyman/help-the-candyman-make-his-come-back?ref=category_featured
(last visited July 13, 2016).

44. *See* Deborah Netburn, *Pebble Smartwatch Raises $4.7 Million on Kickstarter Funding Site*,
L.A.Times.com, April 18, 2012, *at* http://articles.latimes.com/2012/apr/18/business/la-
fi-tn-pebble-smart-watch-kickstarter-20120418 (last visited June 8, 2017); *see also* David
McGrail, *"Crowdfunding" a Chapter 11 Plan*, Am. Bankr. Inst. J., Feb. 2013, at 30 (reporting
Oculus Rift "raised about $2.5 million").

45. *See, e.g.*, Indiegogo, *Haste the Day: New Album*, *at* https://www.indiegogo.com/projects/
haste-the-day-new-album#/ (last visited July 13, 2016); Indiegogo, *We The Kings—Our 4th
Album*, *at* https://www.indiegogo.com/projects/we-the-kings-our-4th-album#/ (last visited
July 13, 2016).

46. *See* Kiva.org, *How Kiva Works, The Long Version*, *at* https://www.kiva.org/about/how/even-
more (last visited July 13, 2016).

47. *See* Prosper.com, *Legal Compliance, Lender Requirements*, *at* https://www.prosper.com/plp/
legal/compliance/ (last visited July 13, 2016); Lending Club, *Prospectus* (August 22, 2014),
at https://www.lendingclub.com/fileDownload.action?file=Clean_As_Filed_20140822.
pdf&type=docs (last visited July 13, 2016). For an overview of online peer-to-peer lending, see Eric C. Chafee & Geoffrey C. Rapp, *Regulating Online Peer-to-Peer Lending in the
Aftermath of Dodd-Frank*, 69 Wash. & Lee L. Rev. 485 (2012), and Andrew Verstein, *The
Misregulation of Person-to-Person Lending*, 45 U.C. Davis L. Rev. 445 (2011).

48. Securities Exchange Act of 1934, § (a)(4) ("The term 'broker' means any person engaged in
the business of effecting transactions in securities for the account of others").

49. *See* 15 U.S.C. § 78o(b)(8); *see also* Norman S. Poser & James A. Fanto, Broker-Dealer
Law and Regulation (4th ed. 2016 Supp.) at §§ 4.01[F], 5.01-02.

50. *See, e.g.*, Poser & Fanto, *supra* note 49, at 12.02 (net capital requirements), 19.01 (suitability), 21.01 (market manipulation).

51. *See* Rules Governing the Offer and Sale of Securities Through Crowdfunding Under Section 4(a)(6) of the Securities Act, codified in scattered sections of 17 C.F.R, available in Federal Register format at 80 F.R. 71387 (Nov. 16, 2015).

52. *See* Securities Act § 4(a)(6)(B).

53. *See* JOBS Act, §§ 302, 304. For a general discussion of funding portals, *see* Joan MacLeod Heminway, *The New Intermediaries on the Block: Funding Portals Under the CROWDFUND Act*, 13 U.C. Davis Bus. L.J. 177 (2013).

54. *See* Hurt, *supra* note 8, at 251–58 (collecting criticisms of the regulations when proposed); *cf.* Financial Industry Regulatory Authority, *Funding Portals We Regulate*, *at* http://www.finra.org/about/funding-portals-we-regulate (listing funding portals that have been created despite these challenges).

55. *See* Exchange Act § 3(a)(80).

56. *See* Regulation Crowdfunding, at 386 n. 1334, *at* https://www.sec.gov/rules/final/2015/33-9974.pdf (last visited July 13, 2016).

57. *Compare* Regulation Crowdfunding Rule 204 *with* Securities Act § 4A(b)(2).

58. *See* US Securities and Exchange Commission, *About: The Investor's Advocate: How the SEC Protects Investors, Maintains Market Integrity, and Facilitates Capital Formation, at* https://www.sec.gov/about/whatwedo.shtml.

59. *See* Therese Maynard, *Spinning in a Hot IPO—Breach of Fiduciary Duty or Business as Usual?*, 43 Wm. & Mary L. Rev. 2023 (2002) (identifying particularly flagrant abuses of this power in the "hot" IPO market of the early 1990s).

60. *See* Andrew A. Schwartz, *Crowdfunding Securities*, 88 Notre Dame L. Rev. 1457 (2013).

61. Michael B. Dorff, *The Siren Call of Equity Crowdfunding*, 39 J. Corp. L. 493, 521 (2014); *see also* Steven Bradford, *Crowdfunding and the Federal Securities Laws*, 2012 Colum. Bus. L. Rev. 1, 105–109 (2012).

62. *See* Hurt, *supra* note 8 at 251 (describing the current "outlook for equity crowdfunding" as "doubtful," attributed by proponents to the costly and burdensome regulatory regime the SEC imposed).

63. Kansas moved first. *See* Invest Kansas Exemption, K.A.R. 81-5-21 (effective Aug. 12, 2011; amended Jan. 4, 2016). For a more comprehensive list of intrastate crowdfunding approaches by state, see North American Securities Administrators Association, *Intrastate Crowdfunding Legislation*, *at* http://nasaa.cdn.s3.amazonaws.com/wp-content/uploads/2014/12/NASAA-Crowdfunding-Index-5-23-2016.pdf (last visited July 13, 2016).

64. While sites might be designed to block access to users from outside the state, the simplest and cheapest Internet solicitation design—one viewable by anyone—would take an issuer outside the intrastate exemption.

65. *See* Exemptions to Facilitate Intrastate and Regional Securities Offerings, at 12, *at* https://www.sec.gov/rules/proposed/2015/33-9973.pdf (last visited July 14, 2016).

66. *See* 17 C.F.R. § 230.147A; *see also* Securities and Exchange Commission, *Exemptions to Facilitate Intrastate and Regional Securities Offerings*, Release Nos. 33-10238; 34-79161 (Oct. 26, 2016), *available at* https://www.sec.gov/rules/final/2016/33-10238.pdf (describing the changes worked by the new rules).

67. *See* Hurt, *supra* note 8, at 258–60 (arguing this element will make crowdfunding particularly attractive to social enterprises).

68. DrinkerBiddle, *Drinker Biddle Crowdfunding Report—FINRA's First Enforcement Action and Updated Data Analysis*, Jan. 30, 2017, at 2, *at* http://www.drinkerbiddle.com/insights/publications/2017/01/crowdfunding-report (last visited Apr. 6, 2017).

69. *See* I.R.C. §§ 511–14 (taxing otherwise exempt charitable entities on "unrelated business income"); § 170 (allowing a deduction for corporations' charitable contributions, subject to a 10 percent limit).

70. For a discussion of the difficulty of assigning a social enterprise's expenses to either the ordinary and necessary business expense or charitable contribution category and suggested reforms, see Lloyd Hitoshi Mayer, *Taxing Social Enterprise*, 66 Stan. L. Rev. 387, 408–409, 439–40 (2014). *See also* John Tyler, Even Absher, Kathleen Garman, & Anthony Luppino, *Producing Better Mileage: Advancing the Design and Usefulness of Hybrid Vehicles for Social*

Business Ventures, 33 Quinnipiac L. Rev. 235, 311–31 (2015) (describing a similar problem for individuals faced with limitations on deducting "hobby" losses).

71. I.R.C. § 162(a). The IRS recently offered guidance that a benefit corporation may deduct contributions it makes to charities as ordinary and necessary business expenses under § 162(a) if the contribution is "for institutional goodwill advertising to keep the corporation's name before the public" but did not address expenditures made to pursue social good. Internal Revenue Service, General Information Letter 2016-0063 (June 2, 2016), *available at* https://www.irs.gov/pub/irs-wd/16-0063.pdf.

72. 290 U.S. 111 (1933).

73. *Id.* at 112.

74. *Id.* at 115.

75. *Id.* at 116.

76. Victor Fleischer, *"For-Profit Charity": Not Quite Ready for Prime Time*, 93 Va. L. Rev. Online 231, 232 (2007), *at* http://www.virginialawreview.org/sites/virginialawreview.org/files/fleischer.pdf.

77. I.R.C. § 1(h) provides a lower tax rate for "capital asset[s]," and § 1221 lists a variety of types of property omitted from this privileged category. Our proposal would add SE(c)(3) shares to this list. Limiting this to gains is possible and would reduce the risk of abusive tax planning involving SE(c)(3) losses.

78. *See* I.R.C. § 1(h)(11) (treating dividend income as "net capital gain" taxed at capital gain rates).

79. Thomas C. Schelling, The Strategy of Conflict 135 (1980).

80. Jon Elster, *Don't Burn Your Bridge Before You Come to It: Some Ambiguities and Complexities of Precommitment*, 81 Tex. L. Rev. 1751, 1783 (2003).

81. Michael Abramowicz & Ian Ayres, *Commitment Bonds*, 100 Geo. L.J. 605, 607–608 (2012). In this way, the SE(c)(3) regime shares much in common with what Abramowicz and Ayres call "compensating commitment bonds," in which the right to receive the penalty for default is sold to a third party. The third party's upfront payment encourages would-be promisors to undertake promises in the first instance.

82. *See* Thomas C. Schelling, *Enforcing Rules on Oneself*, 1 J. L Econ. & Org. 357 (1985) (describing the two factors: precision and enforceability).

83. *See* Louise Story et al., *Wall St. Helped to Mask Debts Shaking Europe*, N.Y. Times, Feb. 14, 2010, at A1.

84. Edward D. Kleinbard, *The Congress Within the Congress: How Tax Expenditures Distort Our Budget and Our Political Processes*, 36 Ohio N.U. L. Rev. 1, 3 (2010).

Chapter 6

1. This oft-repeated maxim has been widely attributed to management guru Peter Drucker.

2. This concept is variously credited as Goodhart's Law and Campbell's Law, and originated from critiques of government policies pegged to metrics.

3. *See* Kevin Davis, Benedict Kingsbury, & Sally Engle Merry, *Introduction*, *in* Governance by Indicators: Global Power Through Quantification and Rankings at 3, 6 (Kevin Davis, Angelina Fisher, Benedict Kingsbury, & Sally Engle Merry eds., 2012) (defining particular types of evaluative metrics as "indicators").

4. *See* Kate Ruff & Sara Olsen, *The Next Frontier in Social Impact Measurement Isn't Measurement at All* (May 10, 2016) *at* http://ssir.org/articles/entry/the_next_frontier_in_social_impact_measurement_isnt_measurement_at_all?utm_source=Enews&utm_medium=Email&utm_campaign=SSIR_Now&utm_content=Title (last visited July 19, 2016).

5. *See* Amit Bouri, *How Standards Emerge: The Role of Investor Leadership in Realizing the Potential of IRIS*, Innovations, 145, 146 (Special Issue for SOCAP11, 2011).

6. IRIS, *History*, *at* https://iris.thegiin.org/about/history (last visited July 11, 2016).

7. Global Impact Investing Network Website, *About*, *at* https://thegiin.org/about/(last visited July 11, 2016).

8. *See* Allman, *supra* Chapter 4 note 12, at 208; Sarah Dadush, *Impact Investment Indicators: A Critical Assessment*, *in* GOVERNANCE BY INDICATORS, *supra* note 3, at 392, 402.

9. *See* IRIS, *Metrics*, *at* https://iris.thegiin.org/metric/4.0/PI2845 (last visited July 11, 2016).

10. *See* IRIS, *Download Full Catalog*, *at* https://iris.thegiin.org/metrics/downloads (last visited July 20, 2016).

11. *See* IRIS, *Social Performance for Microfinance*, *at* https://iris.thegiin.org/microfinance-metrics (last visited Dec. 13, 2016).

12. *See* IRIS, *Health Working Group*, *at* https://iris.thegiin.org/about/working-group/health-working-group (last visited Dec. 13, 2016).

13. *See* IRIS, *Data Brief: Focus on Beneficiaries*, *at* https://iris.thegiin.org/research/iris-data-brief-focus-on-beneficiaries/summary (last visited July 20, 2016).

14. *See* The GIIN, *IRIS Data Brief: Focus on Beneficiaries*, (March 2014) at 2, 9, *at* https://thegiin.org/assets/documents/pub/iris-data-brief-focus-on-beneficiaries.pdf (last visited July 11, 2016).

15. Good Beta Finance Website, *Home*, *at* http://www.goodfinance.org.uk/impact-matrix/filter/102 (last visited July 11, 2016).

16. Global Reporting Website, *About GRI*, *at* https://www.globalreporting.org/information/about-gri/Pages/default.aspx (last visited July 11, 2016).

17. Sustainability Accounting Standards Board, *Vision and Mission*, *at* http://www.sasb.org/sasb/vision-mission/ (last visited July 11, 2016).

18. *See* Michael B. Dorff, *Assessing the Assessment: B Lab's Effort to Measure Companies' Benevolence*, 40 SEATTLE U.L. REV. (515, 520 (2017) (arguing an ideal assessment tool would succeed across four dimensions: simplicity, validity, vision, and inclusiveness).

19. To review these and other sample questions, see B Impact Assessment, *Step 1: Assess Your Impact*, *at* http://bimpactassessment.net/how-it-works/assess-your-impact (last visited April 11, 2017) (scroll to portion of page titled "See Sample Questions" and click through to see the quoted samples and others).

20. *See* Dorff, *supra* note 18, at 523, 534–35.

21. *See* B Impact Assessment, *Assess Your Impact*, *at* http://bimpactassessment.net/how-it-works/assess-your-impact (last visited July 11, 2016).

22. *See* B Corporation, *Performance Requirement*, *at* https://www.bcorporation.net/become-a-b-corp/how-to-become-a-b-corp/performance-requirements (last visited July 11, 2016). Certified B Corps that are wholly owned subsidiaries or public companies are subject to a mandatory on-site Certification Evaluation during each two-year certification term.

23. *See* B Corporation, *Improve Your Impact*, *at* http://bimpactassessment.net/how-it-works/improve-your-impact (last visited July 11, 2016).

24. *See* B Analytics, *Fund Ratings: Methodology*, *at* http://b-analytics.net/products/giirs-ratings/fund-ratings-methodology (last visited July 11, 2016).

25. *See* Global Impact Investing Ratings System, *How GIIRS Works*, *at* http://giirs.nonprofit soapbox.com/about-giirs/how-giirs-works/166 (last visited July 11, 2016).

26. *See* GIIRS, *Our Partners*, *at* http://giirs.nonprofitsoapbox.com/about-giirs/our-partners (last visited July 11, 2016) ("Whenever possible GIIRS has integrated IRIS metrics and definitions into its rating system. By using IRIS metrics, GIIRS is helping ensure that the metrics and definitions within its rating system have been vetted and accepted by the larger impact investing industry").

27. *See, e.g.*, Dadush, *supra* note 8, at 403; GIIRS, *What Is a GIIRS Impact Rating?*, *at* http://giirs.nonprofitsoapbox.com/about-giirs/how-giirs-works/159 (last visited July 20, 2016).

28. *See* Social Return on Investment, *What Is the Relationship Between IRIS and SROI*, *at* http://www.socialvalueuk.org/resource/iris-and-sroi/ (last visited July 20, 2016).

29. *See* Brian Trelstad, *The Elusive Quest for Impact: The Evolving Practice of Social-Impact Measurement*, 583–603, *in* FRONTIERS OF PHILANTHROPY (Lester M. Salamon, ed. 2014) (reviewing and analyzing a number of such efforts, their development and future challenges).

30. *Cf.* Jeffrey B. Liebman, Social Impact Bonds (Feb. 2011) 15–16, *at* https://cdn. americanprogress.org/wp-content/uploads/issues/2011/02/pdf/social_impact_bonds.pdf (last visited July 11, 2016) (outlining the comparable importance of measurable outcomes and reliable assessment for social impact bonds to work effectively).

31. *See* The Smart Campaign, *Index*, *at* http://www.smartcampaign.org/index.php (last visited July 11, 2016).

32. *See* The Friars Club, *Members*, *at* http://friarsclub.com/members/ (last visited July 11, 2016).

33. *See* Sam's Club, *Sam's Club Membership*, *at* http://www.samsclub.com/sams/pagedetails/content.jsp?pageName=aboutSams (last visited July 11, 2016).

34. *See* Mary Kay Gugerty & Aseem Prakash, in *Voluntary Regulation of NGOs and Nonprofits: An Introduction to the Club Framework*, in Voluntary Regulation of NGOs and Nonprofits (Gugerty & Prakash eds. 2010) at 3, 20.

35. *See* B Lab, *Participate in an Ad Campaign*, *at* https://www.bcorporation.net/become-a-b-corp/why-become-a-b-corp/participate-in-ad-campaign (last visited July 11, 2016).

36. *See* B Corporation, *B Lab, Generate Press*, *at* https://www.bcorporation.net/become-a-b-corp/why-become-a-b-corp/generate-press (last visited July 11, 2016).

37. *See* B Lab, Home, at https://www.bcorporation.net/ (last visited Jan. 5, 2017).

38. *See* B Corporation, *Performance Requirements*, *at* https://www.bcorporation.net/become-a-b-corp/how-to-become-a-b-corp/performance-requirements (last visited July 11, 2016).

39. B Corporation, *What Are B Corps*, *at* https://www.bcorporation.net/what-are-b-corps (last visited July 11, 2016).

40. *See* Dorff, *supra* note 18, at 537–39.

41. *See* US Small Business Association, *Program Overview*, *at* https://www.sba.gov/sbic/general-information/program-overview (last visited June 8, 2017).

42. *See* US Small Business Association, *Expanding SBAs Impact Funding*, *at* https://www.sba.gov/sbic/general-information/key-initiatives/impact-investment-fund/new-2014-expanding-sbas-impact-fund (last visited July 11, 2016).

43. *See* US Small Business Association, *Impact Investment Fund Policy*, *at* https://www.sba.gov/sites/default/files/articles/SBA%20Impact%20Investment%20Fund%20Policy%20-%20September%202014_1.pdf (last visited July 11, 2016).

44. *See* SVX, *Issuer Manual*, at 17–18, *at* http://s3.amazonaws.com/svx.staging/comfy/cms/files/files/000/000/173/SVX_Issuer_Manual-original.pdf (last visited June 8, 2017) (listing "SVX platform access requirements").

45. *See* MaRS Centre for Impact Investing, *The SVX*, *at* http://impactinvesting.marsdd.com/strategic-initiatives/svx-formerly-the-social-venture-exchange/ (last visited Apr. 11, 2016).

46. *See also* Sarah Dadush, *Regulating Social Finance*, 37 U Pa. J. Int'l L. 1, 202 (2015) (noting the use of metrics by SVX, but also praising their embrace of narrative reporting to ensure beneficiaries' stories are being told).

47. *See id.* at 146, 191–214; Brett H. McDonnell, *Benefit Corporations and Public Markets: First Experiments and Next Steps*, 40 Seattle U.L. Rev. (717, 739–41 (2017) (suggesting the promise of social stock exchanges as regulators).

Chapter 7

1. *See* D. Gordon Smith, *The Exit Structure of Venture Capital*, 53 UCLA L. Rev. 315, 345 (2005); Ronald J. Gilson, *Engineering a Venture Capital Market: The American Experience*, 55 Stan. L. Rev. 1067, 1087–90 (2003).

2. *See* Usha Rodrigues, *Securities Laws' Dirty Little Secret*, 81 Fordham L. Rev. 3389, 3400 (2013).

3. D. Gordon Smith, *Team Production in Venture Capital Financing*, 24 J. Corp. L. 949, 952 (1999); *see also* Gilson, *supra* note 1, at 1078–81.

4. *See* Smith, supra note 1, at 348–50.

5. *See* Jesse M. Fried & Mira Ganor, *Agency Costs of Venture Capitalist Control Structure*, 81 N.Y.U. L. Rev. 967, 981–82 (2006); *see also* Ronald J. Gilson & David M. Schizer,

Understanding Venture Capital Structure: A Tax Explanation for Convertible Preferred Stock, 116 Harv. L. Rev. 874, 879 (2003) (noting the "ubiquity" of convertible preferred stock in VC deals).

6. *See* Gilson, *supra* note 1, at 1076.

7. *See* Jacob Gray, Nick Ashburn, Harry Douglas, & Jessica Jeffers, Great Expectations: Mission Preservation and Financial Performance in Impact Investing (2015) (reporting on surveyed investors' concerns and perceptions about their ability to secure mission-aligned exits), *at* http://socialimpact.wharton.upenn.edu/wp-content/uploads/2013/11/Great-Expectations_Mission-Preservation-and-Financial-Performance-in-Impact-Investing_10.7.pdf (last visited July 20, 2016); Global Impact Investing Network & J.P. Morgan, Eyes on the Horizon 33–36 (2015), *at* https://thegiin.org/assets/documents/pub/2015.04%20Eyes%20on%20the%20Horizon.pdf (last visited July 20, 2016) (similar).

8. *See* Gilson, *supra* note 1, at 1086–87.

9. *Cf.* Darian M. Ibrahim, *The (Not So) Puzzling Behavior of Angel Investors*, 61 Vand. L. Rev. 1405, 1440–42 (2008) (describing negative signal sent by overly onerous angel investment terms in traditional start-ups).

10. Michael Moody, *"Building a Culture": The Construction and Evolution of Venture Philanthropy as a New Organizational Field*, 37 Nonprofit & Voluntary Sector Q. 324, 332 (2008) (quoting C. E. Gray & S. Speirn, *Introduction*, in Defining Virtue: Five Key Elements of Venture Philanthropy and Five Years of Documented Results (Menlo Park, CA: Center for Venture Philanthropy and Peninsula Community Foundation (2004)).

11. *See* Ben Cohen & Jerry Greenfield, Ben & Jerry's Double-Dip 97–101 (1997).

12. *Id.* at 101–103.

13. *Id.* at 20.

14. *See* Brad Edmonson, Ice Cream Social: The Struggle for the Soul of Ben & Jerry's 138–68 (2014).

15. *See* Revlon, Inc. v. MacAndrews & Forbes Holdings, Inc. 506 A.2d 173 (1986).

16. Unocal Corp. v. Mesa Petroleum Co., 493 A.2d 946, 955 (1985).

17. Vt. Stat. Ann., tit. 11A § 8.30(a)(3).

18. For an exhaustive review and point-by-point refutation of this conventional wisdom, *see* Antony Page & Robert A. Katz, *The Truth About Ben & Jerry's*, Stan. Soc. Innovation Rev. 39 (Fall 2012).

19. *See* William Safire, *On Language; Beware the Junk-Bond Bust-Up Takeover*, N.Y. Times Magazine (Jan. 27, 1985) (musing on the emergence of these new techniques and terminology).

20. *See* Edmonson, *supra* note 14, at 170–80.

21. *See id.* at 170.

22. *Id.* at 171.

23. *See id.* at 185–252.

24. *See* Martine Geller, *Unilever Says Its Socially Responsible Brands Outperform Rest*, Reuters, May 4, 2015, *at* http://www.reuters.com/article/us-unilever-sustainability-idUSKBN0NQ02G20150505; *see also Unilever's CEO on Making Responsible Business Work*, Harvard Business Review, May 2015, *at* https://hbr.org/2012/05/unilevers-ceo-on-making-respon.

25. *See* Unilever, Press Release, *Statement Regarding Announcement by The Kraft Heinz Company of a Potential Transaction*, Feb. 17, 2017, *at* https://www.unilever.com/news/press-releases/2017/Statement-regarding-announcement-by-The-Kraft-Heinz-Company.html (last visited Apr. 17, 2017).

26. Unilever, Press Release, *Unilever Review*, Feb. 22, 2017, *at* https://www.unilever.com/news/press-releases/2017/Unilever-review-170222.html (last visited Apr. 17, 2017).

27. Unilever, Press Release, *Accelerating Sustainable Shareholder Value Creation*, Apr. 6, 2017, *at* https://www.unilever.com/news/press-releases/2017/Accelerating-sustainable-shareholder- value-creation.html (last visited Apr. 7, 2017).

28. *See* Page & Katz, *supra* note 18 at 40; David Gelles, *Gobbled Up, but Still Doing Good for the World*, N.Y. TIMES, Aug. 25, 2015, at BU3.

29. Jay Coen Gilbert, *How to Sell Without Selling Out*, Sept. 20, 2016, *at* http://www.bthechange. com/stories/impact/transparency/selling-without-selling/.

30. *See, e.g.*, John Foraker, Taste of General Mills Blog, *General Mills and Annie's—a Six Month Update*, Mar. 4, 2015, http://www.blog.generalmills.com/2015/03/general-mills-and-annies-a-six-month-update/ (last visited July 6, 2016) ("The headline *thus far* is that we are not at all diluting what Annie's has come to stand for over the past 25 years") (emphasis added); CLOROX COMPANY, 2008 ANNUAL REPORT TO SHAREHOLDERS AND EMPLOYEES 2-3, https://s21.q4cdn.com/507168367/files/doc_financials/annuals/2008/ar08_complete.pdf (last visited July 6, 2016) (highlighting acquisition of Burt's Bees as important component of Clorox's plan to enhance its presence in the sustainable products category).

31. *See* B Lab, *Plum Organics*, *at* https://www.bcorporation.net/community/plum-organics (noting Campbell's support of its Delaware PBC structure) (last visited July 6, 2016).

32. Michael J. De La Merced, *After Sale to Bain, Tom's Chief Wants to Expand Global Reach*, N.Y. TIMES, Aug. 21, 2014, at B4.

33. *See* STEVEN C. ALBERTY, 3 ADVISING SMALL BUSINESSES § 46:1 (2016) (describing the typical tax-driven preferences of buyers and sellers in small business sales).

34. *See id.* § 45:27.

35. *See id.* § 45:45–46 (noting that all-cash purchases of small businesses are "unusual").

36. *Id.* § 45:44.

37. *See id.* §§ 45:54–57.

38. *See generally* JUDY WICKS, GOOD MORNING, BEAUTIFUL BUSINESS (2013).

39. *See id.* at 258.

40. For a corporation to sell all or substantially all of its assets, a majority of shareholders must approve. *See, e.g.*, DEL. GEN. CORP. L. § 271 (2010); MODEL BUS. CORP. ACT § 12.02 (2010). For an LLC to do so, all owners must consent. *See, e.g.*, REVISED UNIFORM LIMITED LIABILITY COMPANY ACT § 407 (2006). Different types of partnerships are governed by different rules, but unanimous consent is the most frequent requirement there as well. *See, e.g.*, UNIF. PART. ACT § 9(2) (1914); REV. UNIF. PART. ACT §§ 301(2), 401(j) (1984).

41. *See, e.g.*, REVISED UNIFORM LIMITED LIABILITY COMPANY ACT § 502(A)(3).

42. *See* ALBERTY, *supra* note 33 §§ 21:1 et seq.

43. *See* JAMES D. COX & THOMAS LEE HAZEN, 2 TREATISE ON THE LAW OF CORPORATIONS §§ 12:1–2 (2015).

44. *See id.* §§ 12:2–7.

45. *See id.* § 14:1.

46. *See* ALBERTY, *supra* note 33, § 21:2.

47. *See* JAMES J. FISHMAN, STEPHEN SCHWARZ & LLOYD HITOSHI MAYER, NONPROFIT ORGANIZATIONS 73 (5th ed. 2015).

48. *See, e.g.*, DEL. GEN. CORP. L. § 275 (2010); MODEL BUS. CORP. ACT §§ 14.02, 14.03 (2010). LLC statutes vary considerably across jurisdictions, but all permit dissolution by consent of the members; again, a filing is generally required. *See* LARRY E. RIBSTEIN & ROBERT R. KEATINGE, 1 RIBSTEIN & KEATINGE ON LIMITED LIABILITY COMPANIES §§ 11:5–6 (2016). No filing is required to dissolve a partnership, and the rules for dissolution differ depending upon the type partnership involved. *See* J. WILLIAM CALLISON & MAUREEN A. SULLIVAN, PARTNERSHIP LAW & PRACTICE §§ 16:1 et seq. and 26:1 et seq. Statutes also permit owners some discretion to vary the dissolution process by agreement.

49. For an example of the default duties applied to members of LLCs, which may be varied by an operating agreement, see REVISED UNIFORM LIMITED LIABILITY COMPANY ACT §§ 110(d)–(e), 409 (2006).

50. *See* 1-1 COLLIER ON BANKRUPTCY ¶¶ 7.01-05 (15th 2015).

51. *See id.* ¶ 1.03[4].

52. *See* Marrama v. Citizens Bank, 549 U.S. 365, 367 ("The principal purpose of the Bankruptcy Code is to grant a 'fresh start' to the 'honest but unfortunate debtor'") (quoting Grogan v. Garner, 498 U.S. 279, 286, 287, (1991)).

53. A recent statute provides for some consideration of noncreditor interests, but only in extremely narrow situations. *See* 11 U.S.C. §§ 333, 704(a)(12) (providing special rules for bankruptcies of healthcare businesses, including the appointment of an ombudsman to consider patient concerns and requiring a trustee to use best efforts to transfer patients of a liquidating entity to new providers). For an extended argument that bankruptcy decisions should consider community interests, see KAREN GROSS, FAILURE AND FORGIVENESS (1997).

54. *See* 7-1100 COLLIER ON BANKRUPTCY ¶ 1100.01, 1100.06 (15th 2015).

55. *See* 1-15 COLLIER ON BANKRUPTCY ¶ 15.04[2][a].

56. *See* 7-1129 COLLIER ON BANKRUPTCY ¶ 1129.01.

57. *See id.* ¶ 1129.03.

58. *See id.* A complex exception—sometimes termed a corollary—to the absolute priority rule allows some equity owners who contribute new value to a reorganizing entity to retain ownership interests. *See id.*

59. *See* 1-1 COLLIER ON BANKRUPTCY ¶ 1.07[3][b] (describing accelerated small business process); ALBERTY, *supra* note 33, at 47:61 (noting that even simple reorganizations can cost close to or over six figures).

60. *See* 1-1 COLLIER ON BANKRUPTCY ¶ 1.04[2].

61. 11 U.S.C. § 303(a) (omitted language further excepts farmers) (emphasis added).

62. *See* Reid K. Weisbrod, *Charitable Insolvency and Corporate Governance in Bankruptcy Reorganization*, 10 BERK. BUS. L.J. 305, 347–50 (2014).

63. *See* RESTATEMENT (THIRD) OF TRUSTS § 67.

64. *See, e.g.*, REVISED MODEL NONPROFIT CORPORATION ACT § 14.06(a)(6).

65. *See* Henry B. Hansmann, *The Role of Nonprofit Enterprise*, 89 YALE L.J. 835 (1980).

66. *See, e.g.*, 39 U.S.C. § 3626 (postal rates); MARILYN E. PHELAN, NONPROFIT ORGANIZATIONS: LAW & TAXATION § 14:08 n. 13 (West 2000) (describing states retaining qualified charitable immunity).

67. *See* NORMAN M. ABRAMSON ET AL., BOGERT ON TRUSTS & TRUSTEES § 342 (2015).

68. *See* Julie Battilana, Matthew Lee, John Walker, & Cheryl Dorsey, *In Search of the Hybrid Ideal*, STAN. SOC. INNOVATION REV. 51, 52 (Summer 2012).

Conclusion

1. *See* Cassady V. Brewer, *A Novel Approach to Using LLCs for Quasi-Charitable Endeavors (a/k/a "Social Enterprise")*, 38 WM. MITCHELL L. REV. 678, 696 (2012) (noting that the statutory requirements for L3Cs were crafted "to encourage private foundations . . . to make certain expenditures that qualify as program-related investments").

INDEX

Index